MW00389655

CRITICAL CONDITIONS: FIELD DAY ESSAYS AND MONOGRAPHS

Edited by Seamus Deane

1. *The Tree of Liberty*, Kevin Whelan
2. *Transformations in Irish Culture*, Luke Gibbons
3. *Mere Irish and Fíor-Ghael*, Joep Leerssen
4. *Remembrance and Imagination*, Joep Leerssen
5. *Crazy John and the Bishop*, Terry Eagleton
6. *The Keeper's Recital*, Harry White
7. *The Present Lasts a Long Time*, Francis Mulhern
8. *Poets and Politics*, Marc Caball
9. *Ireland After History*, David Lloyd
10. *Ireland's Others*, Elizabeth Butler Cullingford
11. *Circe's Cup*, Clare Carroll
12. *Revival*, P.J. Mathews
13. *Native and Natural*, Peter McQuillan
14. *Golden Ages and Barbarous Nations*, Clare O'Halloran

Critical Conditions: Field Day Essays

Foreign Affections

Essays on Edmund Burke

Seamus Deane

UNIVERSITY OF NOTRE DAME PRESS
in association with
FIELD DAY

Published in the United States in 2005 by
University of Notre Dame Press
310 Flanner Hall
Notre Dame, Indiana 46556
www.undpress.nd.edu

And in Ireland by
Cork University Press
University College Cork, Ireland

Library of Congress Cataloging-in-Publication Data

Deane, Seamus, 1940–
Foreign affections : essays on Edmund Burke / Seamus Deane.
p. cm. — (Critical conditions ; 15)
Includes bibliographical references and index.
ISBN 0-268-02570-3 (alk. paper)
1. Burke, Edmund, 1729-1797—Contributions in political science. 2. Liberty—History—18th century. 3. Great Britain—Colonies. I. Title. II. Series.

JC176.B83D43 2005
325'.341'01—dc22 2004051736

For Iseult

“But to transfer humanity from its natural basis, our legitimate and home-bred connections; to lose all feeling for those who have grown up by our sides, in our eyes, of the benefit of whose cares and labours we have partaken from our birth: and meretriciously to hunt abroad after foreign affections; is such a disarrangement of the whole system of our duties, that I do not know whether benevolence so displaced is not almost the same thing as destroyed, or what effect bigotry could have produced that is more fatal to society.”

Edmund Burke. ‘Tracts relating to Popery Laws’ (1765) *Writings and Speeches* IX, 461

CONTENTS

PREFACE

Almost all of the essays collected here are concerned with some aspect of Edmund Burke's accounts of the French and American Revolutions and his accompanying analyses or commentary on the themes of liberty, empire and political faction. They also provide a companion narrative, piecemeal in the Burkean way, of the various disputes about the estrangement from natural feelings and affections that modernity seemed to threaten or enforce. Burke's reading of the French Revolution and of British imperial policies gave these disputes a novel urgency, so much so that human feeling thereafter emerged as a topic for which a history could be written. That history itself then became an integral feature of the defence of what Burke called liberty and of the widespread conservative assault on faction, despotism and the new world of theory and modernity. The affiliations between these, later to be taken as "natural', were largely created by Burke.

Eighteenth-century Europe, and, centrally, the profoundly dissonant histories of Ireland and Britain, provide the setting for debates that are dominated by the question 'Is liberty compatible with colonial rule?' Although Burke (and Swift) posed this question more sharply in relation to Ireland earlier than it was posed to the Thirteen Colonies or India, Burke's answer did not alter in time, although its assurance weakened. The answer was yes, except in those places where colonial rule had escaped the rule of law and gave the opportunity or excuse for a corrupt faction to aggrandize itself by the violent exercise of arbitrary power and unappeasable greed.

The confidence of Burke's answer seemed initially to be merited by the triumph of principle in the loss of the American colonies. But ultimately, he had to secure his position by at least sometimes condemning colonial as well as always condemning revolutionary violence. But in the case of others dealt with here, especially Tocqueville and Acton, colonial atrocity is condoned or supported while revolutionary violence (not by any means always directed against colonial power) is condemned out of hand. This is not merely an indication of individual blindness. It is, I suggest, constitutive of the liberal anti-revolutionary position on violence and 'progress', which Burke did so much to create and to which he yet remained and remains alien.

These essays, then, are occasional studies of various writers who sought and fought for an idea, even an ideal, of traditional authority which they felt was menaced, if not entirely overcome, by the hostile forces of a new world that had emerged as a consequence of the designed and revolutionary deformation of the old.

ACKNOWLEDGEMENTS

All but one of the following essays have appeared in earlier form. Most have been in part rewritten and updated. Some essays have been conflated with others for the sake of survival. I would like to thank the editors of the various journals involved for permission to republish and the various institutions and organizations for the invitation to address them and to allow versions of the lectures given to be published here. These include the Eighteenth-Century Ireland Conference, University of Aberdeen, University of Cardiff, University of Notre Dame, American Conference for Irish Studies, University College, Dublin, International Association for the Study of Irish Literature. My thanks also to my graduate classes and my colleagues in the Keough Institute for Irish Studies at the University of Notre Dame. Special thanks to Mary Burgess, Chris Fox, Luke Gibbons, Jim Smyth, Nathan Wallace, and Kevin Whelan. And to Emer Nolan.

The following list contains all the essays and talks that in whole or in part are drawn upon here.

"Burke and the French Philosophes," *Studies in Burke and his Time* X, no. 2 (Winter, 1968–69), 1113–1137.

"John Bull and Voltaire: The Emergence of a Cultural Cliché," *Revue de Littérature Comparée* XLV (Octobre–Decembre, 1971), 582–594.

"Lord Acton and Edmund Burke," *Journal of the History of Ideas* XXXIII, no. 2 (April–June, 1972), 325–335.

"Swift and the Anglo-Irish Intellect," *Eighteenth-Century Ireland* 1, no. 1, 1987, 9–22.

"The Reputation of the French *Philosophes* in the Whig Reviews between 1802 and 1824," *The Modern Language Review* 70, no. 2 (April, 1975), 271–290.

"Edmund Burke and the Ideology of Irish Liberalism" in R. Kearney ed. *The Irish Mind* (Dublin: Wolfhound Press, 1985), 141–156.

"Edmund Burke (1729–97)" in S Deane, A. Carpenter and J. Williams eds., *The Field Day Anthology of Irish Writing* 3 vols., (Derry: Field Day, 1991), I: 807–853

"Montesquieu and Burke" in *Ireland and France; a bountiful friendship* ed. Barbara Hayley and Christopher Murray (Savage, Maryland: Barnes and Noble, 1992), 17–29; revised version in Graham Gargett and Geraldine Sheridan eds., Ireland and the French Enlightenment 1700–1800 (London: Macmillan, New York: St Martin's Press, 1999), 47–66

"Swift: Virtue, Travel and the Enlightenment" in Christopher Fox and Brenda Tooley eds., *Walking Naboth's Vineyard* (University of Notre

Dame Press, 1995), 17–39; another version, 'Virtue, Travel and the Enlightenment," in Michael O'Dea and Kevin Whelan eds., *Nations and Nationalisms; France Britain and Ireland and the eighteenth–century context. Studies in Voltaire and the Eighteenth Century* no. 335, (Voltaire Foundation, Oxford, 1995), 275–296

"Factions and Fictions: Burke, Colonialism and Revolution" *Bullán* IV. no. 2 (Winter 1999/Spring 2000), 5–26

"Newman and Ireland: Converting the Empire" (University College, Dublin, Millennium Lecture, 2000)

"Burke and Tocqueville: New Worlds, New Beings" in Robert Savage Jr. ed. *Ireland in the Century* (Dublin, Four Courts, 2003) 130–50; and in *boundary* 2 31, 1 (Spring, 2004), 1–23

"Freedom Betrayed: Acton, Burke and Ireland" in *Irish Review* 30 (Spring/Summer 2003), 13–56

1. LIBERTY
The Universal Event

I

It is so routine to declare that Edmund Burke attacked the universal appeal of French revolutionary claims and defended those of national and provincial traditions, that it is easy to underrate his own understanding of what true universality was. For him, as for Christian thinkers in general, there were universal events, of which the arrival of Christianity was the first. Thereafter, events that revealed their universality through their very specificity would have included, in his view, the Glorious Revolution of 1688 in Britain and the American Revolution. There was no inescapable discord between the particular and the universal; the logic of their relationship was exhibited in the nature of such events. They were highly specific historical occasions but their meaning and appeal went beyond the time and circumstance of their birth. However, it was also true that there were other events which seemed to be the obverse of these. The Reformation and the French Revolution were for him the outstanding examples here, because they both shattered a previously established universal system and produced in its place an assemblage of difference which they nevertheless paraded as the new and emancipated form of rational universality. All of these events were, in Burke's view, repetitions of one another without being identical one with the other. Such patterning seemed to him characteristic of historical process and its connection to universal revelation.

The crisis of his career was formed by the attempt to universalise the British-American form of liberty by emphasising its particularity and contrasting it with, one the one hand, its corruptions in Ireland and India and, on the other, with the fake universality of French liberty which, in his view, dematerialised the particularity of human experience and offered in its stead a lethal ideational purity.

It is also routine to say, in one way or the other, that Burke did not clarify the philosophical foundations of his thought, either because he was a practising politician and not that way inclined, or because his thought was so confused and his ready betrayal of principle so stark, that the murk surrounding these foundations should be seen as strategic mystification or as a demonstration of what he himself called the Sublime.[1] For some commentators, the more decisive Burke is about his conclusions, the more shabby or cryptic his motives or principles. Yet, it is revealing that Burke's reputation oscillates so wildly, from that of political hack to that of great political philosopher. He was perhaps both, either at the same time or at different times.

Burke quickly understood that the French Revolution, merely by virtue of the fact that it had happened, had already made the invention of opposing 'traditions' the only possible alternative to it and that, in this invented form, they were already products of the Revolution itself. The same was true of colonial domination; it had to be opposed by defence of the hallowed traditions it had destroyed, but once tradition was articulated as an alternative or as a form of resistance, it could only operate effectively by being defined against its destroyer. Counter-revolution or national resistance could succeed in one sense against their enemy, but they could not reinstate the world that was lost; they could only pretend to do so, while actually inaugurating a new world.

However, the larger problem was that, in redefining themselves as Irish or Indian or as English or British, the local counter-revolutionary cultures would make such a fetish of their local integrity that they would lose any claim to universal dimension. Counter-revolution or restoration could be successful to the degree that it particularised itself as an antidote against fake universalism. But the result might be a monadic culture that made insularity and eccentricity, or some combination of its own internal relations, the only – or at least the most favoured or most available – means by which people could situate themselves. They would as a result always be within that culture but have difficulty in finding a way to apprehend much beyond it. In relation to Empire, it would mean that England or Britain would attempt to reinvent versions of itself all over the globe. In religious terms, it would mean that a local variation of Protestantism would claim universality for itself. Burke sought to reinforce these national specificities without making a fetish of their provincial nature.

Contrastingly, John Henry Newman, for instance, found it impossible to renovate this system intellectually, in part because Protestantism was, by its nature and its history, given to localism and fission and incapable of achieving universality. For him, universality was only available through Catholicism. England was lost to Catholicism but the Empire might be saved for it, although by giving Ireland a role in that conversion, he knew – but how well, one wonders? – he would, in the short term at least, intensify the local prejudices, anti-Irish and anti-Catholic, he hoped to dislodge. However, Newman stayed at least within hailing distance of Burke's conviction that liberty was the historical achievement and the political concept that could illumine the world from London, just so long as liberty was not annexed by liberals and, in his view, perverted into liberalism. For him, liberalism was the political dominant of the degraded modern condition in which the reign of Protestantism's mystique of 'private judgement' had reached a terminal extremism; buoyed by political and economic success, this world-wide provincialism was finally being confronted by a revived Catholicism which, as in the Catholic University experiment in Ireland, would begin the conversion of the new pagan empire to a realisation of what true universality and authority meant. More effectively than any other inheritor of Burke's view of the post-revolutionary world, Newman insisted that it was not only the French, but also the British polity that claimed for its local historical development a speciously exemplary character. Empire of whatever kind – Roman, Ottoman, French or British – was not universality; it was, in fact, its simulacrum.[2]

Still, the immediate question in relation to Burke remains. Given the late (post-revolutionary) intensification of his apologia for the traditional British system as the epitome of liberty and of his assault on the colonisers of India and Ireland, was it possible to reconcile that domestic system with colonisation or Empire? If the defence of one and the attack on the other were both merited, was there not a hopeless irreconcilability here, of a constitutive, not a contingent nature? Burke, of course, untiringly argues against this; the issue is always to be understood as one of secure principle allergic only to the criminal behaviour of those who pretend to act in accord with or for the sake of it. The belief that the extension of liberty to the globe at large was a duty consorted easily with the assertion that British liberty conformed to human nature while French 'liberté' violated it. French revolutionary universalism was really the Proteus of French royal absolutism undergoing an astonishing shape-change. Burke thought that by remaining immune to its deceptions he would finally expose its fundamental nature and compel from it the bloody future that it betokened. British suspicions of the French did not need to be aroused, since they never slept. What was necessary, in his view, was to prevent the confiscation by the French and their allies in Britain and Ireland of the claim for the newly-minted Parisian doctrines of British liberty's appeal to human nature.

In Burke's view, when a criminal like Warren Hastings or any of the choice bigots of the Anglo-Irish establishment ruled in the name of British liberty, the whole question of liberty's role in a global civilising enterprise was certainly threatened. It was not, however, undermined; liberty, in Burke's understanding of it, was the essential feature of the civilising purpose of Empire. Once cleaned of its pollutions in Ireland and India, it could resume the career which had begun in the Glorious Revolution and was then renovated in the American War of Independence. Internal and imperial harmony were for him always interlinked and the promotion of this interlinkage formed the basis of policy:

> . . . the effort to make liberty and authority mutually responsible can be said to constitute the core ambition of Burke's political rhetoric. In this context responsibility defines the optimally beneficial relation between government and people on the one hand and national sovereignty and the extended empire on the other.[3]

But after 1789, liberty was threatened, not just by its internal corruptions at home and abroad, but by an ideological reformulation that was a brilliant travesty of what it had been, as appalling to him as it was appealing to others. This was liberty redesigned for easy export, all its inbuilt home-bred characteristics erased. It was in the face of this predatory version of French liberty that, Burke claimed, English liberty lost all its resilience and lapsed into a state of cataplexy which he called upon it to abandon. Liberty did not mean freedom from restraint, nor the exercise of the radically free will. This was a denial of the compact into which humans were born, a claim for arbitrary rule against the rule of law; it was this that, even before the French Revolution happened, Hastings had perpetrated in India:

> Law and arbitrary power are at eternal enmity. Name me a Magistrate, and I will name property. Name me power, and I will name protection. It is a contradiction in terms, it is a blasphemy in religion, it is wickedness in politics to say that any man can have arbitrary power. Judges are guided and governed by the eternal laws of justice to which we are all subject. We may bite our chains if we will, but we shall be made to know ourselves, and be taught that man is born to be governed by law; and he that will substitute will in the place of it is an enemy to God.[4]

II

In 1827, thirty years after Burke's death, and two years before Catholic Emancipation, Francis Jeffrey, the pioneering editor of *The Edinburgh Review*, published an essay-review of John O'Driscol's *The History of Ireland*. In this he justified the Union of 1800, chiefly on the grounds that it had abolished the local tyranny of the Protestant Ascendancy and replaced it with metropolitan rule; it 'has shut up the main fountain of corruption and dishonour; and palsied the arm and broken the heart of local insolence and oppression. It has substituted . . . the wisdom and honour of the British government and the British people, to the passions and sordid interests of a junto of Irish borough-mongers. . .' The completion of the Union would be Catholic Emancipation. The choice was stark, according to Jeffrey. Either Ireland 'must be delivered from the domination of an Orange faction, or we must expect . . . to see her seek her own deliverance' by independence, perhaps 'effected by the help of a French army and an American fleet . . . and an Irish Catholic republic installed with due ceremony in Dublin'.[5] In this argument, still recycled today in relation to Northern Ireland on the advantages of Direct Rule over the domination of the local sectarian faction, there is a clear political preference for the metropolitan over the provincial; with this kind of centralising rule, the Union, it was argued, would hasten the modernisation of Ireland and emancipate it from the benighted faction that had retarded its growth. Jeffrey was one among many who pointed to the Union of Scotland and England as the example to follow.

This political-economic argument co-existed then, as it still does, with a 'cultural' argument that also owed something in its early form to Burke. According to it, Ireland or India or any such place should have its damaged or threatened traditions repaired and encouraged, so that its specific cultural identity could be asserted and nourished. These arguments, usually reduced to recommendations, could work in concert or they could produce conflict. When in concert, they agreed that if a colony was to be politically redeemed by London from the hands of a faction, it could have all the cultural integrity it wanted, just so long as that was accompanied by political integration and its widely advertised chief attractions – liberty, progress, science, a role in global history. These would provide the main outlines of development, while culture could crayon in the local colorations, all of which would be 'typical' of the nation or region. In such a reconciliation, traditional custom and habit could accompany the metropolitan developments in science, economics and politics and thereby prevent their flight into the abstractions of theory. Without that, theory would become 'inhuman'; and tradition would, in consequence, be compelled into a defence of the archaic and even – in a condition of crisis – of the dionysiac powers that lay beyond the reach of the rational élites but remained a defining possession of the people. Burke sought a language that would create a harmony between these antinomies before they became permanent.

To some readers, Burke's weakness, to others his strength, is his capacity to find in subjectivity a universal dimension. For him, impartiality was founded in partiality, not in its repression. Certainly in the genre of the public letter he found an opportunity to profess personal attachment as a basis for political wisdom. Letter-writing, naturally given to intimacy, had several literary variations – the public letter, the epistolary novel, the memoir, diaries, the publication of a selected or collected correspondence, or the letter(s) of real or fictive travellers whose adopted personae meditated on issues of general import, sometimes reporting on foreign cultures or indirectly or directly on their own. The descriptive sketch or the tour could also modestly indicate its anecdotal or impressionistic status as information while establishing its loyalty to the actual and specific. There is in such works an increasing momentum of feeling against the kinds of abstraction that are needed for the purposes of generalisations. Even the more political forms of commentary did not entirely abandon the personal protocols that inevitably dominated letter-writing or autobiographical ventures. They obviously persist in Burke's *Reflections on the Revolution in France*, in which the new France is taken to be the foreign country under analysis and they play an important role in *Democracy in America*, which is a traveller's report on a new country and on a condition that could possibly be Europe's future.

Such writing looks for ways by which the subjective element might be taken by its readers as the basis for a profound wisdom rather than for an impressionistic observation. Mme de Staël claimed that for such commentary there must be an effective combination of closeness and distance; this was critical for the writing of history. As she put it in her *Considérations sur les principaux événements de la révolution* (1818), 'Mon ambition serait de parler du temps dans lequel nous avons vécu, comme s'il était déjà loin de nous.'[6] She often attempted to see what the present would look like in the eyes of posterity and, for her, the position of a foreign observer was as approximate and as available a substitute for posterity as could be found. Such distance allowed her to see the English and French revolutions of the preceding 130 years as the third epoch in the advance of the human spirit towards its fulfilment – the epoch of representative government. For Alexis de Tocqueville, the enchanted phrase was 'equality of conditions' and for him too the rhetorical as well as the imaginative requirement was to see the phenomena of which he wrote in close and intense detail as well as in the larger perspective of a movement which was embodied in the detail and which the detail embodied. The ensemble of immediacy with distance was much sought in historical writing in both England and France in the wake of the French Revolution and Burke's mode of evoking an immemorial past to ratify a present political system was widely influential in that regard.[7] The historical novel or the national tale, particularly in Scotland and Ireland, explored and to a degree exposed the difficulties involved in achieving such harmony, although they usually managed at the very least to endorse it as a hope that could be rationally entertained.

The sentimental novel was different. Following Jean-Jacques Rousseau, the chief English sentimental novels of the 1790s, like Robert Bage's *Hermsprong; or, Man as He is Not* (1796) Mary Wollstonecraft's *Maria; or The Wrongs of Women* (1798) William Godwin's *Things as They Are: or, The Adventures of Caleb Williams* (1794) even in their titles intimated the struggle between inherited and anachronistic attitudes associated with ideas of male aristocratic honour, inherited wealth and religious belief, as against the new sincerity of feeling associated with emancipation and the achievement of ethical character. The peculiar intensites of Rousseau's reverie, a true generic innovation, were never realised in these works; instead they were dully replaced by heartfelt preaching.

Elements of what we find in these kinds of fiction belong to the ethos of United Irish politics, although no novelist embodied it in any of the national parables of the period. The United Irishmen argued that political and commercial liberation would make an ethical society possible in Ireland; this was central to their attempt to overcome both the Protestant sectarian bigotry that was the basis for colonial rule in Ireland *and* the Catholic readiness to accept colonial rule if only it were cleansed of this bigotry. Burke resisted the notion that anti-Catholicism was necessary to the colonial system in Ireland; it was, in fact, what, in contemporary circumstances, disfigured it, even though that system had been initially and necessarily so aggressively Protestant. Take power from the bigots, he argued, and liberty would finally reach Dublin, although he could not envisage where it might then be housed – certainly not in the Irish Parliament at College Green nor in the back-street parliament of Taylor's Hall where the United Irishmen met.[8] The principle of 'toleration' for Catholics had already been conceded in the Empire by the Quebec Act of 1774 and the Canada Act of 1791, but Canada was far away and recently-acquired, Ireland was close and long-resistant to coercion, conquest and even blandishment. Union was a project that might produce separation; the Ascendancy or its successor faction, the Orange Order,[9] might have driven the cause of independence by the very ferocity of its attempts to stifle it in either its 'French' radical or its Irish nativist form.

On the other hand, there was a possibility that cultural difference, now newly understood as a defining because endangered characteristic of the oppressed rather than of the oppressor, could be made a ground for political change. Such a possibility was especially strong in Ireland given the enduring sectarian basis of the system there. The antiquarian researches and debates of the eighteenth century,[10] especially in and after the revolutionary decade of the 1790s, were animated by a specifically Protestant anxiety to dismiss as 'romantic' the notion that there was in the deep past of Ireland any legitimate claim to a 'civilization' that could be said to be prior to, or even more, to have been mutilated by the blessed advent of 'British liberty'. Burke's interest in the topic was on occasion cited to give authority to the repudiation of such claims.[11] They seemed especially dangerous and, by extension, specious, when linked to the arguments for Catholic Emancipation. Any scientific or impartial investigation of cultural difference was fine if it validated rule over but not by Catholics.

The rhetoric of the historical novel, with its biased distinction between the 'scientific' and the 'romantic', owes a good deal of its resources – limited as these are – to antiquarian debate. But the historical novel and the 'national tale' were successful in bringing the fierce debates about the various civilizational sources of the Catholic and Protestant, British and Celtic communities from the enclaves of professional (or not so professional) scholarship to a much wider readership and in a much more palatable, if processed, form. By the 1820s, the 'romantic' support for national traditional communities, like the Greek, the Polish and the Irish, stifled within the Ottoman, Russian and British empires respectively, had altered the local debate so profoundly, that the (now plural) liberties of those admitted within the British system had begun to lose their appeal and appear merely local advantages, compared to the Liberty sought by the emancipated national community. Were Liberty's clothes to be stolen so brazenly by O'Connell's peasantry? Worse, were they going to parade in them specifically as Catholics, whose religion was now to be associated with the realisation of democratic freedoms in Europe?

III

Burke had first-hand knowledge of Ireland, scarcely any of France and none at all of the Thirteen Colonies of America or of India. His effective first-hand knowledge was of Britain and the changing nature of her relation to these places and of theirs to Britain. He attempted to give an account of the specific nature of the British nation-state and of what Philip Bobbitt has recently called the 'state-nation', the nation-state as an imperial power. His ambition seemed to be to overcome the contradiction or at the very least the paradox that bedevilled this dual condition. In Bobbitt's words,

> The nationalism of the state-nation, which created the imperial state, focussed the will of the nation in serving the state, building in a kind of paradox at the inception: the great state-nations existed to promote liberty and equality, constitutionalism and the rule of law; and yet in order to aggrandise the State, which was the deliverer of national identity and political liberty, other nations were subjugated and alien institutions imposed upon them.[12]

Burke attempted to argue that this paradox was avoidable; it was not a necessity but a corruption or misunderstanding of Empire. He thought it possible to extend 'British liberty' to the Empire but unwise to think of liberty itself as a universal right. The successful extension of liberty was for him an exercise in prudence; the universalisation of it as an idea for humankind was an exercise in delusion. He sought to defend it against the charge of provincial inadequacy by claiming that it was because of a failure in policy not because of any inherent limitation that it had not been realised elsewhere – in America because of ineptitude fed by corruption, in Ireland because of the unexampled bigotry of Protestant rule and in India because of the violence and greed of the East India Company. In each case, the dominance of a vicious faction usurped the idea and travestied the constitutional forms of British liberty. Force would achieve subjugation but liberty could win consent. Sovereignty or authority required subordination, but a subordination readily bestowed, not a submission continuously enforced.

Burke had been quite clear, at least since the quarrel with the Thirteen Colonies, on his 'idea of an Empire'; it is 'the aggregate of many States, under one common head' in which it often happens 'that the subordinate parts have many local privileges and immunities'. To confuse a claim to these with a threat to authority or imperial unity was foolish in itself and more likely to be disastrous in its consequences, for would it not teach the 'subordinate parts' of the Empire that the central government 'against which a claim of Liberty is tantamount to high-treason, is a Government to which submission is equivalent to slavery?'[13] Imprudence on the part of central government could make local privilege into the basis for an argument against despotism and for liberty. The unity of Empire was always a chimera; Ireland had always been separate and dependent. In this system, 'Every thing was sweetly and harmoniously disposed through both Islands for the conservation of English dominion, and the communication of English liberties.'[14] This was the argument for unionism before there was a formal union, especially one preceded by the bloodletting of 1798. The English, or the old republican system in its true form was 'an empire of laws, not men'[15], and this differentiated it wholly from the French or Jacobin 'empire of doctrine'[16] or the rule of those factions and cabals who ruled in their own interest and at the expense of the public weal. It hardly mattered if their imprudence led to despotism or their despotism expressed itself as imprudence. The effect on liberty was damagingly the same.

Burke attacked these groups as early as 1770 in his 'Thoughts on the Present Discontents'[17] and then, in an ever-intensifying and widening range of condemnation, in their Irish, Indian and ultimately French versions – revolutionaries, financiers, robbers, men of letters, bigots, creators of cults. It was the 'empire of laws' that was to give appeal and legitimacy to the rule of the miltary-commercial empire. The importance of the Hastings trial for Burke was that the very principles of justice were being contested there. Hastings had broken all rules and all laws; 'the solid established rules of political morality, humanity and equity'; 'the law of Nature' and 'the Law of Nations'; 'the Laws, statutes and Acts of Parliament of Great Britain, either in their Letter or in their spirit'; and 'the laws, rights usages, institutions and good customs' of the country.[18] Only Justice, 'which existed before this world . . . will revive the fabric of this world', even in the midst of the French Revolution;[19] his attack on it and on Hastings were of a piece.

The evidence was against Burke; certainly if, in so many countries of the Empire, British liberty was so readily exchanged for factional despotism, its claim to universality was weakened. Yet the cumbrous detail of his defence of the principle against its imperial violators would probably seem merely stifling by now had he not transmuted his argument, via the French Revolution, into a critical ideological dispute in the war for world domination between France and Britain. One of the wonders of his rhetoric is its deployment of the most operatic and dazzling effects in order to defend the idea of the plainness of truth, the dull but candid nature of the British people and their 'tone of rusticity', which not only distinguishes them, as ever, from the conceited and vocationally sophisticated French but also from all those, like Hastings and his minions, who indulge in the 'politeness of extortion' or 'the delicacies of bribery'.[20] Political, financial and intellectual dishonesty needs infinite resource in order to turn good leaden dullness into its finely-spun fool's gold.

This long debate was not unattended by monotony, but what gave it its peculiar and even perverse dynamic was the recognition, dim and faint at times, that it was taking place in the shadow of violence, revolutionary and imperial. The initial concentration on one at the expense of the other was not solely an exercise in propaganda. It was part of the claim that any true universality could not be constitutively violent, that any violence attendant upon it was the consequence of a local corruption or a contingency which would, in time, fade. The future would be with the empire of liberty even if, in the short or medium term, it was surrendered to revolutionary freedom.

That was Burke's hope, although it seemed scarcely tenable by the time he died.

There was, moreover, the matter of equality's dangerous liasions with liberty, which Tocqueville, more than Burke, recognised had become central to European and American political development. He and Lord Acton, in their different ways, absorbed much of what Burke had said about the French Revolution and then reinterpreted it in the light of their view of the American Revolution as the truly universal event of the modern era. That did require a plausible account of a natural or creatable compatibility between freedom and equality which Tocqueville seemed to concede was needed but which neither he nor any other liberal of his generation managed to provide – either for Europe or, least of all, for the European colonies, especially for the 'natives' of those. The understanding of Liberty as something reified, idealised, personified, is central to its history as a a concept; and, so conceived, it discovered, late in the liberal day, that it had in Equality a companion it had earlier spurned or failed to recognise, but to which it seemed, because of the American and French revolutions, to be inescapably, even fatally, tied for an unforeseeable future.

2. SWIFT AND BURKE
'THE TERRITORIES OF THE HEART'

Swift's *Gulliver's Travels* and *A Modest Proposal* parody and incorporate a whole range of moral-political issues that were then and later to remain at the heart of the work of other Irish writers – Francis Hutcheson and Burke above all. The decisive, early formulations of these issues were achieved in England, by the Third Earl of Shaftesbury and Bernard Mandeville; they included, in their opposing repertoires, interconnected reflections on travel literature, on economic theory, on atheism, despotic power and, most of all, on what Hutcheson called 'national love'. The main emphasis here is on the adaptation of the debates on these issues to what ultimately becomes a diagnosis of fanaticism and its effects on the colonial relationship between England and Ireland.

Shaftesbury and Hutcheson; Travel Literature and the Principle of Benevolence

In the section 'Advice to an Author' in *Characteristics of Men, Manners, Opinions, Times*, Shaftesbury attacks the current taste for light reading, that is, reading as a relaxation:

> The more remote our pattern is from anything moral or profitable, the more freedom and satisfaction we find in it. We care not how Gothic or barbarous our models are, what ill-designed or monstrous figures we view, or what false proportions we trace or see described in history, romance or fiction . . . Our relish or taste must of necessity grow barbarous, whilst barbarian customs, savage manners, Indian wars, and wonders of the terra incognita, employ our leisure hours and are the chief materials to furnish out a library.[1]

But then this attack on the current vogue for travel literature, takes another and more telling turn:

> It must be something else than incredulity which fashions the taste and judgement of many gentlemen whom we hear ensured as atheists, for attempting to philosophise after a newer manner than any known of late. For my own part, I have ever thought this sort of men to be in general more credulous, though after another manner, than the mere vulgar. . . . I can produce many anathematised authors who, if they want a true Israelitish faith, can make amends by a Chinese or Indian one. If they are short in Syria or Palestine, they have their full measure in America or Japan. Histories of Incas or Iroquois,

> written by friars and missionaries, pirates and renegades, sea-captains and trusty travellers, pass for authentic records and are canonical with virtuosi of this sort. Though Christian miracles may not so well satisfy them, they dwell with the highest contentment on the prodigies of Moorish and Pagan countries.They have far more pleasure in hearing the monstrous accounts of monstrous men and manners than the politest and best narrations of the affairs, the governments, and lives of the wisest and most polished people.[2]

The modern traveller, therefore, sets out from home and, in order to gain the reader's attention, proceeds from 'monstrous brutes to yet more monstrous men'; it is by dwelling on the 'monstrous' that the travel-writer gains attention and reputation.[3] The worst thing about these philosopher-travellers, in Shaftesbury's view, is that they do not condemn 'unnatural vices and corrupt manners' such as they find in foreign climes, but instead portray them as natural, thereby abolishing in the name of the 'natural' a long-established and crucial moral distinction. But 'Virtue is of the same fixed standard', he warns; 'Nature will not be mocked.'[4] Still, if we represent monstrosities as natural, should we not counter this current trend by taking our models of perfection from the Bible? The answer is no, because the biblical models, being divinely formed, are beyond our powers of imitation and we should merely deform them by trying to represent them in fiction.

So, in Shaftesbury's essay, we find a readership caught between a corrupting taste for exotic deformity and an inability to represent models of divine excellence. The only recourse is 'to make a formal descent on the territories of the heart'.[5] There the human world will be re-established in all its normative benevolence. These remarks long anticipate Robinson Crusoe and Gulliver; but their immediate interest lies in the association Shaftesbury makes between extreme atheistic opinion and exotic travellers' tales; between the credulity of those who will admire a patchwork of foreign and strange religions rather than adhere to the Christian faith and thereby also adhere to the traditional distinctions beween virtue and vice, rather than falling into a moral indifferentism which is to be justified by an appeal to Nature and with that, a denial of the universality of both moral ideas and of what he is famously to call the moral sense.

Twelve years later, Hutcheson, in his *Inquiry into the Original of Our Ideas of Beauty and Virtue*, resumes Shaftesbury's theme in the Second Treatise, 'Concerning Moral Good and Evil', and gives even stronger emphasis to the objection that writers of travels are sparing in their accounts of the 'natural affections, the Familys, Associations, Friendships, Clans of the Indians' and are gruesomely detailed in their accounts of things like human sacrifice or cannibalism. This he sees as strange in countries that make much of their Protestant memories,

> nations no strangers to the Massacre at Paris, the Irish rebellion, or the Journals of the Inquisition. These they behold with religious Veneration; but the Indian

> sacrifices, flowing from a like perversion of humanity by Superstition, raise the highest abhorrence and amazement. What is most surprizing in these Studys, is the wondrous credulity of some Gentlemen of great Pretensions in other matters to Caution of Assent, for these marvellous memoirs of Monks, Friars, Sea-Captains, Pirates; and for the Historys, Annals, Chronologys, received by oral tradition, or hieroglyphicks.[6]

Hutcheson goes beyond Shaftesbury in his anxiety to demonstrate that the fashionable taste for the exotic or gruesome obscures what these foreign races have in common with Europeans, most especially in relation to their benevolent actions. This is, for him, the crucial information, whereas for the travellers, and for the readership, it is uninteresting. Moreover, he finds it necessary to establish a second line of defence against the implications of these foreign and remarkably unbenevolent practices. If a society kills off its old people or its surplus children, then that might be a measure justifiable in terms of the public good and self-interest. But it can scarcely be called appealing.

> If a deform'd or weak race could never, by Ingenuity or Art, make themselves useful to mankind, but should grow an absolutely unsupportable burden, so as to involve a whole State in Misery, it is just to put them to death. This all allow to be just, in the case of an over-loaded boat in a storm. And as for killing of their children, when Parents are sufficiently stocked, it is perhaps practis'd, and allow'd from Self-love; but I can scarce think it passes for a good action anywhere.[7]

We can see in these comments by the two most renowned benevolist philosophers of the age the emergence of a philosophical commentary on the moral implications of travel literature which has a bearing both on *Gulliver's Travels* and *A Modest Proposal*. Hutcheson is especially important as the most distinguished moral philosopher of the Dublin Philosophical Society in the mid-seventeen twenties.[8] He, more than Shaftesbury, is constantly attempting, especially in his second treatise, to assert the prevalence and the uniform working of the moral sense, the principle of disinterested benevolence, in the most contrastingly different situations. In exposing the fact that the alliance in most people's minds between, say, signs of social status – clothes, coaches, food – and what he calls moral abilities, is unjustified, he poses the question:

> How many would be asham'd to be surpriz'd at a dinner of cold meat,who will boast of their having fed upon Dogs and Horses at the siege of Derry? And they will all tell you, that they were not, nor are ashamed of it.[9]

If we think that eating dogs and horses is excused on the grounds of its being a good or heroic action, we will not apologise for it; but if eating good food is a sign of selfishness, we may be embarrassed to be caught with cold meat on our plate. Hutcheson wants to show that many of our inherited moral attitudes are in fact derived from an idea of the figure we cut in other people's eyes. Similarly, the view we have of others determines our behaviour towards them. So if we think them bestial, or beyond redemption, vicious or the like, we will treat them tyrannically or with contempt, as the Romans did their slaves, and the Greeks the barbarians. But to regard others in this light is to offend against the claims of universal benevolence, to pervert the operation of sympathy which depends on the recognition of our similarity with others. The more kindly disposed we are towards others, the more readily we fulfil our God-given nature and the less likely we are to justify acts of oppression towards them. The egoism of the individual or that of the group have a similar withering effect on sympathy, or the principles of humanity, which Hutcheson amalgamates with one another. This kind of ethical thinking, in which 'the duality of the regulative principles in human nature' is taken to be fundamental, inevitably has a political and literary dimension to it.[10] Politically, it allows for a reformulation of fanaticism and despotism, both of them characterised by extreme selfishness or egoism and, in literary terms, Swift is one of many authors who struggles against but finally concedes to the force of this dual system, creating figures who seem to be monstrous versions of human nature itself or caricature versions of what was then plausibly but shallowly taken to be human nature.

So Hutcheson proceeds to his famous account of and attack upon despotic power:

> The Characteristick of Despotick Power is this, 'That it is solely intended for the good of the governors, without any tacit trust of consulting the good of the Governed.' Despotick Government, in this sense, is directly inconsistent with the Notion of Civil Government.[11]

This was to become a well-known formulation in America before the War of Independence. Given the nature and number of references in Hutcheson's works to Irish Protestant history, it is easy to recognise its application to Ireland also, although his wish to assert Scottish equality with England in the Union is just as tangible. Hutcheson, like so many writers in the commonwealth tradition, sees no moral basis for the concentration of power in the hands of a self-perpetuating élite. The dispersal of power is a security for liberty. Civil society has, as its aim, in Knud Haakonssen's words, 'an institution for the moral improvement of mankind'; virtue is its preoccupation, happiness one of its consequences.[12] So we see in Hutcheson and in his mentor Shaftesbury, a sequence in which the current taste for travel literature, the moral implications arising from its treatment, the association between it and atheism, the general suspicion of fashion and the kinds of moral attitude associated with that, and, finally, the contradiction between universal benevolence and despotic power, are all interlinked. Here, I believe, we have a counterpart to the writings of Swift, as well as a contemporary commentary upon their implications.

Mandeville: Luxury and Vice

Shaftesbury and Hutcheson attacked the new vogue for travel literature, fully conscious of the fact that modishness in taste was a new social reality. This modishness was consistently linked, throughout the century, with moral instability and both were widely considered to be products of 'luxury'. More brilliantly than anyone else, Swift had caricatured the links between the religious and the social situation by choosing fashion in clothes as one of the basic tropes in *A Tale of a Tub*. But it was Bernard Mandeville who actually analysed the connection between clothes and consumption. Like Thomas Hobbes, with whom he shared notoriety, Mandeville was an exponent of political hedonism, the doctrine that the good is identical with the pleasant. He follows Hobbes in his denial that the indulgence of appetite is vanity and therefore morally reprehensible. Instead, he proposes that appetite is natural, and that the satisfaction of appetite is the dynamic which drives the social system. Social status is achieved by emulative consumption.[13] In the early eighteenth century, this manifested itself most prominently in the buying and wearing of clothes. A man was what he wore, what he appeared to be. The social system was designed to satisfy appetites and to produce wealth, not to adhere to pre-ordained moral principles.Thus prostitution should be allowed in a society where sexual desire was regulated by marriage; gin-drinking was not an evil, since it helped to consume surplus grain-stocks.[14]

The Epicurean tradition achieves one of its most famous and paradoxical formulations in the subtitle of *The Fable of the Bees* (1714; vol. II, 1729) – *Private Vices, Public Benefits*. This was not only anathema to Swift, who had already attacked the Epicureanism of Sir William Temple in *A Tale of a Tub*; it was also an attitude repudiated by the benevolist utilitarians, most especially by Hutcheson, who were anxious to prove (although they never did) that there was something other than self-love as the motive for human action and something other than self-interest as the most plausible explanation for it.[15] Yet Mandeville's doctrines have in this context a richer satiric potential because they lead him to promote, as a feature, even a necessary feature, of the economic system, the creation by the typical agent within it of a *persona,* whose existence is manifested in the clothes she or he wears. This is indeed an all-consumer and all-consuming existence. Such a *persona* is in Swift a satiric strategy. What is common in each case is the production of a world of illusion, or of one in which the distinction between the real and the illusory is problematic. What is different is that the Mandevillian world of illusion is the real world of society; the Swiftian world of illusion is the crazed (although actual) world of the virtuoso, the expert, the fanatic. Mandeville is, in fact, defending as natural a society in which fashion is a sovereign power; for Swift, this society, in claiming to be natural, thereby reveals its sinful and radical lunacy.[16]

However, Mandeville's formulation contains another paradox which has its counterbalance in Swift's writings. The indulgence of appetite, or selfishness, 'vice' in the conventional terminology, promotes 'luxury'. The production of wealth is sustained by consumption. Yet luxury is itself the product of work and it is accompanied by poverty and squalor. Mandeville readily acknowledges the co-existence, in contemporary London, of these two contrasting worlds and gives a very Swiftian account of the relationship between them. The London of the court and the London of Gin Lane are functions of one another. The opulence of one and the fetid dirt of the other are necessarily related. The mediating consolation is provided by the consumer himself:

> There are, I believe, few People in London, of those that are at any time forc'd to go a foot, but what could wish the Streets of it much cleaner than generally they are; whilst they regard nothing but their own Cloaths and private conveniency; but when once they come to consider, that what offends them is the result of the Plenty, great Traffick and Opulency of that mighty City, if they have any Concern in its Welfare, they will hardly ever wish to see the Streets of it less dirty.[17]

The consumer converts dirt into luxury by indulging his appetite. What is in Mandeville a metaphor of the economic system is in Swift a metaphor of the degradation of the moral system. The relationship between the two is as close as it is ironic.

It becomes even closer when we consider that Mandeville's economic analysis of the relationship between the two Londons is similar to Swift's recognition of the economic relationship between the two interconnected worlds of England and Ireland. The opulence of one and the poverty of the other were, he recognised, causally related. English policy in Ireland, since the 1690s, had damaged Irish commerce for selfish English purposes.[18] It is appropriate that his first Irish *persona* should be that of the Drapier, a figure whose clothes both disguise who he really is and identify the interests which he represents. Swift's satiric techniques, so Mandevillian in their form, are increasingly deployed in his Irish pamphlets to portray the corruption of an economic system which is Mandevillian in its substance. This does not imply any acceptance by Swift of Mandeville's system. Rather, it is the prevalence of that system which confirms the triumph of immorality in the public world and which rouses in him the cold fury of *A Modest Proposal*.

Hutcheson and the Doctrine of Benevolence

Hutcheson's objections to travel writers and to Mandeville had a common basis – both denied, in effect, the existence in man of the moral sense, that faculty or capacity which renders benevolence pleasing to us and is a guarantee of the natural relationship between moral goodness and aesthetics. For him, altruism and the beautiful were one. Hutcheson's work, especially in the interpretations which extended its influence, was consistently taken to be a rebuke to those political-moral ideologies which, in pretending to a harsh moral realism about the inescapability of self-love as the basis for their analyses, justified various forms of despotism and denied the affective and moral bases for toleration and political consensus. His was an early form of that doctrine of the sympathetic imagination which was to reappear in the Romantic era in the writings of Percy Bysshe Shelley and William Hazlitt, both of whom reacted strongly against the eighteenth-century theorists of self-love, of whom Mandeville was to them one of the most formidable.[19] Hutcheson was among the first to accuse Mandeville of Epicureanism and libertinism, claiming that his economic doctrines were no more than a disguise for this:

> Since then *Intemperance*, or *Pride*, were scarce ever understood to denote all Use of any thing above bare Necessities, all Conveniency of Life above *Hottentots*, why any one should affect to change their Meaning, is not easily guessed, unless it be with this View. *Luxury*, *Intemperance*, and *Pride*, in their common meaning are *Vices* but in this *new Meaning* are often innocent, nay *virtuous* and without them, in this new Sense, there can be no *Consumption of Manufactures*. Common Readers however will still imagine that these Sounds denote *Vices* and finding what they confusedly imagine as vitious is *necessary to publick Good*, they will lose their Aversion to *moral Evil* in general, and imagine it well compensated by some of its Advantages.[20]

Hutcheson's defence of the 'common forms' of morality is consistent with his doctrine of benevolence and his repudiation of both exotic theory and exotic tales which tend to undermine these and replace them with eccentricities which are then claimed to be natural. For him, selfishness, superstition, eccentricity and barbarous practices are all deviations from the benevolent norm. The common affections and habits of mankind are evidence of the prevailing force of benevolence. Particular circumstances, however, can distort the action of this force and produce various forms of anti-social behaviour. This was especially true in Ireland, where sectarian and political divisions coincided.

This coincidence has been identified by David Berman as a characteristic preoccupation of Anglo-Irish thinkers in general.[21] He has described in some detail how the freethinking of John Toland's famous work, *Christianity Not Mysterious* (1696), aroused a particular ire in the breasts of men whose whole political and social position depended upon the preservation of a link between certain forms of Christian belief and the retention of political power. Men as various as William King, Edward Synge, Peter Browne and others adopted the famous Molyneux problem to produce the theory of what Berman calls 'theological representationalism'. This succeeded in making Christianity sufficiently mysterious to justify the Anglican supremacy in Ireland as a rationally defensible position. In its pinchbeck way, this argument perhaps provides the cover needed for its political aim; my more limited goal is to look at another issue to which theological representationalism may bear some resemblance. In one light, that issue is Luxury; in another light, it is the exotic; their shared characteristic is that they are both beyond the range of common forms and common readers. By their connection, something abnormal is touted either as normal in itself or as a force which has the power to subvert the traditional ideas of what constitutes normality. This is, in effect, Hutcheson's argument against Mandeville and travel literature. Its particular Irish application derives from his description of the relationship between universal benevolence and 'narrow views', or the lesser and more selfish form of benevolence in which most people are encased. He is speaking of what he calls national love:

> Here we may transiently remark the Foundation of what we call national love, or Love of one's native country. Whatever Place we have liv'd in for any considerable time, there we have most distinctly remark'd the various affections of human nature; we have known many lovely characters; we remember the associations, friendships, familys, natural affections, and other human sentiments: our moral sense determines us to approve these lovely dispositions, where we have most distinctly observ'd them; and our benevolence concerns us in the interests of those persons possess'd of them. When we come to observe the like as distinctly in another country, we begin to acquire a national love towards it also; nor has our own country any other preference in our Idea, unless it be by an association of the pleasant ideas of our youth, with the Buildings, Fields and Woods where we receiv'd them. This may let us see how Tyranny, Faction, a Neglect of Justice, a corruption of Manners, and anything which occasions the Misery of the subjects, destroys this national love, and the dear idea of a country.[22]

He then goes on to attack what he calls the 'diversity of systems' to which men foolishly confine their benevolence. Thus, those who raise the spirit of party or faction, those who 'cantonise men into several sects for the defence of very trifling causes', those who 'love the Zealots of their own sect' for the 'Fury, Rage, and Malice against opposite sects' impair our moral sense and almost destroy in us the capacity to distinguish between good and evil. Further, such party or sectarian feeling allows us to treat others as base and almost inhuman and ratifies the most despotic and cruel behaviour towards them.

Hutcheson is clearly talking about the political world which Swift knew; but he is also talking about the country to which they both belonged and the deforming of reason and feeling for the sake of preserving sectarian and party distinctions. It is at this point that Hutcheson's political philosophy, or the political implications of his moral philosophy, touch upon the theological debates which Berman has described as central to Irish philosophy at this time. For in each case, the issue was the validity or otherwise of sectarian distinctions for the sake of preserving and justifying despotic political power. Hutcheson denies its validity and, in describing the growth of benevolence, from near relationships to national love, to the love of other nations and thence to the principle of universal benevolence, provides both an alternative to and a critique of the existing system, redolent of Toland's radical, but more ostensibly theological approach in *Christianity Not Mysterious*. This critique reaches a culmination in the late writings of Burke. Before turning to him, it is time to situate Swift more clearly in relation to the issues so far discussed.

Swift and Benevolence

It hardly needs restating here, in any detail, that in the *Tale of a Tub*, Swift attacked modern corruptions in religion and learning in alternating sections, depicting Puritanism and Catholicism as two forms of monomaniac corruption which contrast with the temperate moderation of Anglicanism. In their methods, they also correspond in many ways to the techniques of modern pedants and virtuosi in learning. We know too that the substance of many of his arguments and attitudes was quite conventional, drawn from the writings of the Anglican rationalists in particular (especially Ralph Cudworth and Henry More), and that Swift's uniqueness lies in the brilliance with which he adapts these standard arguments – developed earlier to combat Catholicism and Puritanism when they had posed a threat to the seventeenth-century political system – to his own purposes.[23] By a reductive process of degradation, he renders his opponents both absurd and disgusting; yet so subversive is his technique that the informing irony destabilises even the norm which he is ostensibly supporting. For the moment, however, all that need be established is Swift's hatred for the capacity of human reason to find ingenious ways of defending irrational or purely selfish modes of behaviour on the ground of reason itself. The world of the *Tale* is one in which the most serious issues are trivialised into the most derisory disputes. Religion has, as its central analogy, fashion in clothes; and this is consistently associated with the physiological processes of the body's power to consume and excrete.

When Swift was exiled to his native city, and realised the depressing relationship between the economic power and wealth of London and the dirt and disease of Dublin, Mandeville's and Hutcheson's ideas came to play the same role in his later writings as had those of the Anglican rationalists in the *Tale*. In identifying the political and economic considerations which dominated the Irish, or, more exactly, the Anglo-Irish situation, Swift showed his readiness to 'cantonise' – in Hutcheson's word – the two nations in Ireland. He refers to William Wood's surprise at the insolence of the Irish in refusing his coin and adds:

> . . . where, by the Way, he is mistaken; for it is the true English People of Ireland who refuse it; although we take it for granted, that the Irish will do so too, whenever they are asked.[24]

Still, the contrasting worlds of Dublin and London, Ireland and England, and the enhancement of the contrast in terms of the opposition between money and dirt, opulence and poverty, provides Swift with the strategy for his anti-Mandevillian crusade on behalf of Ireland against the depredations of England. Ireland is both a part of the kingdom and a foreign territory. In Ireland, conditions are so monstrous that they are inconceivable to the English. His English correspondents at times assumed, as David Nokes has pointed out,[25] that Swift was either exaggerating or being professionally gloomy in his descriptions of the place, his loathing for it and his sense of isolation within it. But it is surely perfectly possible to see that the idea of a British territory which is foreign, a home country which is monstrously different, like and yet unlike, is both a radical experience for Swift and a basis for the strategies of *Gulliver's Travels*. Further, just as he turned the arguments of the rationalists in the *Tale* to his own purposes, so too he turns the attitudes and arguments of Shaftesbury and Hutcheson to his own purposes in the *Travels*. For here he picks up their central objections – that the taste for the exotic, the fashionable, the rare and the gruesome was damaging, in that it flattered Europeans into believing that they (with their bloody record) were in some way superior; and it flattered the virtuosi into believing, as (like Gulliver) they credulously would, that every foreign system was a product of nature and ultimately superior to their own. Swift, in other words, establishes the so-called normal traveller, God's own Englishman of the Robinson Crusoe persuasion, as the gull who cannot see that he has travelled into versions, first of his own country and then into aspects of his own imagination, always taking the fantasies of the mind to be realities and taking realities (like his wife, family, etc.) to be fantasies. What is also interesting is to see the degree to which Gulliver is almost entirely robbed of the role of *homo economicus* which Daniel Defoe had assigned to Crusoe. He is a *persona* whose most conspicuous consumptions will be of the customs and habits of others, until he becomes that which he consumes and is revealed to be no more than a Yahoo with pretensions to Houyhnhnm status.

The only points about Gulliver which I want to look at in this instance concern those aspects of his 'character' which we may call benevolist. He is indeed both an inverted and, as we may gather from the subversive and prefatory 'Letter from Captain Gulliver to his cousin Sympson', a disappointed benevolist:

> Pray bring to your mind how often I desired you to consider, when you insisted on the motive of publick Good; that the Yahoos were a species of Animals utterly incapable of Amendment by Precepts or Examples: and so it hath proved . . .[26]

He goes on to admit that it is only the revival in him of 'some corruptions of my Yahoo nature' which have allowed him

> to attempt so absurd a project as that of reforming the Yahoo race in this Kingdom; but, I have now done with all such visionary schemes for ever.[27]

On other occasions in the text, as at the close of chapter 1 of Book II, he addresses the reader with an ostensible avowal of his public responsibilities:

> I hope the gentle Reader will excuse me for dwelling on these and the like particulars; which, however insignificant they may appear to grovelling vulgar minds, yet will certainly help a Philosopher to enlarge his thoughts and Imagination, and apply them to the Benefit of publick as well as private life; which was my sole design in presenting this and other Accounts of my Travels to the world . . .[28]

When we check to see what the particulars are, we discover that he is referring to the episode in which Gulliver kills the giant rat and then is obliged, with great embarrassment, to let his mistress know that he needs to 'discharge the necessities of Nature', the which he is able to do between two leaves of sorrel. His benevolent intentions are grotesquely caricatured by the incidents related. Monstrous creatures, human pride and the humiliations of the human body are composed here into a characteristic parable, in which the exotic, the dirty and the ridiculous are ironically offered to us as an example of the way in which private vices can be identified with public virtue or benefit. Gulliver, like the travellers criticised by Shaftesbury and Hutcheson, is titillating the reader by choosing to relate extraordinary events; but the inversion consists in the fact that Gulliver is unwittingly exposing the absurdity of his own pretensions in demonstrating the discrepancy between the two aspects of human pride and humiliation. Swift's conception of the uniformity of human nature is in savage contrast to that of the benevolists. It is always and in all places essentially corrupt but, equally, in all places and at all times disguised under the fiction of disinterested benevolence. By the close of Book II, Gulliver has convinced himself, if not us, that the King of Brobdingnag's universal benevolence is a chimera and shows a want of knowledge of the true world. In doing so, he exposes his own shortcomings and the improbability of disinterested benevolence as a virtue that could be recognised, even were it to exist, in the European world.

If we are to have greatness and an expanding eonomy, we need vice. To show someone benevolent like the King of Brobdingnag through Gulliver's eyes, is to demonstrate the inutility of virtue; but, of course, it is also to destroy, simultaneously, the benevolist and the Mandevillian positions to admit the utopianism of one and the essential depravity of the other. By the time we come to *A Modest Proposal*, the link between ideas of public utility and moral depravity has been firmly established; the mad economist of that pamphlet, who is also perfectly rational in his development of his initial premisses, is speaking there of a country, Ireland, in which the only available remedy for its economic ills is precisely the kind of cannibalism which Hutcheson and

Shaftesbury had described as characteristic of the gruesome and morally subversive detail of the traveller's tale. Hutcheson in particular had unwittingly anticipated Swift's basic notion – that the killing of surplus children could in fact be defended on the grounds of self-interest as a rational procedure, although it could hardly be called good. Hutcheson was here reaching the limits of his own benevolist philosophy and Swift delights in exposing the interchangeability of benevolence and self-love, between murder which is rationally justifiable even if not aesthetically pleasing for a projector who appeals to our sense of taste by imagining the various appealing ways in which Irish children could be served up, fit to please the most Epicurean of palates.

It could therefore be said that Swift's Irish pamphlets derive at least some of their startling force from the skill with which he adapts elements which we find in Shaftesbury, Mandeville and Hutcheson. The basic manoeuvre is to see Ireland as an extraordinary place; one of the remote nations of the earth, a site for the traveller's tale; the subsequent manoeuvres all flow from that. He follows the established pattern in relating the most exotic, extraordinary situations: this is a country that the English will look upon as they did upon Lilliput or Houyhnhnmland. But as the *Travels* indicate, these strange places are, in various ironic ways, versions of England and Europe. The difference in the Irish pamphlets is that the strange world of the Modest Proposer is not a fiction but a reality. There is no need of allegory; but Swift, as usual, inverts things by allowing us to see that an allegorical method can be used to give to reality the appearance of the fictive, just as the very real virtuoso economist can be seen as an allegorical version of human pride or, more precisely, of the unreal man of the Mandevillian universe, in which economic greatness is dependent literally upon an increase in consumption which can only be achieved by the annihilation of all traditional moral attitudes. It is impossible to be both great and virtuous. An expanding economy needs vice. Therefore Ireland's dilapidated economy needs a proportionately greater measure of viciousness in order to restore it to health. All this is done in the name of benevolence.

Ireland was a scandalous demonstration of what Mandevillian theory could create and justify. It was a standing rebuke to any Hutchesonian theory of benevolence. It was a country threatened by quacks, incompetents, fanatics, sentimental moralists, experts. It was also a country divided into sects, 'cantonised' in a particularly damaging manner. Swift's political attitudes did not permit him to see any alternative to this situation, even though Hutcheson had already supplied a covert critique of it in his *Inquiry*. This issue was to be taken up by Burke, even though in doing so, Burke was to adopt some of Swift's techniques as well as his hostility to the extremes of reason and feeling.

Burke: Liberty and Benevolence

One of Burke's earliest projects was his uncompleted Tracts (unpublished until 1819) on the Popery Laws, written in the 1760s. In the course of his opening argument, he criticises Temple and the First Earl of Clarendon, for the view they had given of the Irish rebellions of the seventeenth century. The Temple he mentions here is Sir John Temple, author of *The History of the Irish Rebellion* (1646) and father of Sir William Temple, Swift's patron.[29] What Burke begins to do here, and later develops in other contexts, is to portray Ireland as a country suffering from 'unparallel'd oppression'[30] and plagued by the presence within it of a faction – chiefly the Irish Anglicans – who identify their own interest against that of the mass of the people. In other words, in Hutcheson's terms, their benevolence is restricted in precisely that manner which fosters zeal for a sect in proportion to the hatred or contempt members of that sect show towards outsiders. But it is in his writings on the French Revolution and on the Ireland of the 1790s, that Burke gives full expansion to these views. They are well known in themselves but less so in their similarity to and compatibility with what Hutcheson and Swift had written in their accounts of fanaticism and its perversion of common or natural feelings.

In the first place, Burke follows Hutcheson in his sponsorship of the affections and love which are characteristic of that 'narrow scheme of relations', that 'little platoon'[31] into which we are born and which thereafter remains the stabilising factor in the general political system. Affection, love, natively rooted, expands to include the whole system of relations which form civil society. This can only happen, he says (following Hutcheson), where the early associations are pleasant. In order to love our country, our country ought to be lovely. Where injustice prevails, these affections are damaged and our natural benevolence is soured. This has happened in Ireland. But in an important variation on the Hutchesonian theme, he attacks the new system of universal benevolence, of which Rousseau is the originator, because it preaches universal philanthropy without teaching local love. This is a schematic version of benevolence detached from actual experience. From Rousseau, Burke proceeds to all the other French intellectuals – and sometimes to their British counterparts – as people who have, like Swiftian projectors, established systems of universal improvement and utility which neither pay attention to nor have any respect for the realities of the moral world; which are indeed anxious to extirpate those realities and the moral and religious systems which have defined and supported them.[32]

So in Burke we see a new sequence of connections established: in the first place, between atheism (never to be tolerated), and visionary schemes offered for the public benefit; in the second place, denial of the actual circumstances of European countries, especially France and Ireland, for the sake of preserving the appeal of utopian politics. In the third place, there was a reaffirmation of a necessary relationship between doctrines of self-love and the practice of licentiousness and Epicureanism, or of 'libertinism' in its increasingly political sense. All these culminated in – or perhaps derived from – the collapse, which Hutcheson had remarked in relation to Mandeville, of all ideas of good and evil and their replacement by a fake system of universal benevolence which would, as in *A Modest Proposal*, lead to a justification of atrocity. Atrocity would be presented as an exercise in social utility by a fanatic intellectual who was anxious at any cost to impose his beliefs on others. In Ireland, Burke saw that the poisoned relationships between Catholics and Protestants would create a situation in which these revolutionary doctrines would readily take hold, especially through the Catholics, who would prefer these against what he liked to think was the deformed version of the British system that had done nothing but cause them suffering. In the end, Burke recommended the redemption of Ireland from revolutionary doctrine and fanatics through the extirpation of the 'junta of robbers' who formed the nucleus of the Protestant Ascendancy. It was a question of extending to Ireland the genuine liberty of the British political system in order to preserve it from the spurious liberty of the French intellectuals and their universalist claims.

British liberty did indeed have a narrow theological and historical-geographical basis in the island of Great Britain but that did not confine its abiding principle. The epithet 'British' did not qualify the range of the word 'liberty'; it identified the place where the idea had finally – after much wandering among 'the ingenious nations of antiquity who inhabited the south of Europe' – found 'refuge in the Atlantic ocean'[33] in a form that was reproducible in widely different circumstances and conditions. The combination of the political form and the principle was, in Burke's view, what made British liberty unique, although if any paradox was to be admitted at all, it was that one element of its uniqueness was its very reproducibility. This was an original from which many copies could be struck. It was the product of a historical compromise and was best reproduced by a similarly delicate process and structure of modified continuity. In that view, the American Revolution was a successor to the Glorious Revolution, while the French Revolution, which sought to disengage principle from historical experience and claim it entirely for philosophy, was its inversion.

It was in Ireland, though, that the question of the applicability of the system of British liberty outside the island of Britain was most tellingly posed – and would continue to be. America was a special case; its political population was British, while its native inhabitants and black slaves could be effortlessly ignored. India was a commercial tyranny. But in Ireland the Catholic majority could not be ignored, so it was, politically and culturally, extinguished. When British liberty went abroad, even that short distance across the Irish Sea, it remained the exclusive preserve of the colonists. The Irish advocate, John Philpot Curran, in his defence of the United Irishman Hamilton Rowan in 1794, ironically observed in court that

> England is marked by a natural avarice of freedom, which she is studious to engross and accumulate, but most unwilling to impart; whether from any necessity of her policy, or from her weakness, or from her pride, I will not presume to say, but so is the fact; you need not look to the east, nor to the west; you need only look to yourselves.

> . . . If it acquired [required?] additional confirmation, I should state the case of the invaded American and the subjugated Indian, to prove that the policy of England has ever been to govern her connexions more as colonies than as allies . . .[34]

Burke would not have defended Rowan but he could hardly have disputed Curran's point here. Yet he would have insisted that English 'avarice' did not define but contradicted the spirit of British liberty. America had fought for British liberty when it fought for independence from Britain; it was not at all a revolution in the French sense. Indeed it was only later, especially after 1789, that the War of Independence became widely known as the American Revolution.[35] In James Harrington's phrase, the system of British liberties was 'an empire of laws and not of men'.[36] Hence the evil effects of faction; factions exercised powers for their own sake, often in the name of liberty but in contradiction of it. They ignored or parodied or suspended the law in their pursuit of selfish interests. This was domination; it was, in the republican tradition, freedom from domination that constituted liberty and it was the law that exempted people from arbitrary rule.

No political philosopher has emphasised more than Burke the importance of affection for the preservation of a political system. It is likely that he incorporated into the British polity features of the Irish Catholic political culture that he remembered from his youth, with its specific emphasis upon family and clan loyalties.[37] Additionally, the affection given by a populace that has no formal political existence is a mute (or not wholly articulate) form of participation; a community's 'feeling' of belonging to a political system and of a political system belonging to it is, for Burke, an important process of mutual reinforcement. It was the more attractive to him because in Ireland he saw the ill-effects of its absence and that itself was the more painful because of the intensity of the loyalties within the old Irish system that were so alienated by Ascendancy rule. In this regard, Burke made an important contribution to the debate on the necessity of reconciling traditional 'feudal' forms of communal feeling with modern individual and rational forms of liberty.

However, it exaggerates the situation to read Burke's defence of 'feeling' as entirely of a piece with the 'Romantic' reaction since associated with figures like Sir Walter Scott or William Wordsworth. They are indeed companionate in many ways, but there is an earlier tradition of political thinking that gives affection an important political role in the support of liberty and against the bigotries of selfish interest, whether that is of a sectarian or party kind. Before the French Revolution, the most serious threat to liberty was regularly considered to be the spirit of faction, a belief that governed Burke's own thinking on internal and colonial issues. This traditional republican analysis had been re-equipped by Hutcheson's updated benevolist version which provided it with a more elaborate and closely worked moral foundation and vocabulary. Still Hutcheson's indebtedness to the political thought of men like Toland and Harrington, as well as Shaftesbury, is unmistakable. So too is

Burke's. This can be readily acknowledged without denying the difference that did make itself decisively clear after 1790.

According to Harrington,

> A Common-Wealth is nothing else but the National Conscience. And if the Conviction of a Man's private Conscience produces his Private Religion, the conviction of the National Conscience must produce a national Religion.[38]

The bulk of the commentary on Burke's idea of British liberty, or of Liberty as such, sits uneasily with the important distinction between liberty as a private matter, that demands as a right non-interference from arbitrary power, and liberty as public participation.[39] Burke, like Harrington and Hutcheson, insists on a relationship between private and national concience even though he, no more than they, is not able (nor wants to) show this philosophically. Instead, like them, he is ready to demonstrate it historically, from ancient or from British history. Law creates freedom, it does not constrain it; the complexity of accumulated case law attends and attests to the variety of human experience. It has axiomatic force which he finds preferable to conceptual rigour and transparency. Indeed transparency is precisely what is not wanted in a political system because that would rob it of the mysterious quality that resides in the processes of historical growth and that gives to power that awe-inspiring quality that induces reverence as well as provoking a submission that is freely given.

Perhaps it is at this juncture that Burke's many affiliations with the republican tradition and with the benevolists fade away. There may be resemblances between his view of the French Revolution and, say, John Toland's view of the Cromwellian dictatorship and the misnamed commonwealth; he is closer to Harrington than to Hobbes or Sir Robert Filmer in his view of the law and of the linkages between private and national freedom. But it is when the dispute between Burke and contemporaries, like Richard Price, Joseph Priestley or Thomas Paine, is opened out in the 1790s that the role of mystery or secrecy in Burke's thought is fully revealed in contrast to their ache for transparency. It is not entirely unfair to say that he makes a mystique of power. But it is more to the point to say that he has an aristocratic concept of secrecy that relies on the belief in an arcanum of knowledge available only to a select few and even then not necessarily wholly revealed to them. This is a knowledge that the mass of the people have an intuitive sense of, although no cognitive access to it. It expresses itself in the theatrical splendours of monarchy and of aristocracy but these splendours are themselves mediated versions of the divinity that doth hedge a king (or queen).

Despite the intense effort on Burke's part to resacralise political power and to make consent seem like an exercise in mystification, many elements survive from the earlier phase of his thought, the American, so to say, as opposed to the later French phase. They remain prominent in the writings on India and Ireland. The late attacks of 1792 on the Penal Laws in Ireland are of a piece with his earlier writings; they remain almost entirely free of the new version of political obedience that he forged for his anti-revolutionary philosophy. As in the case of America, he still cited the basic republican doctrine to which Hutcheson had given a heightened lustre. Liberty exists only when there is no arbitrary power, even when not exercised. 'The mildness by which absolute masters exercise their dominion, leaves them masters still.'[40] Hutcheson and Swift (although in the latter's case from an entirely different political position) would have agreed with that and with its bitter pertinence to one of the central deformities of the colonial system in Ireland. The Irish and Indian cases were so severe that they threatened the constitution itself. In America, Burke could say, 'We lost our Colonies but we kept our Constitution.'[41] But in keeping the Irish or Indian colonies, his anxiety was that such a boast could not safely be made.

3. MONTESQUIEU AND BURKE

Burke, Montesquieu and Ireland

Montesquieu's great work, *L' Esprit des lois* was published in 1748; the first English translation, by Thomas Nugent, appeared in 1750. There was a Dublin reprint 'with corrections and additions communicated by the author' in 1751, again in 1767, and a further two in 1792. Thomas Nugent, was possibly known to Burke, and was once thought to be connected to Burke's wife's family. Burke certainly knew Lord Charlemont, who met Montesquieu in 1754 and 1755. It is in the first of these meetings that Montesquieu expressed his view of the Irish situation. Charlemont reports:

> In the course of our conversations, Ireland, and its interests, have often been the topic; and upon these occasions, I have always found him an advocate for an union between that country and England. 'Were I an Irishman', said he, 'I should certainly wish for it; and, as a general lover of liberty, I sincerely desire it; and for this plain reason, that an inferior country, connected with one much her superior in force, can never be certain of the permanent enjoyment of constitutional freedom, unless she has, by her representatives, a proportional share in the legislature of the superior kingdom.'[1]

This is not a view which Burke would have shared; but he would have agreed with Montesquieu's criticisms of the conquest of Ireland, the confiscation of her lands, the Navigation Acts that crippled her trade and the Penal Laws against Catholics.[2]

It is also well known that Burke's Catholic relations, the Nagles of County Cork, with whom he lived for five years – 1735–40 – had connections with France. Indeed, there were especially close connections between County Cork and the Irish College at Bordeaux, which was itself close to Montesquieu's home. In addition, there were close trading links between Cork and Bordeaux in which Montesquieu, in his capacity as a wine exporter, played a part.[3]

Recent research on Burke's connections with County Cork and, specifically, the Blackwater Valley, has emphasised the moulding influence upon him of the experience of the Catholic families who lived there under the dominion of the Protestant regime that asserted its power in a memorable and scandalous manner on four celebrated occasions, by the murder, judicial or otherwise, of four men – Sir James Cotter in 1720, Morty Oge O'Sullivan in 1754, Arthur O'Leary in 1773 and, most notorious of all, Father Nicholas Sheehy in 1766.[4] Louis Cullen has gone so far as to say that Eoghan Rua O Súilleabháin and

Burke share the same (political) language and views and that they are 'those of the Blackwater'.[5] It would, then, be possible to claim that it was this specific experience that governed Burke's general view of the Protestant 'junta' in Ireland; this is what lies behind the assault on the Protestant Ascendancy that is most fully and angrily formulated in the 1792 'Letter to Sir Hercules Langrishe'.[6] The passage in which Burke remembers the events of 1761–66 deserves quotation in full:

> I do not desire to revive all the particulars in my memory; I wish them to sleep for ever; but it is impossible I should wholly forget, what happened in some parts of Ireland, with very few and short intermissions, from the year 1761 to the year 1766, both inclusive. In a country of miserable police, passing from the extremes of laxity to the extremes of rigour, among a neglected, and therefore disorderly populace – if any disturbance or sedition, from any grievance real or imaginary happened to arise, it was presently perverted from its true nature (often criminal enough in itself to draw upon it a severe appropriate punishment), it was metamorphosed into a conspiracy against the state, and prosecuted as such. Amongst the Catholics, as being, by far, the most numerous and the most wretched, all sorts of offenders against the laws must commonly be found. The punishment of low people for the offences usual amongst low people, would warrant no inference against any descriptions of religion or of politicks. Men of consideration from their age, their profession, or their character; men of proprietary landed estates, substantial renters, opulent merchants, physicians and titular bishops, could not easily be suspected of riot in open day, of nocturnal assemblies for the purpose of pulling down hedges, making breaches in park walls, firing barns, maiming cattle, and outrages of a similar nature, which characterise the disorders of an oppressed or a licentious populace. But when the evidence given on the trial for such misdemeanours, qualified them as overt acts of high treason, and when witnesses were found (such witnesses as they were) to depose the taking of oaths of allegiance by the rioters to the king of France, to their being paid by his money, and embodied and exercised under his officers, to overturn the state for the purposes of that potentate; in that case, the rioters might (if the witness was to be believed) be supposed only the troops, and persons more reputable, the leaders and commanders in such a rebellion. All classes in the obnoxious description, who could not be suspected of the lower crime of riot, might be involved in the odium, in the suspicion, and sometimes in the punishment, of a higher and far more criminal species of offence. These proceeedings did not arise from any one of the Popery laws since repealed, but from this circumstance, that when it answered the puproses of an election party, or a malevolent person of influence to forge such plots, the people had no protection. The people of that description have no hold on the gentlemen who aspire to be popular representatives. The candidates neither love, nor respect, nor fear them individually or collectively. I do not think this evil (an evil amongst a thousand others) at this day entirely over; for I conceive I have lately seen some indication of a disposition perfectly similar to the old one; that is, a disposition to carry the imputation of crimes

> from persons to descriptions, and wholly to alter the character and quality of the offences themselves.[7]

Because the 'sequence of gentry episodes of blood' just listed 'had no parallels elsewhere',[8] Burke's wide-ranging indictment of the whole system may be said to have derived from a local and untypical regional experience. This is possible. But it is also the case that the Blackwater Valley episodes could be seen as locally enhanced examples of the whole political system in Ireland and that Burke is the first to identify that system as characteristic of the colonial structures that Britain had to learn to incorporate within the British constitution. Without such incorporation the way was open to various forms of coercive, despotic rule which ominously heralded the revolutionary despotism that was to take power in France in the final decade of the century.[9]

Since Burke also linked the Protestant Ascendancy's brutalities in Ireland (or in the Blackwater Valley) with those of Warren Hastings in India and those of the Jacobins in Paris, it would seem to be an implication of Cullen's argument that his apocalyptic political vision of the 1790s owes a remarkable debt to his knowledge and experience of the plight of Cork Catholics, including his own relations, over a period of about sixty years. While it could hardly be said that Hastings or the Jacobins behaved in a manner that was untypical either of British colonialism or of radical revolutionaries, the suspicion still lingers that his Irish experience exercised such a determinant influence on Burke that he read international politics in the light of it. If he was wrong in general about the Protestant Ascendancy, perhaps he was wrong on the other issues too; or perhaps he was right about them and wrong about the Ascendancy? It would be of a piece with the view that Burke manifested a notable level of paranoia in the 1790s, not only in his vision of an isomorphic Irish-French-Indian structure of internal corruption within their various polities, but also with his belief in an external conspiracy of Illuminati, philosophes and Freemasons to overthrow altar and throne in Europe.

In effect, if there is substance in this account, Burke is not to be taken seriously as a political thinker, especially on Irish affairs. As an intellectual, or as a rhetorician, or as a hired gun for the Whigs, or as an apologist for the Irish Catholics, the French emigrés or the Begum of Oudh, he is too partisan to be reliable. For reliability, some less partisan witness must be found, although it is a puzzle to know just what definition of partisanship would allow one to discover such a commentator. Of course, it has always been a feature of Burke's reception, both in his own time and since, that he has been regarded as a suspect witness to and analyst of the events of his own time. Caricatured endlessly as a closet Catholic, who had been educated at Saint-Omer outside Paris by the Jesuits, or as a bourgeois apologist for an aristocratic order that he at once despised and admired, Burke has constantly been, in one incarnation, subject to local assaults on his religious beliefs, his national allegiance, his 'outsider' pathology; in another, he has been canonised as the most profound analyst of Revolution and of the alteration that the French Revolution inaugurated in Europe and the world.[10]

Montesquieu, on the other hand, has always enjoyed the reputation of being a sage, a founding figure in political and social science, and a reliable, if not always satisfactory, commentator on the French and European political systems before the French Revolution. In him, more than in any other figure, the best qualities of the philosophe and the *érudit* were said to be combined. Burke, indeed, contributed in no small measure to this version of Montesquieu's reputation in the English-speaking and in the European world, supported early in this by Gibbon's 1761 *Essai sur l'étude de la littérature*. He made his admiration clear as early as 1757, when he praised Montesquieu as a genius of the first order in his *Abridgement of English History*. Thirty-four years later, he praised him again, more fulsomely and at more length, in *An Appeal from the New to the Old Whigs* (1791). On the second occasion, Montesquieu was chosen both for his own qualities and for the contrast which he made with the radical and revolutionary thinkers, Rousseau most prominent among them. It was, by then, beginning to be a standard feature of counter-revolutionary writings to ascribe to the radicals a shallow egoism and to the *érudits* a profound scholarship and respect for the complexity of human affairs. The scandal of revolutionary thought was that it was so simplistic and authoritarian in its schematic purity; in the case of Rousseau, it was also, according to Burke, the product of an eccentric and diseased sensibility which claimed for itself a universality that was both absurd and frightening. It is ironic that Burke deployed arguments against Rousseau that were to be used against himself, especially arguments or polemics that ascribed the formulation of a political philosophy to the psychology, even the pathology, of its creator.

Even though Burke was anxious to enhance this contrast between Montesquieu and the other pre-revolutionary French philosophes, he did not, on that account, give a wholly tendentious account of Montesquieu's thought. He learned from Montesquieu – especially from *L' Esprit des lois* and from the *Considérations sur les causes de la grandeur des romaines et de leur décadence* – the art of analysing political systems in relation to their prevailing circumstances and also of achieving the formulation of general laws that governed these systems and made history intelligible. In many ways, Burke's own writings aspire to the same admixture of laboriously detailed research on particular issues and wise *sentential*, although he did not share Montesquieu's confidence in the illumination that the discovery of first principles would shed on human affairs. But, for all the differences between them, Burke was influential in establishing the view that Montesquieu had offered an analysis of the *ancien régime* in France that demonstrated how it could have been effectively reformed without revolution. He consistently refused to see Montesquieu as one of those men of letters whose ideas had helped to destroy traditional France. Central to Montesquieu's achievement, as Burke saw it, was the defence of traditional aristocratic rights and an appeal to the example of the mixed constitution of England for the liberation of France from centralised monarchical control.

Montesquieu and Burke: Britain and France

A brief account of the principles of Montesquieu's political thought would identify the following features: an ever-changing relationship between what he calls 'raison primitive' and positive law and custom; the existence of a specific 'principe' which characterises the main forms of moderate political systems – democracy, aristocracy and monarchy; a belief that man is determined only to a limited degree by the physical laws of nature; and a melancholy conviction that political systems have a natural tendency towards despotism. This last point is exemplified for him in the fall of Rome and in the history of France in the seventeenth and eighteenth centuries. He shared the contemporary conviction that the decline of the Roman Empire was a dire warning to all European states, France most of all. This is countered by his apotheosis of England, of the 1688 Revolution and of the British constitution, which he famously described (or misinterpreted) in Book XI, chapter six of the *Lois*. It was, of course, pleasing to Burke and to many others in England that Montesquieu should have seen the British constitution as the ideal system for the production of liberty.

> Il y a une nation dans le monde qui a pour objet direct de sa constitution la liberté politique. Nous allons examiner les principes sur lesquels elle la fonde. S'ils sont bons, la liberté y paroîtra comme dans une miroir.[11]

The question that concerns us here is the use to which Burke put Montesquieu's version of the British constitution, his account of the decline of France into despotism and his analysis of the 'esprit général' which characterised all nation states. Since he was writing, for part of the time, after the French Revolution, it is understandable that Burke should have given prominence to features of Montesquieu's writings which supported his own anti-revolutionary stance.

Montesquieu's famous separation of the three powers – executive, legislative and judical – is, in itself, a formulation which has within it an implied tribute to the idea of complexity. The three powers are not always separate from one another; but, in Europe, they are rarely confounded in one person. When they are, we are looking at the phenomenon of Oriental despotism, the antithesis of English liberty.

> Dans la plupart des royaumes de l'Europe, le gouvernement est modéré, parce que le prince, qui a les deux premiers pouvoirs, laisse à ses sujets l'exercice du troisième. Chez les Turcs, où ces trois pouvoirs sont réunis sur la tête du sultan, il règne un affreux despotisme.[12]

When the powers are separate, there is a risk of paralysis; but, as he argues in the same section of the *Lois*, Montesquieu believed that since they were obliged to operate 'par le mouvement nécessaire des choses', they would operate in concert. The reciprocal interactions between the three would produce a 'concordia discors'. Friction was both inevitable and necessary, for the rivalry between the powers assured that no one would predominate. The result was 'une union d'harmonie'.[13] Competing ideologies, a struggle for the rights pertaining to one or other branch of government, stimulated the health of the political system. Only within and through this complicated arrangement could the complexity of the society find adequate expression.

Although Montesquieu does render his account of political systems in an almost diagrammatic form, it does not follow that he gives theoretical purity priority over specific circumstances. In his *Lettres de Xénocrate à Phères*, he claims the ruler who believes in theory and in perfection will often be more struck by a political fault or evil than by the inconvenience of repairing it. But it might be necessary to tolerate it, for the people may regard certain practices which are rationally inconsistent with the theory of a government as equivalent to laws, simply because they have been ratified by habit, by time and, perhaps, were at one time, ratified by reason itself. Logical consistency is not a virtue at all times. The people cannot 'changer d'esprit dans un moment'. This line of thinking leads Montesquieu towards his formulation of the 'esprit général' and is, I suggest, the element in his thought which Burke made central to his own political philosophy. The lack of uniformity in a European system of moderate government is not, therefore, a flaw. Uniformity is attainable only under despotism:

> Un gouvernement despotique, au contraire, saute, pour ainsi dire, aux yeux: il est uniforme partout: comme il ne faut que des passions pour l'établir, tout le monde est bon pour cela.[14]

Complexity, on the other hand, can be classified into four categories which are never, in practice, distinct from one another; these correspond to the four major divisions of *L' Esprit des lois*. The first contains political systems and forms (Books I–XIII); the second, physical and climatic influences (Books XIV–XVIII); the third, social forms (Books XIX–XXVI); the fourth, historical influences and examples (Books XXVII–XXXI). Central to the whole argument is Book XIX, which discusses the 'esprit général'. It is central because in it we learn the main differences between moderate and despotic systems. Despotism has neither past nor future; it is the instant product of the individual will. Moderate governments are essentially evolutionary systems, belonging in part to the physical world of nature and the historical world of culture. They are susceptible to analysis for an account of their different forms but they are organisms of such delicacy that any sudden intervention, any upsetting of the fragile balance of powers which generates their growth, leads to ruin and, inevitably, to the rigidities of despotism.

This is a brilliant reordering of the distinction between Europe and the Orient. In the revolutionary era, Burke exploits this to the full, seeing the revolution as precisely that kind of intervention in the historically evolved European system that will lead to its downfall and its replacement by the regime of the despotic instant, regimes that have no respect for custom, habit, affection or complexity, in which all powers are confounded in one person whose whim thereby becomes law. The French Revolution, so viewed, is something non-European, Oriental not Occidental, a repudiation of the idea of complexity and, with that, of moderation – although Burke also says the converse of this when he denounces the description of the French monarchical system as though it were an Oriental despotism.[15] The pursuit of theoretical purity is indulged at the expense of traditional habit and yet the consequent uniformity, no matter how stern it may be, is ultimately rooted in one person's will. Burke read Montesquieu's version of Oriental despotism as an advance sketch for the despotic revolutionary government of France, even though Burke knew better than most that Montesquieu's version of the Orient was a European fiction that was used to justify French and British imperial warmongering in Asia, a point forcibly made by Anquetil-Duperron in his *Législation orientale* of 1778.[16] However, the application of Montesquieu's version of Oriental despotism to the France of Louis XIV was more appealing to Burke, since it could so readily be adapted as a description of the forces that brought about the catastrophic extinction of the France of Louis XVI. (Yet it must be said that Burke declared Montesquieu's description of Indian civilisation as without laws was plainly wrong when Montesquieu was cited by Hastings to sanction his own behaviour in India).[17] The adaptation is one-sided, since it emphasises the idea of absolute and unmediated will and underplays the paralysis and silence of the Montesquiean despotism, the fear that produces tranquillity. What Burke saw was a despotism that annulled a historic and complex culture and replaced it, not with inertia, but with a frenzied and voracious energy. Still, he stayed close to Montesquieu's view of despotism as a system that produced not order but uniformity. As order was to liberty, so was uniformity to tyranny.

Montesquieu is regarded as one of the founders of sociology because he developed a theory of a culture as an integrated system, the product of general causes operating within a specific set of circumstances.

> Plusieurs choses gouvernement les hommes: le climat, la religion, les lois, les maximes du gouvernement, les exemples de choses passées, les moeurs, les matières; d'où il se forme un esprit général qui en résulte.[18]

Given that, what might be regarded as vices from the point of view of another culture may have a particular function or be part of an intricate system in another. The traditional fidelity of the Spaniard, for instance, has a connection with his traditional laziness. The conscious reforming activity of the legislator in attempting to correct a vice might seriously impair the whole system in which the 'vice' is embedded. It is necessary to accept imperfection or, perhaps, complexity, since imperfection is not easily ascribed within a system that functions to any one of its parts. So, let man be; 'qu' on nous laisse tels que nous sommes'.[19]

This is not merely a defence of abuse. But it does mean that Montesquieu has to make a distinction between moral and political values. There might be some characteristics of a people (for example, laziness, drunkenness) which are not morally admirable but that might be politically useful. It is hard to say to what extent Montesquieu was covering himself against a clerical attack when he wrote this:

> Je n'ai point pour diminuer rien de la distance infinie qu'il y a entre les vices et les vertus: à Dieu ne plaise! J'ai seulement voulu faire comprendre que tous les vices politiques ne sont pas des vices morales; et c'est ce que ne doivent point ignorer ceux qui font des lois qui choquent l'esprit général.[20]

The apparent dominance of political influences over those of physical circumstances does not subvert the account, for it would seem that Montesquieu envisaged the replacement of physical by political and moral influences as a sign of a highly developed civilisation. The more advanced the civilisation, the less was it subject to purely physical laws – although there was, in the end, no absolute escape from them possible. The point is that he can be read as saying that we live in such a complex balance of forces that change should be only rarely or tenderly attempted. The conservative bias of his thought is certainly pronounced in the short term; in the long term, there is at least the suggestion of an eventual transformation. Burke evidently looked at the short term implications and made them, in his own writings, the ground for his long-term scepticism about the human capacity for improvement.

More immediately important for Burke was Montesquieu's analysis of what had gone wrong in mid-century France and what was needed to put it right. Much of what Burke says in the *Reflections on the Revolution in France* (1790) about the old French system – its capacity for an improvement which would have fallen short of revolution and yet would have gone far beyond revolution in bringing about the changes needed – owes its substance to Montesquieu. In Book IV of *L' Esprit des lois*, Montesquieu dealt with old feudal laws of the Franks in such a way as to make it plain that he favoured the recovery by the contemporary aristocracy of the privileges which had been lost under the despotic rule of Louis XIV. He used the feudal system as a historical support for the aristocratic case, more urgent in this, perhaps, because he was himself a comparatively new member of that thrustful section of the aristocracy, the *nobles de la robe*. This was visible to the extreme royalists who attacked Montesquieu after the Restoration: le Comte de Saint-Romain, in his *Réfutation de la doctrine de Montesquieu sur la balance des pouvoirs* (1816) saw the Charter of 1814 as a victory for 'la transcendance de la royauté'. I mention this here because this royalist position seems to be close to that of Burke and his glorification in the *Reflections* of the French royal family. Yet Burke was too much a man of 1688, too much the long-term opponent of George III and the King's friends, to sponsor the cause of monarchy in so outright a fashion. He was perfectly willing to dispel the shadow of divine right from monarchy when he was defending the rights of parliament against monarchical encroachment, but he was also perfectly capable of reintroducing it as a historical memory in order to counteract the iconoclastic and secular spirit of the revolution which denied all divine inspiration or guidance in human affairs. Like Montesquieu, he believed that the remedy for the political ills which were the heritage of Louis XIV could have been cured by the reintroduction of the rights of the *parlements* and of the aristocratic powers which had formerly intervened between the direct power of the king and the people. France was, in the view of both men, on the way to becoming a despotism but it still had the corporate bodies and the traditions which, reinvigorated, could restore it to its former status as a 'moderate' European government.

As we have seen, 'European' was a key word here. It helped enhance the contrast with the 'Orient' (represented for most Europeans by Turkey) and with the ancient world, of which the so-called Orient was an extension. Europe had been formed in its essential features by the Roman Empire, for it, unlike the Asiatic despotisms, had allowed a diversity which did not deny a fundamental unity. Montesquieu's political theory of the balance of powers within a state was matched by his notion of a balance of European powers or nation-states which was just as delicate and as necessary:

> L'Europe n'est plus qu'une Nation composées de plusieurs; la France et l'Angleterre ont besoin de l'opulence de la Pologne et de la Muscovie, comme une de leurs Provinces a besoin des autres: et l'Etat qui croît augmenter sa puissance par la ruine de celui qui touche, s'affoiblit ordinairement avec lui.[21]

What distinguished modern Europe from the Roman Empire was the arrival of Christianity. It had two effects, according to Montesquieu. In the first place, the despotic paternalism of the Romans was broken by the new Christian emphasis on celibacy; by that, the extreme dependence of children on their parents was reduced. This, in turn, led to the emergence of a greater diversity in Europe, since that which had been ancestrally established before Christianity had subsequently less hold than on the new generations. On the other hand, Christian celibacy encouraged the contemplative life, which Montesquieu thought unsuited to the development of a healthy social system and it undermined the status of the married state, thus unwittingly ratifying the behaviour of those libertines who avoided it.[22] Montesquieu goes on to contrast Christian contemplatives with the Stoics who combined a distaste for the grosser pleasures of this life with a committed sense of duty to society at large. These stoical virtues were, he argues, transposed from the classical world to Protestantism in the Christian world. The liberty of the Protestant states of Europe seemed to him to be a natural product of their more independent form of the Christian religion, their more invigorating (more northerly) climate and to vary only in degree in relation to the particular form of Protestantism that prevailed – Lutheran or Calvinist. Catholicism, found in the more languid climates of the *midi*, and visibly ruled by a single figure, was less productive of liberty.[23] Its closest political analogue was monarchy and France was the country in which the political form and the religious influences had been most notably combined to produce a system which was manifestly less free than that of Protestant England with its modified monarchy and its various independent religious sects. The heading of the fifth chapter of Book XXIV – 'That the Catholic religion better suits a monarchy and that a Protestant religion is better adapted to a republic' – gives away more than the actual discussion which follows. This investigation of the linkages between Europe's Protestant North and Catholic south, taken up in relatively casual form in Burke's writings, is not fully developed until the writings of Mme de Staël in the first two decades of the nineteenth-century.[23]

Burke's Montesquieu and the French Revolution

Turning to Burke, then, we can see in what respects Montesquieu's writings proved useful to him in his crusade against the French Revolution. The defence of historically accredited aristocratic rights against the increasing despotism of the French monarchy, the glorification of the British Constitution, the general defence of complexity culminating in the formulation of the idea of an integrated culture, the identification of Europe as an exemplary instance of such a culture, heavily dependent on its Christian inheritance and wholly distinct from the culture of the Orient – all of these elements recur in his writings both before and after the French Revolution, although their predominance increases markedly after 1789. Yet all of them operate in Burke in a different manner and, obviously, for a different purpose.

Montesquieu's elaboration of the 'esprit général' and its relation to the nation-state as such, and to the European community of nations, is transformed by Burke into something at once vaguer and more powerful in its appeal. Europe was indeed, in his view, a historical entity, containing a diversity of nation-states which, despite their differences, had many fundamental principles and values in common. The system of internal bonding that gave a nation its coherence was a local version of the system that gave Europe its cultural integrity. When he speaks of this, Burke does not reproduce Montesquieu's diagrammatic descriptions of the balance of internal powers in a constitution. In fact, he believed (rightly) that Montesquieu had seen in the British Constitution a separation of powers that did not exist. What he does do, instead, is to seize upon the notion that the constitution operates like something that is natural, not man-made; it lacks symmetry, it lacks manifest clarity and yet it works in mysterious but successful ways:

> To avoid the perfections of extreme, all of its several parts are so constituted, as not alone to answer their several ends, but also each to limit and control the others; insomuch that . . . you will find its operation checked and stopped at a certain point . . . From thence it results, that in the British constitution, there is a perpetual treaty and compromise going on, sometimes openly, sometimes with less observation. To him who contemplates the subordinate material world, it will always be a matter of the most curious investigation, to discover the secret of this mutual imitation.[25]

The secret is, of course, not discoverable. Montesquieu may have thought the constitution beautiful; Burke sees it as sublime. Everything that is central to the functioning of a nation-state, as Burke understood it, is either secret or virtual. Even when he denounced the failure of the British system in Ireland, he did so on the grounds that it failed to give to the Irish that 'virtual representation' which, in the England of rotten boroughs and oligarchic rule, was the most they could ever expect to have. But that was also the most that was needed in a proper system. In the *Second Letter to Sir Hercules Langrishe* (1795), he declared:

> Virtual representation is that in which there is a communion of interests, and a sympathy in feeling and desires between those who act in the name of any description of people, and the people in whose name they act, though the trustees are not actually chosen by them.[26]

A nation in which such processes takes place is a 'moral essence, not a geographical arrangement'.[27] It makes its presence and its nature clear but by indecipherable means. In fact, the nation is clearly what it is because its principle of bonding and of derivation is beyond analysis. For anything that is amenable to analytic scrutiny is not secret, not mysterious. Burke indicates time and again that mystery is the source of all our human enterprise. It is closely related to affection, to moral sense, to the workings of political arrangements, to historical processes and to the spirit of a people. But what it is in itself cannot be formulated; to attempt to do so is impious as well as foolish. Moral essence is constituted by natural aristocracy and natural aristocracy is the virtual expression of common feeling. The proof of this is simple. If it is true, the nation survives; if not, the nation is destroyed.

Montesquieu's 'esprit général' is thus transformed into an almost mystical notion that informs and is expressed in historical experience. During the revolutionary era, Burke applied to the idea of the European system of nations the same notions of secrecy, virtuality and sublimity as he had to the 1688 settlement in England. It was a system that, in its diversity, sustained a fundamental unity; in its divisions, it retained an underlying interdependence.

Christianity bound Europe into one common culture and within a single providential destiny; the sectarian distinctions between the various religious factions were ultimately less important than their similarities. Protestantism, the national religion of England, could not survive the destruction of Catholicism, the national religion of France.

> This religious war is not a controversy between sect and sect as formerly, but a war against all sects and religions. The question is not whether you are to overturn the catholick, to set up the protestant. Such an idea in the present state of the world is too contemptible. Our business is to leave to the schools the discussion of the controverted points, abating as much as we can the acrimony of the disputants on all sides. It is for christian Statesmen, as the world is now circumstanced, to secure their common Basis, and not to risque the subversion of the whole Fabrick by pursuing these distinctions with an ill-timed zeal.[28]

Further, the whole system of manners that characterised Europe derived from that common Christian heritage. Chivalric modes of conduct, towards women, between warriors, in relation to prisoners, the whole ethical system that had Christian morals as its ground and support, would disappear with the defeat of religion.

> The hell-hounds of war, on all sides, will be uncoupled and unmuzzled. The new school of murder and barbarism, set up in Paris, having destroyed (so far as in it lies) all the other manners and principles which have hitherto civilized Europe, will destroy also the mode of civilized war, which, more than anything else, has distinguished the Christian world.[29]

Montesquieu had also claimed that Christian Europe purged war of its more barbaric cruelties.[30] But Christianity and feudalism, investigated by him as historical phenomena that had a bearing upon the present, were revised by Burke as forces in which a transcendent power operated by mysterious means to preserve, in Europe, a culture which was the product of a history in which God was immanent.

Therefore in relation to revolutionary France, Burke could easily adopt the principle of an appeal to complexity and, like Montesquieu, to the 'concordia discors'. When he does so, there is always in addition an appeal to the latent providential design which, since it is visible in the historical past must also be concealed in the present. Diversity, variety and complexity, by intricate processes, produce harmony and order.

> In your old states you possessed that variety of parts corresponding with the various descriptions of which your community was happily composed; you had that action and counteraction which, in the natural and in the political world, from the reciprocal struggle of discordant powers, draws out the harmony of the universe. These opposed and conflicting interests which you considered so great a blemish in your old and in our present constitution, interpose a salutary check to all precipitate resolutions.[31]

The harmony he speaks of here is self-generated; it is not created by 'precipitate resolutions' nor is it elicited by any form of interference which is not itself in accord with the 'spirit' of the constitution and the nation. Burke did promote the idea of gradual reform and, as far as pre-revolutionary France was concerned, he was obliged to admit the necesssity of it. Yet he was not merely cautious and gradualist in his approach. To tinker with the established system was wrong unless the adjustments were designed to preserve, not to reduce or annihilate, the presence within all parts of the system of its abiding spirit. Therefore he was worried by the writings of men like J.L. de Lolme, William Blackstone, Dean Tucker and Adam Ferguson on the British constitution because – influenced to a degree by Montesquieu – they tried to apply the notion of the separation of powers with a strictness and consistency that seemed to him anomalous in relation to such a mysteriously derived and complex entity. De Lolme argued against the predominance of the legislature; Blackstone for the power and prerogative of the king. The balance of powers seemed to Burke 'a contrivance full of danger',[32] particularly because Blackstone, the most prestigious of these constitutional commentators, seemed to advocate the priority of the king, something against which Burke had long fought since his early days as a Rockingham Whig.[33] In England, as in France, there was one guiding principle for reform: stay in accord with the spirit of the constitution and the nation.

To do so was, in Burke's view, analogous to preserving an inheritance. The legal metaphor is apt, since he often referred to the system of legal precedent as the surest guide to any attempted legal change or innovation. But, in complete opposition to a radical reformer like Jeremy Bentham, Burke admired and cherished the unwieldy and disorganised bulk of legal precedent. As always, asymmetry was a mark of complexity. The French Revolution would replace this with symmetry, order and the perniciously egoistic opinions of the individual, disguised as principles of right, claiming a theoretical purity while actually being individually eccentric.

> And first of all, the science of jurisprudence, the pride of the human intellect, which, with all its defects, redundancies, and errors, is the collected reason of ages, combining the principles of original justice with the infinite variety of human concerns, as a heap of old exploded errors, would no longer be studied. Personal self-sufficiency and arrogance . . . would usurp the tribunal.[34]

The new theory of the individual was the chief enemy. Individualism, as a political project, repudiated the past and looked upon its inheritors in a spirit of vengeance.

Thus, Burke objected to the persecution of the clergy by the revolutionaries on the grounds that it is unjust to punish men for the sins of their ancestors, even if those men are the beneficiaries of former injustices. He wanted to preserve what he called 'the fiction of ancestry in a corporate succession' and to do that, he had to see the nation, as he saw the French monasteries and the French clergy, as a corporate body.

> Corporate bodies are immortal for the good of the members, but not for their punishment. Nations themselves are such corporations. As well might we in England think of waging inexpiable war upon all Frenchmen for the evils which they have brought on us in the several periods of our mutual hostilities.[35]

But Burke's appeal to English legal history has a further implication. All his citations of Magna Carta, Coke, Bracton, the men of 1688, are designed to convey an essential point about the English character – that the English have always chosen the appeal to precedent and to history over the appeal to abstract principle and universal rights. But he wants to go further, especially in the revolutionary years. He wants to claim that this specific trait of the English is 'natural', that it is human in the most fundamental sense. Those who yearn for abstract principle are those who belong to no community; they live in a state of psychic anarchy and therefore seek justification for themselves in the promulgation of doctrines which would annihilate the very idea of historical community and continuity. They have no access to, are not enfolded within, the 'esprit général'; for them, existence is an experiment. The revolutionary is in love with risk; the conservative is in love with precedent.

Out of this emerges a final paradox. France had, in Burke's view, exchanged a species of despotism for a species of anarchy. Montesquieu had characterised despotism as the *régime* of the instant moment, founded on personal will, eccentric in its origin but appallingly uniform in its manifestations. It was this version of despotism that Burke ascribed to revolutionary France and he seemed to believe it a matter of indifference whether it was called despotism or anarchy. Revolution as such was flawed by an inherent contradiction. It spoke of liberty and created dictatorship; it reduced human diversity to the demands of uniform and universal principles; it regarded human existence as a problem and not as a mystery. Worst of all, it liberated people into barbarism in the name of progress. It persuaded them to give to the abstract idea of the State an allegiance which would never have been demanded of them by the Nation. The war against France was, as he wrote in a letter of 1793 to the Duke of Buckingham, 'a war to civilize France, in order to prevent the rest of Europe being barbarised'.[36] Europe was in danger of becoming a drear Oriental waste, a despotic system which allowed of no difference or distinction, and where power exercised the function which had once belonged to authority.

In *L' Esprit des lois,* Montesquieu had described the perfect despotism. In it he claimed,

> Il n'y a point de tempérament, de modifications, d'accomodements, de termes, d'equivalents, de pourparlers, de rémontrance; . . . l'homme est une créature qui obéit à une créature qui veut.[37]

In 1795, writing to William Elliott, Burke admitted the charge of 'the jockey of Norfolk', Thomas Paine, that he had defended the British constitution in its entirety,

> . . . loaded with all its incumbrances, clogged with its peers, and its beef; its parsons and its pudding; its commons, its beer; and its dull slavish liberty of going about just as one pleases . . .[38]

That was just the point. The constitution of England, the old constitution of France, the system of European civilisation, with all their respective faults and flaws, their incoherence and their disorderly arrangements, were in accord with the unpredictable and complex nature and history of the human person. Ultimately, there was no order that man could discern but there was an order of which he could have a sense, an awareness. When this was replaced by man-made order, when all the circumstantial and specific aspects of geography, history and precedent were removed, then the order which was the consequence could only be artificial and despotic. In its thoroughness it would be more symmetrical; equally, it would in its functions and consequences be more anarchic. To be human, we had to assent to our place in a wider community, of the dead, the living and those to come. To be revolutionary, we had to assent to the titanic will of the here and now, embodied in a particular leader or group. To give such assent is to cease to be fully human. It is a surrender of civilisation to barabarism, of actual experience to abstract principle. Montesquieu's characterisation of the French despotism of the seventeenth and eighteenth centuries was adjusted by Burke to fit the authoritarianism of the French Revolution. Human nature itself was being altered. It would have been wiser and better to leave it as it was, doing as it pleased. What Burke and the revolutionaries made of Montesquieu is an exemplary instance of the reinvention of a political text for diametrically opposed purposes.

Burke's Montesquieu and Ireland

It is in the light of this particular interpretation of Montesquieu that Burke's view of Ireland may be reconsidered. He was suspicious of the concentration of power in the hands of any group or person whose interests were hostile to those of the people at large. In the *Second Letter to Sir Hercules Langrishe* (1795), he defined the common element that linked Protestant Ascendancy in Ireland, what he called 'Indianism' and Jacobinism:

> Whatever tends to persuade the people, that the *few*, called by whatever name you please, religious or political, are of opinion that their interest is not compatible with that of the *many*, is a great point gained to Jacobinism.[39]

This does not at all mean that Burke was in any remote sense sympathetic to democracy. Rather the reverse; concentration of power, by alienating the people, risked provoking the kind of insurrection that could lead to democracy. Reform in France was necessary in order to prevent that. This was increasingly Burke's view of the Irish situation as it developed in the 1790s. But it is equally the case that Burke's view of revolutionary France bears a remarkable resemblance to the view of Ireland he had held since his youth. A country ruled by a faction; a country subjected to a revolution in which an old religion had been dispossessed; a country in which a juridically established religious sectarianism was practised by a 'plebeian' oligarchy, pretending to aristocratic rights and privileges, in ignorance of the common cause of Catholicism and Protestantism against atheistic revolution – such a country was Ireland and, in secular mimicry, such a country was revolutionary France. 'The State of France', Burke declared in *Remarks on the Policy of the Allies*, is perfectly simple. It consists of but two descriptions – The Oppressors and the Oppressed.'[40] This is also the situation in Ireland where

> every franchise, every honour, every trust, every place down to the very lowest and least confidential (besides whole professions), is reserved for the master cast.[41]

This is a telling point. Burke wanted to see something similar to the British class system established in Ireland. But that could not happen because of the caste system that operated there, under the principle of a 'universal exclusion'[42] of the Catholics that was against the spirit of the British constitution but was exercised by the Protestants in Ireland who

> considered themselves in no other light than that of a colonial garrison, to keep the natives in subjection to the other state of Great Britain.[43]

Burke takes the colonial situation in Ireland as a model for the revolutionary situation in France. Despite the differences, he sees one as an early version of the other. Where the difference is most marked, in the foundation of the former on a principle of exclusion on religious grounds, he incorporates that too in his lament for the weakening of Christian Europe in the face of international atheistic revolution, brought on by precisely that kind of sectarian bigotry that so disfigured Ireland and debarred it from the benefits of the British constitution. Britain enjoyed the traditional benefits of a traditional, hereditary class system, with all its complex checks and balances between interests which the constituion preserved in a delicate, yet stable, equilibrium. Ireland had all the disadvantages of a caste system, in which there were only oppressors and oppressed and in which traditional habits and customs were starved of constitutional and juridical support.

There has been much commentary on the class–caste distinction in relation to France and England in the vast literature on the French Revolution, but little or no attention has been paid to Burke's inflection of this distinction in relation to Ireland. The best-known of all such commentaries is de

Tocqueville's *L'Ancien régime* (1856). Tocqueville's remarks on both Montesquieu's version of the British political culture and Burke's reading of the Revolution have a direct bearing upon this issue. Tocqueville believed that Montesquieu had only glimpsed the element that distinguished England from all other European states that had inherited the feudal system. In England, caste had been replaced by class; there was intermarraige between nobles and the merchant class.

> It was much less its parliament, its freedom, its press, its jury, which made England even then so different from the rest of Europe, but rather something much more effective, and much more peculiar. England was the only country where the caste system had not merely been changed but really destroyed. In England, nobles and commoners together engaged in the same business, pursued the same professions, and, what is still more important, married each other.[44]

This is pertinent to Tocqueville's accusation that Burke did not see what the French Revolution meant; the dissolution of the feudal system and the common law of European nations:

> Burke does not realise that what stands before his eyes is the revolution which will abolish the old common law of Europe; he does not understand that it is its sole purpose.[45]

These comments go straight to the heart of the relationship between Burke and Montesquieu. Whatever Montesquieu may have said of England and its constitution, he evidently used England as an example for France. His purpose in so doing was to reinstate the power of the nobility, to place effective intermediary bodies between the king and the people; in effect, to restore the power and privileges of his class. Burke was at one with Montesquieu on this. However, he believed that in England the intermediate bodies, which restrained any tendency towards despotism on the part of the king, were more complexly formed than their counterparts in France. His diagnosis is similar to that of Tocqueville, in that he identifies a division in eighteenth-century France between, on the one hand, the 'men of letters' and the 'moneyed classes' and, on the other, the political classes of the nobles, clergy and monarchy. In England, that division had been reconciled. Burke recognised that the British system had in effect brought the landed aristocracy and the mercantile class together within the political system. The social division remained; but it did not produce a corresponding political division. That was the difference. The constitution, in which the three powers were in fact intermixed and not separated, was a contrivance that enabled a conciliation between competing interests. By an intricate system of checks and balances, the product of many trials over a long history, the constitution provided a miraculous stability. It made virtue and commerce compatible one with the other.

However, in the revolutionary period, Burke modified his view of the difference between France and England in relation to their respective caste and class systems, as Tocqueville described them. In *Thoughts on French Affairs* (1791), he repeated his earlier charge that

> The monied men, merchants, principal tradesmen, and men of letters . . . are the chief actors in the French Revolution.

But then he goes on to say:

> I once thought that the low estimation in which commerce was held in France, might be reckoned among the causes of the late revolution; and I am still of opinion, that the exclusive spirit of the French nobility, did irritate the wealthy of other classes. But I found long since, that persons in trade and business were by no means despised in France in the manner I had been taught to believe.[46]

This leads on to the declaration that England is not quite so different from France as has been imagined. Men of wealth and talents might be excited to revolutionary action there as in France.

> In England a security against the envy of men in these classes, is not so very complete as we may imagine. We must not impose upon ourselves.[47]

Tocqueville does not take account of this alteration, however strategic it may be thought to be, in Burke's view of the caste and class systems in England and France. What is consistent in Burke is his opposition to any faction that might upset the traditional system of checks and balances that were characteristic of the British social and political system. The powers of the king, if permitted to inflate, as during the period of the American War and the King's Friends, could threaten to become despotic. Similarly, in colonial circumstances, like those obtaining in India or in Ireland, a faction in which all power was invested could emerge and become a caste, in Tocqueville's sense. This caste could be based on money, as in the case of Warren Hastings and the East India Company; or on religion, as in the case of the Protestant Ascendancy in Ireland. The despotism of such castes was a threat to the constitution. The Jacobin party in Paris was the most recent and formidable example of such a despotic group.

In other words, Burke saw in Montesquieu's reading of French politics a version of what he saw in the American crisis, in Ireland, in India and in revolutionary France – the arrogation of power into the hands of an élite group that was indifferent or hostile to the plight of those deprived of it. Such a concentration was possible because of the destruction of those intermediate bodies that, in complex and subtle ways, dispersed power throughout the whole system and thereby made liberty available and despotism impossible. The Penal Laws in Ireland constituted a grimmer internment camp than the gilded palace of Versailles; but their purpose was the same – the political and judicial demoralisation of a community or class that claimed part of that power for itself. Burke's Blackwater Valley experience may have helped mould his attitude towards the Protestant Ascendancy; Montesquieu was one of those thinkers who helped him to theorise it. The Ascendancy had produced the perilous situation of Ireland in the 1790s; the Indian faction had produced devastation in India and the impeachment of Hastings; the King's Friends had lost the American colonies in war; the Jacobins had destroyed France and threatened to destroy Europe and civilisation. All of these groups acted against the spirit of the cultures they spoliated; all of them were locked within an ideology that provided a rationale for greed and power. Because of the Ascendancy, Ireland was anomalous in the British system; because of the Jacobins, revolutionary France was anomalous within the European system. One was a constitutional monarchy that produced despotism, the other an absolute monarchy that produced revolution.

Much of Burke's effort as a politician and as a political theorist was to understand the paradoxes produced by these situations. After his death, two of the measures widely recommended in the 1790s as a solution to the political crises of the time were put in effect. But, despite the Union – a measure he had never anticipated with enthusiasm – and the Bourbon restoration, which he might have greeted more warmly, the paradoxes remained. In 1829, the year of Catholic Emancipation and within months of the July Revolution in Paris, Eyre Evans Crowe described France as 'une monarchie absolue, temperée par des chansons' and Ireland as 'une monarchie constitutionelle, temperée par des gendarmes'.[48] This is apt. Burke had always understood the relationship in Ireland between coercion and Catholic subjugation; it was the more complex one, between coercion and emancipation, that eluded him. He knew that the British system, as he and Montesquieu both described and understood it, had never transplanted successfully outside the Great Britain of the eighteenth-century. Above all, it had never done so to Ireland, the realm nearest to it. He came to the point of recognising that Ireland's relationship to Britain was, at one level, an internal relationship that could be understood in terms of the British realm; at another level, it was a colonial relationship that could only be understood in terms of the Empire. Burke negotiates between these positions, increasingly anxious to find a language in which to clarify them in face of the threateningly new and highly developed language of revolutionary France.

4. VIRTUE, TRAVEL AND THE ENLIGHTENMENT
SWIFT, DIDEROT, BURKE

I

> Car c'est quasi le même de converser avec ceux des autres siècles, que de voyager. Il est bon de savoir quelque chose des mœurs de divers peuples, afin de juger des nôtres plus sainement, et que nous ne pensions pas que tout ce qui est contre nos modes soit ridicule et contre raison, ainsi qu'ont coutume de faire ceux qui n'ont rien vu. Mais lorsqu'on emploie trop de temps à voyager, on devient enfin étranger en son pays; et lorsqu'on est trop curieux des choses qui se pratiquaient aux siècles passés, on demeure ordinairement fort ignorant de celles qui se pratiquent en celui-ci.[1]
>
> Descartes, *Discours de la méthode* (1637)

As Descartes reminds us here, travel happens in both time and space. We can travel in the past as much as in foreign lands. Although travelling in foreign parts can help towards a sounder judgement of home and its practices, travelling in the past, through study, can make the traveller a foreigner in his or her own time and space. For some, the strangeness of other times or territories made it difficult to believe in any universal norms. The literature of travel and its satiric accompaniments cannot escape this issue. Yet for all the anxiety it betrays about the claims of European civilisation, it is difficult to find any European writer of the eighteenth-century Enlightenment, however that is understood, who did not believe that freedom was the highest expression of political virtue, a good in itself that would appeal to humankind, whatever the circumstances. Further, it should be extended across the world as an inevitable prelude or accompaniment to human progress, civilisation or happiness, or to a consolidated version of all three. This belief could accompany even the most caustic accounts of European colonial enterprises. The pleasure the French took in having helped the Americans achieve their independence from Britain perhaps over-stimulated their view of American independence as *the* event in world history that showed the incompatibiltiy between liberty and subjugation, but it also encouraged the belief that liberty could be exported and might have a career open to the talents of the New World more promising than it could have in the crowded and muffled circumstances of the Old. After the Seven Years War of 1756–63, it was clear that the European powers had a global reach and the consciousness of this began to have its effects on the writing of history (William Robertson's *History of America* (1777), on travel literature (Denis Diderot's *Supplément au voyage de Bougainville*, written 1772, published 1796), and on the early versions of world-systems theory of which the most notable example is the best-selling collection of essays edited by the Abbé Raynal, *Histoire des deux Indes* (1770).

History, or travel in time or time-travel, usually fastens on a period that clearly contains the central problems of its own present. One period of historical time especially fascinated many writers of the European Enlightenment – the period that saw the passage of Rome from a city of virtue to a great and ultimately decadent Empire. A simplified version of the two great historians of this transition – Montesquieu and Edward Gibbon – would claim that Rome fell to the barbarians because it lost its republican virtue and that it did so because the republic expanded and degenerated into an Empire. The loss of virtue was not permanent. The barbarian invasions to some extent restored what Gibbon calls 'a manly spirit of freedom'.[2] Both he and Montesquieu conceded that this restoration was not identical with what had been lost. Further, in modern conditions, with the rise of commerce and with the supposedly new phenomenon of movable property, virtue must survive, if at all, on the basis of something other than the arms-and-agriculture economy that Rome and the Goths had developed. Virtue, whether it was to be associated with the form or *principe* of a system of government, like the Roman republic, or with an economic and social system, was a tender plant that depended upon particular conditions for its survival. The virtue of the old Roman republic could not be reborn in its original form, although it was endlessly recycled as an ideal. Indeed, the notion that an original ideal was the same as a historically precedent achievement is one of the issues concealed in the Enlightenment's understanding of virtue as a cultural phenomenon that was always, in some sensed, tinged with a sense of loss. Virtue in its truest sense belonged to the simplest forms of agrarian-military society. Advanced commercial societies could not hope to reproduce that achievement, even though they could provide notable compensations, among which the growth and expansion of liberty would be the most considerable.[3]

Montesquieu, even more than Gibbon, emphasises another feature of the decline of Rome that is pertinent here. As the Empire expanded, its system became so complicated that it was beyond the range of any individual or group to understand the interrelation of all its parts. There was not only an intensification of the evils that attend upon luxury, like the apathy and irresponsibility that characterised for him this early version of a consumer society. In addition, there was a failure to recognise the incompatibility between the original republican form of government and the new commercial economy that the Empire had perforce developed. This lack of synchrony between political and economic systems is one that gave both Montesquieu and Gibbon pause. It raised the question, which neither of them answered, if there was in existence (even theoretically) a political system that was consonant with an expanding commercial economy and, further, if such existed, would a description of it be possible? These problems were confronted most directly by the Scottish philosophers of civil society, Ferguson, Adam Smith, John Millar, Robertson and David Hume. But before looking briefly at them, I want to pause at a short essay by Hume, called simply 'A Dialogue', that closes the 1777 edition of his *Enquiries Concerning the Human Understanding and Concerning the Principles of Morals.*

The dialogue is between the author and his friend Palamedes. Palamedes begins by telling a travel story, about a strange country, called Fourli, where he found everything that he and his culture considered ethically normal was astonishingly inverted. It turns out that he is teasing his comrade; the country is ancient Greece and the incidents he recounts are founded on episodes in Greek and Roman history. Part of the point of the dialogue is to establish that conceptions of virtue vary according to the cultures from which they emerge. Equally, though, Hume wishes to claim that 'different customs and situations vary not the original ideas of merit . . . in any very essential point. What he calls 'the merit of riper years' is the same everywhere and 'consists chiefly in integrity, humanity, ability, knowledge, and the other more solid and useful qualities of the human mind'.[4] Palamedes agrees but then brings up the question of what he calls 'artificial lives and manners', instancing Diogenes and Pascal, with a side-swipe at Dominic and Loyola. These two remarkable men, one Stoic and critical, the other superstitious and contemptuous of life, form a contrast and yet have won universal admiration. So, he asks,

> Where then is the universal standard of morals which you talk of? And what rule shall we establish for the many different, nay contrary sentiments of mankind?

The answer is remarkable:

> An experiment, said I, which succeeds in the air, will not always succeed in a vacuum. When men depart from the maxims of common reason, and affect those artificial lives, as you call them, no one can answer for what will please or displease them. They are in a different element from the rest of mankind; and the natural principles of their mind play not with the same regularity, as if left to themselves, free from the illusions of religious superstition or philosophical enthusiasm.[5]

Thus virtue depends for its survival on particular historical circumstances; its career is fraught with danger and its 'original' form can never be perfectly reproduced. In this dialogue, travel into the past is openly (and conventionally) adapted to make a comment upon the present; but the consequence is that, while the principle of cultural relativity is conceded with the left hand, it is retracted with the right hand by the assertion of the universality of certain principles of human nature. Yet that universality must itself be suspended to account for the appearance of extraordinary and admirable people like Pascal and Diogenes. This is not Hume at his most penetrating or persuasive; but it is an instance of the kinds of issues that recourse to the past, travelling in time, raises for those who wish to defend, restore or otherwise rehabilitate the idea of civic virtue in the eighteenth-century. Discussions of the Greek and Roman civilisations, analyses of their decline and ethical puzzles raised by the recognition of different cultures or extraordinary exceptions, are all dominated by the trope of difference between that which is 'common' and that which is 'artificial' or foreign. It is not only civilisations that can betray their native virtue by contracting habits foreign to it; individuals too can do this. At the end of such considerations we wonder if Palamedes' question is answerable at all. Where are the universal principles to be found if the history of humankind shows so many exceptions to them? Why are there so many disasters that are not wholly accounted for by claiming that they resulted from the abandonment of those universal principles? The idea of universality tends to shrink when the heat is on; precisely when its certainty is most needed.

II

The assumption of a detached point of view for the purposes of surveying a society is one of the standard rhetorical resources of travel literature. The observer who can read a society precisely because he or she is not involved in it has two possible sets of criteria by which an estimate or judgement may be made. One is the criterion of the traveller-observer's own society; the other is the criterion of universal principles of human nature. We get a mix of these at times. By the exercise of the first criterion, the observer may become a victim of his or her own observations; by the exercise of the second, the notion that there are such universal principles may be called into question. But if we stay for the moment with the writing of history as a form of time-travel and turn from the history of ancient to that of modern Europe, then we may see how the ground of universality begins more and more to vanish under the feet of those who seek to stand on it. Inevitably, this has severe consequences for ethical thought and in particular for the career of 'virtue'.

Ferguson's *Essay on the History of Civil Society* (1767), Robertson's *View of the Progress of Society in Europe* (1769), Millar's *Origin of Ranks* (1771) and Smith's *The Wealth of Nations* (1776) are the works that I will be referring to in the most general terms for the articulation of this dilemma. Smith makes a well-known and even by then well-rehearsed distinction between the barbarous and the civilised state. In Volume II (Book V, Part III) of *The Wealth of Nations,* he distinguishes them in this manner. In a barbarous state,

> . . . no man can well require that improved and refined understanding, which a few men sometimes possess in a more civilised state. Though in a rude society there is a good deal of variety in the occupations of every individual, there is not a great deal in those of the whole society. Every man does, or is capable of doing, almost every thing which any other man does, or is capable of doing. Every man has a considerable degree of knowledge, ingenuity and invention; but scarce any man has a great degree . . . In a civilised state, on the contrary, though there is little variety in the occupations of the greater part of individuals, there is an almost infinite variety in those of the whole society. These varied occupations present an almost infinite variety of objects to the contemplation of those few, who, being attached to no particular occupation themselves, have leisure and inclination to examine the occupations of other people. The contemplation of so great a variety of objects necessarily exercises their minds in endless comparisons and combinations, and renders their understandings, in an extraordinary degree, both acute and comprehensive . . .[6]

Here is an account of complexity that is still, according to Smith, within range of the detached observer (or gentleman) who can achieve a synoptic view of the whole intricate system. But the question arises, or rather it is raised by Adam Ferguson, whether such detachment bears too great a price? Later in the century we will hear a great deal, especially from Burke, on the dangers of such detachment from human affairs, the risks of closet-philosophers whose speculations are wilder in proportion to their detachment. But Ferguson anticipates Burke (and, let it be said, lays down at least one plank in the platform of the Scottish Common Sense school, especially as represented by Thomas Reid) and subverts in some degree the writings of Hume, Gibbon and Montesquieu, not to mention his own, by isolating the position of the person whose function it is to see society as a whole. Leisured detachment, he says, may itself be only one among a number of social occupations, professionalised specialisms; when, in his phrase, 'reason itself becomes a profession',[7] then detachment itself becomes a fiction. Or, it becomes a disfiguring occupation, removed from the realities of experience and producing only 'the jargon of a technical language and . . . the impertinence of academical forms'.[8] But if that is the case, then how can the history of civil society be written at all? Where is the space? Are some universal principles not necessary, or some synoptic view not a prerequisite, of writing the history of anything? Whence is the detached observer to come; in what rhetorical space can he be sited? This, I suggest, is one of the questions that bedevils travel-writing and makes its rhetorical procedures so elusive; it is also one of the questions that Swift's writings raise with an unequalled force.

If specialisation, of the kind described by Smith and Ferguson, was a new, largely economic, phenomenon, it nevertheless had a more conventional cousin in religious fanaticism.[9] Swift married the fanatic and the specialist to produce the virtuoso. The virtuoso was the contemporary version of the enthusiast, emotionally committed to reason to the point of madness, forgoing theologies of damnation and salvation for the new and equally lunatic theology or ideology of benevolence, a preacher of social virtue who embodied within himself every vice that threatened civil society.

Taking from Descartes this distinction between foreignness and home, we must remember that to be a foreigner at home is one of the most pronounced dangers of travel – of whatever kind. A passage from *The Drapier's Letters* – Letter VI, 'To Lord Chancellor Middleton' – has a bearing here: Swift is declaring that the Drapier, far from alienating the 'Affections of the People of *England* and *Ireland* from each other . . . hath left that Matter just as he found it.' He continues:

> I have lived long in both Kingdoms, as well in Country as in Town; and therefore, take myself to be as well informed as most Men, in the Dispositions of each People towards the other. By the People, I understand here, only the Bulk of the common People; and I desire no Lawyer may distort or extend my Meaning.
>
> THERE is a Vein of Industry and Parsimony, that runs through the whole People of England; which, added to the Easiness of their Rents, makes them rich and sturdy. As to Ireland they know little more than they do of Mexico; further than it is a Country subject to the King of England, full of Boggs, inhabited by wild Irish Papists; who are kept in Awe by mercenary Troops sent from thence: And their general Opinion is, that it were better for England if this whole Island were sunk into the Sea; For, they have a Tradition, that every Forty Years there must be a Rebellion in Ireland. I have seen the grossest Suppositions pass upon them; that the wild Irish were taken in Toyls; but that, in some Time, they would grow so tame, as to eat out of your Hands: I have been asked by Hundreds . . . whether I had come from Ireland by Sea: And, upon the arrival of an Irish-man to a Country Town, I have known Crouds coming about him, and wondering to see him look so much better than themselves.[10]

I cite this well-known passage to indicate that Swift had particular reason to be alert to the problems of foreignness and its close intimacy with at-homeness. He was, like the persona of so many works of travel literature, a foreigner at home. But the Irish–English axis of Swift's experience enabled him to uncover a paradox in travel literature that none of the other authors mentioned adverts to at any length. It is this: travel literature has built into it as an integral feature not only the obvious critique of both the society the narrator belongs to and the society he visits but also of the narrator himself. This is not simply to say that the narrator can be exposed in a number of ways by the comments he makes on what is foreign to him and what he presumes to be 'native' or 'natural'. It goes deeper than this. The question Swift poses in *Gulliver's Travels* is about the possibility of 'disinterestedness'. What is the ground for a disinterested narrative? Is impartiality a possible narrative stance for a narrator who comes from a particular society and goes to another? Certainly the Cartesian anxiety that, in adverting too much to the past, or to what is foreign, we may lose contact with the present or with home, poses a real threat to any hope of achieving true impartiality. Such removal is predicated on a lack of interest in the actual, not on disinterestedness. But there is a subtler and more elusive question to be answered when the distinction between past and present, home and abroad, is hard to maintain either in itself or in certain circumstances. England might view Ireland as a foreign territory and yet Ireland was part of the British system – it was both home and foreign as Mexico. But where is the vantage point to be found that will recognise both the kinship and the difference between England and Ireland? If no such ground is available, then the possibility of narrative itself, or narrative of the Enlightenment kind, is brought into question. Europe might look at the world, or the world be brought in to look at Europe. The consequence should be a relativisation of cultures. Eurocentric notions of what is normal should thereby be rebuked. Equally, Asia or any other region of the world should be shown to be equally culture-bound. But if societies are culture-bound in this manner, then impartiality is a fiction – unless we can find a position that is free of such boundedness and limitation. This is exactly what Benevolence claimed to offer – not a culture-bound view of the world but a version of the world's diversity seen from the point of view of the Spectator, whose boast was that he had as his remit the world of human nature. He surveyed mankind from China to Peru and, in doing so, disengaged himself from all of the provincial views that had been produced by particular histories, circumstances and beliefs. Swift attacks this possibility because it necessarily abstracts the individual from the particular in the name of a human nature which is itself a specific product of a specific culture and not, as it claimed to be, a conception of human nature founded upon universal principles. The claim to universality was always rooted in time and place and was, therefore, bogus. There was no vantage point available to any person to survey human kind as such.

In attempting to define a space for 'human nature', some of the most radical writers of the Enlightenment attempted to persuade themselves or their readers that there was within the human person a fundamental instinct for virtue that was constantly stifled by the operation of laws that were founded on the precepts of religion and convention. This argument was conducted in France with much more vigour than in England, even though some of the basic ingredients for the argument were drawn from the English writers of the benevolist school, most especially Shaftesbury. In France, the literary work that, more than any other, focused this problem was Samuel Richardson's *Clarissa* (and *Pamela*, to a lesser extent). The central argument was played out between Rousseau and Diderot. Rousseau had angered Diderot by remarking, in a note to *La Lettre à d'Alembert sur les spectacles* : 'J n'entends point . . . qu'on puisse être vertueux sans religion?'[11] Diderot's reaction to this was complicated, but I want to look here at only a few aspects of it as embodied in the works of the early 1770s, particularly, *Entretien d'un père avec ses enfants, Ceci n'est pas un conte, Sur l'inconséquence du jugement publique, Le Supplément au voyage de Bougainville, L'Entretien d'un philosophe avec la maréchale de xxx* and

Jacques le fataliste. In effect, Diderot argues two chief points. One is that the laws of a society are not necessarily to be obeyed if they contradict our nature or instinct. That which is prior to the law is, he seems to say, superior to it. Virtue is coincident with our instincts. So, in his 'travel book', based on Louis-Antoine de Bougainville's report on the first French voyage to Tahiti (1766–69), Diderot offers an account of a Tahitian culture in which law, custom and religion were based on the needs of human nature. The sexual relation, in particular, and the care of children, were so organised that there was no conflict between desire and law. The dialogue ends with the determination that

> Nous parlerons contre les lois insensées jusqu'à ce qu'on les réforme: et en attendant nous nous y soumettrons.'[12]

This is part of the programme of the philosophes and of the Enlightenment in general. But there is another preoccupation in these works which leads to other and more anxious conclusions. Particularly in *Ceci n'est pas un conte* and in *Jacques le fataliste*, Diderot is concerned with the relationship between the reader and the story, claiming that stories as such are corrupting because they pander to the reader's love of observing the operation of narrative conventions without being in the least incriminated by what they are designed to communicate. Virtue is not inculcated by our reading about Pamela, Clarissa, or the like. He pointed out that many of the standard portrayals of the trials of innocent virtue were in themselves erotic narratives, that aroused in the reader a pleasure that ran athwart their ostensibly didactic purpose. Thus in *Jacques le fataliste* the central story of Jacques' love affairs remains untold, both to the frustration of the master and of the reader. Diderot suggests that the reader invent this for himself, that the fantasy be pursued by readers who have to recognise that the triumph of virtue over vice is merely a convention of narrative that conceals the pleasure we take in the depiction of vice itself. Thus Diderot disestablishes the notion that the telling of a story is a legitimate means of inculcating virtue. Sympathy is not, after all, a means to virtue. The surgeon does not feel sympathy for his patient; if he is a good surgeon, he will simply regard the patient's injuries as a challenge to his own technical skills. In displaying these he will not be caught in the sympathy trap; and he will do more good thereby because he might, as a consequence, effect a cure.[13]

I am not suggesting that Diderot surrendered the hope of finding universal principles of human nature upon which to base his campaign for virtue and sincerity, although there is a case to be argued in that direction. Instead, I am suggesting that he questioned the possibility of discovering this through narrative, precisely because narrative, fixed within its conventions, contained the very partition it wished to erase – the partition between author and reader, or the partition between that which was foreign and exotic – what happened in the narrative – and that which was bound to home, to the self.

This glimpse into Diderot's ideas about human nature serves merely to remind us of something about Swift's narratives and their very different function. These – *Tale of a Tub* and *Gulliver* primary among them – have within them a consciousness of the author–reader relationship that is subversive of the notions underlying the moral parable or *conte* of the kind that we associate with Dr Johnson, Oliver Goldsmith, Voltaire or even Gibbon, whose whole history is founded upon that kind of narrative trust that conceals author–reader relationships. The very form of a story told by author to reader is the form favoured by travel-writing; and it contains within itself the pornographic element that Diderot observed. The reader, faced with the exotic story, and its various resolutions, is not incriminated by it. It may show Gulliver, for instance, to be mad or to be rational; it may show the absurdity of English customs and political practices; or it may show that any society that attempts to base itself on rational principles is a dream and a chimera that leads to sorrow and bitterness in the end. It may remind us of the discrepancy between our capacity for abstract imaginings and the limitations of our bodies. In a sense, this is all irrelevant. The point about travel narratives, and about works like the *Tale,* which are so full of digressions and prefatory material and formal jokes that there is no point of rest, no stable centre, no norm, is that narrative is of its nature prolific, diverse, heterogeneous. Whether the style is baroque or polite, the ruse that is involved is that narrative takes civil society as its object when in fact narrative is itself the very means by which society becomes 'objectivised', reified. It is civil society itself in the form of story and critique; but can it as subject see itself as object? Ireland is both subject and object of England. It is part of the same polity, it gives allegiance to the same prince; yet the Irish are exotics to the English. They see Ireland in conventional terms as a foreign place much given to rebellion; whereas in fact it is home. The English are readers of the narrative that is Ireland, authored in the case of the Drapier's letters by the Drapier himself who is not truly the author but a persona of the author. But then there is no author who is not a persona. Authorship is an assumption of a persona; so is readership. Swift anticipated, in his own peculiar way, the problem which was later to worry Diderot.

However, this is an insufficient gloss on what Swift and the Enlightenment, as represented here by Diderot, are concerned with in the travel literature of the period. It is well established by now that there is a link between the increasing specialisations and opportunities offered by a developing commercial society and the varieties of human possibility – or personality – liberated by such a process. This is often held to be one of the sources of the tension and hostility between 'conservatives' who looked back to some ideal of the commonwealth and its antique virtues and stable, heroic personalities and the new Whig-led, Walpolean corruption and diversity.[14] Travel literature is certainly concerned with diversity, but the relativisation of culture that is one of the possible consequences of recognising the 'otherness' both of foreign and of native cultures (although foreign cultures were often patronised and to some degree cancelled by being regarded as native in another sense) brings with it another issue that some of the Enlightenment analysts of civil society – especially Ferguson, Smith, Mandeville and Montesquieu – often remarked upon. The rise of the specialist, the expert, the subdivision of labour into so many different compartments and the ensuing organisational complexity had made it all but impossible for a society to be understood in one embracing conspectus. Variety and diversity were not merely cultural phenomena for which new literary forms like the novel and travel-writing were created to subserve and register. They had made it all the more imperative – especially in Britain, where industrial and economic changes had begun to accelerate to an unprecedented degree – to assert that within such diversity there was perceptible some harmonising unity.

As John Barrell has pointed out, writers like Thomas Gray and William Collins were not as enamoured of the general conviction of some underlying unity as others – say, as the Alexander Pope who wrote the *Essay on Man*.[15] They were more interested in those communities that were disappearing under the wave of the new prosperity, the great phenomenon of Luxury that Goldsmith too and a score of others lamented so much.[16] The elegiac note that we are accustomed to hear in the most bitter satires of the century is struck for the loss of a community that could be understood, in its structure and in its operation, by those who lived within it. In some respects, this is what Swift admires in his version of Anglicanism. It is not only a middle way between extremes. The extremes are so crazy that they are literally incomprehensible after a while; they develop so wildly and randomly, fuelled by emotional conviction or corrupt reasoning, that they defy any attempt to describe their structure. Anglicanism is the religion of people who live in a comprehensible environment and who, in virtue of that, are balanced people. A society is healthy when it is not overly complex. But complexity of this lethal sort arises, in Swift's opinion, not from a series of market forces, economic developments, national debt and so on – but from human evil. Evil is of its nature complex and prolific. Goodness is simple and univocal.

Gulliver's Travels is a work which combines apparent simplicity – of the narrator – with apparent complexity – of his experiences. It is the relationship between these that is to be understood. Gulliver cannot make sense of his experiences, which become increasingly complex and more foreign. But his failure to do so – which is not the reader's failure – is an indication of his fake simplicity. He is not, need it be said, a character; he is a composite of attitudes that were then conventional. He is, above all, a writer whose narrative is determined by the conventions by which he is formed. These conventions are, in part, social and cultural. In addition, he has a convention of himself as a rational creature. Such conventions govern what he sees. He is always a foreigner in these distant parts, and, as a consequence, they are always already read by him in his own terms. The foreign is always read in terms of home. As usual, Ireland, as seen under English eyes, is the exemplary instance, since it is home and abroad simultaneously.

In a piece like *A Short View of the State of Ireland* (1728) Swift supplies a list of the reasons why Ireland is not prosperous. But the pamphlet begins with the accusation that people have been misrepresenting the true state of the country to the government commissioners from England in order to gain favour, win place and allow the English to permit themselves to believe that all is well. The fact is that

> No strangers from other countries, make this a part of their travels; where they can expect to see nothing but Scenes of misery and Desolation.[17]

But he imagines the commissioners roaming round the country and observing its fertility, productiveness and prosperity. What 'glorious reports' would they make when they went back to England. Then he continues;

> But my heart is too heavy to continue this irony longer; for it is manifest, that whatever stranger took such a journey, would be apt to think himself travelling in Lapland or Ysland, rather than in a country so favoured by nature as ours, both in fruitfulness of soil, and temperature of climate. The miserable dress, and dyet and dwelling of the people. The general desolation in most parts of the kingdom. The old seats of the nobility and gentry all in ruins, and no new ones in their stead. The families of farmers, who pay great rents, living in filth and nastiness upon butter-milk and potatoes, without a shoe or stocking to their feet; or a house so convenient as an English hog-sty to receive them. These indeed may be comfortable sights to an English spectator, who comes for a short time, only to learn the language, and returns back to his own country, whither he finds all our wealth transmitted.
>
> nostra miseria magnus es
>
> There is not one argument used to prove the riches of Ireland, which is not a logical demonstration of its poverty.[18]

In the first place, there is misrepresentation of an actual state of affairs, for corrupt reasons; second, there is a set of paradoxes – arguments for wealth becoming demonstrations of poverty – that seem to make a nonsense of conventional wisdom. And lastly, there is the difference between what a native sees and what a foreigner sees; or the difference that there should be between what a native reports and a foreigner reports. When these are coincident, corruption or stupidity are present.

> If Ireland be a rich and flourishing kingdom; its wealth and prosperity must be owing to certain causes, that are yet concealed from the whole race of mankind; and the effects are equally invisible. We need not wonder at strangers, when they deliver such paradoxes; but a native and inhabitant of this Kingdom, who gives the same verdict, must be either ignorant to stupidity; or a man-pleaser, at the expence of all honour, conscience and truth.[19]

But the telling of lies for whatever reason is not a simple action, although undoubtedly reprehensible. It replaces the thing which is with the thing which is not. It is a misrepresentation that will lead to misinterpretation; and yet, if there is a reason for it, it is at least explicable. But when there is no reason for misrepresentation or misinterpretation, no preferment to be gained, no corrupt purpose served thereby, then the issue is more complex. Gulliver is a native Briton who reports on foreign territories; but the ultimate effect of his experience is to make him a foreigner at home, a man in whom the distinction between native and foreign is lost. When,in the same person, we have Gulliver the Englishman and Gulliver the Houyhnhnm-lover, is there any ground left for disputing his accounts other than claiming that he is an unreliable narrator who uses the language of reason to authenticate his insanity? In such a case, it has to be conceded that the loss of the writer's authority produces a lack of security in the reader. The reader is a native to whom the text has become foreign. Yet the text relies for its meanings on the dismantling of that very distinction between native and foreigner.

Language is not a medium which contains within itself authenticating authority; it is no more than a system of conventions, not founded in nature at all. That is the source of the anxiety in Swift's satires, not merely the manipulation of the persona or suspicion of narrative; but the unsettling effects of language itself that are betrayed by the mad virtuoso like Gulliver or the economist of *A Modest Proposal*, or any of the other mad, despotic writers and commentators that populate Swift's writings.

More than that; *A Tale of a Tub* is a work that provides both criticism of itself and is about the relation of authority to criticism and commentary. The link between travel-writing and literary criticism is this: they both take as an object of commentary and dispute a culture or a text that previously was not seen to be susceptible to such contention. Put it another way; the institution of literary criticism, from John Dryden to Johnson, had as its object the English national culture and literature. Travel-writing had the same object – English, French, Irish national culture. But to convert the unknown to the known, the foreign to the native, the philosophical impasse to a liberating conclusion, to show that there was an ethical system that bound the whole world of human nature together by some set of fundamental principles, led to such confusions that the idea of a universal ethics, intuitively given, had to be abandoned. With that abandonment came the death of virtue.

But it is also true that Swift's Irish writings are the first in either the English or the Irish language to propose the notion that, since Ireland was going to be maltreated so outrageously by England, and since it could not, in consequence, become a distinct and prosperous kingdom – even though it had all the titles and the potential to be so – then Ireland would, by becoming foreign to England, also become the critical commentary for which England would be, so to say, the text. If one was authority, the other was subversion; if one was civilisation, the other was its rebuke, barbarism.

But the link between them is not a contrastive one of opposites but a fearsome one of co-producers. In some respects, this reading of the situation was carried on by Burke. The question why the English system did not migrate successfully across the Irish Sea could, if asked with sufficient sharpness, question the whole basis of that system itself; and if that system could be subjected to radical inquiry, what system could not? Travel literature was only rescued from its descent into the inferno by being transmuted, under different auspices, into the literature of tourism.

There were many forms of travel literature produced in the eighteenth-century – accounts of actual voyages, imaginary voyages, picaresque novels, fantasy tales, historical accounts of non-European territories, histories of the past, especially of the ancient world and, within that, histories of the decline and fall of Rome. Confining ourselves for the moment to those works of literature that use the imaginary voyage as their governing trope, we can see that many of these voyagers – who can be travellers abroad or within their own country and culture – are possessed of a sublime simplicity that seems, at first sight, to be a guarantee of their trustworthiness and their essential virtue. By contrast, among those whom they meet are often found people of very complex dispositions, highly untrustworthy and worldly-wise, sharpers, experts, fashionable people who are, in the broadest sense of the term, virtuosi. The contrast so established between two generic types is not always stable. Swift, for instance, could be said to demonstrate that Gulliver's sublime simplicity is no more than the concealed face of virtuosity. He is a virtuoso at not appearing to be so. But I want to defer consideration of this possibility in order to permit the outlines of the general contrast to appear. On the one hand, we have simplicity and virtue; on the other hand, we have virtuosity and vice. This contrast is not at all confined to travel literature, but it is prominent in that genre. Why this should be so is part of my concern here.

The simplicity of the virtuous person is both the source and symptom of his or her moral stability. The vicious person, on the other hand, is characterised by waywardness, fragmentation, disloyalty, political and social volatility. It may be one of the consequences of the upheavals of the seventeenth-century that English writing begins to produce a portrait gallery of rogues who are identified by their splintered personalities. Samuel Butler's Hudibras, Dryden's Absalom, Pope's Sporus, Swift's author in *A Tale of a Tub*, would be among the most outstanding examples, although at a more relaxed level of discourse we could also mention figures like Richard Steele's Jack Dimple, the pretty Fellow, whose artificial behaviour contrasts with that of Sophronius, the gentleman of 'natural behaviour' (*Tatler*, 28 May 1709) or Dr Johnson's Mr. Sober (*Idler*, no. 31, 18 November 1758), for whom Johnson's hope is 'that he will quit his trifles and betake himself to rational and useful diligence'. These portraits are of people who have tried to become many things and have ended by being nothing, victims of the lust for power, of the dictates of fashion, the hunger for fame, the dread of boredom, the spirit of political faction. They all have immense energy but no fixed principles. They lack a moral character; that is why they have, as a substitute, such exotic personalities. In addition, they are all, in one sense or another, enthusiasts, types of that plague of what Hume called 'puritanical absurdities' that were so fatally allied to the history and conception of English liberty. Hume suspected that the high value given to the individual conscience in English Protestantism promoted and even ratified the eccentric volatility of the personality, creating a political instability that was sustained by the Protestant sects with their sullen and gloomy theologies of independence. He contrasted this with Catholic political passivity, nurtured by the terrors and superstitions instilled by an authoritarian clergy.[20] With Hume, as with Swift and many others, it is clear that the religious divisions of the seventeenth-century provided a typology in which there were two extremes, Catholic and Dissenting, and a moderate 'Anglican' middle way. This, in turn, enabled the attack on the 'virtuosi' to retain a historical dimension that would enrich and polemicise the vocabulary of moral debate, so readily deployed by the literature of this period.

The connection between Protestant dissent and the wilfully individual personality is widely acknowledged. Only slightly less acknowledged is the connection between this species of radical individuality and the 'new' system or ideology of benevolence. The presentation of the benevolist takes a somewhat different form because he is characterised, not by volatile changeability, but by a uniform placidity of disposition. One changes without reason; the other never sees any reason to change. Both are fanatics. One is generally fierce or gloomy; the other implacably benign. The benevolist is more often found in the prose than in the verse of this period. His sense of his own virtue is secure and his simplicity the characteristic manifestation of it. Sir Roger de Coverley, Gulliver, Tom Jones, Dr Primrose, Rasselas, would be typical examples. So decorous, benevolent and good-hearted are they that it may seem anomalous to dub them fanatics. They seem to be sunlit personalities who have emerged out of the darknesses of puritan antinomianism, who have forsaken chiliastic furies and convictions and become 'polite' members of civil society rather than deluded participants in some apocalyptic religious melodrama. They are much given to sententious declarations on human life, the more credible because they are so widely experienced in the ways of humankind, as picaresque or vagabond heroes tend to be. In the case of the irretrievably benevolent, the range of human experience encountered by them is irrelevant. They will emerge from variety in their initial state.

We could put this differently and thereby gain closer access to the issue by saying that there is a rhetorical difference in the treatment of dissenting virtuosos and the virtuosos of benevolence. The figure of the traveller is pledged to the act of discovery, either in the sense of introducing us to something new or in the sense of revealing the known in a new light – examples would include Montesquieu's Uzbek and Rica, Voltaire's Candide,

Goldsmith's Lien Chi Altangi, Defoe's Crusoe, Swift's Gulliver, and the various travellers we meet in the works of the Marquis d'Argens, Horace Walpole, Tobias Smollett and others. For the most part, they manage by making the world conform to their initial convictions. By domesticating what they consider to be strange, they often show us how strange the idea of the domestic is. But, rhetorically, they are presented to us in a language of such decorum that they transmit to us a sense of order – no matter how provincial, provisional or placid it may be – that is unshakable. But the dissenting virtuosi (and they may be Catholic or Protestant, but more often the latter) belong to a rhetorical world in which syntactical, grammatical and semantic control is always at risk. The difference between the rhetorically baroque world of *A Tale of a Tub* and the rhetorically 'polite' world of *Gulliver's Travels* is the obvious example that indicates the scale of the contrast. This imperviously decorous observation of the traveller is all the more impressive and interesting because it includes within its view many exemplary cases of fanaticism, madness, strangeness, eccentricity and experiment. But these oddities, although threatening, are kept at arm's length. They are, after all, 'foreign' to the traveller's native country in the geographical or intellectual sense. They do not belong to the rational world, which is often coincident with Europe, England, or a class or group of people within these. Further, that rational world is conventionally dissociated from the realm of the bodily and appetitive functions. In Swift, the body humiliates reason. Those whose rational processes are assimilated to bodily processes are fanatics; those who wish to proclaim reason's independence of the body are insane. But the traditional distinction between the two realms is, nevertheless, sustained by him and enhanced by the benevolist school of Shaftesbury and Hutcheson, which carefully separated the 'internal sense' of taste from the five physical senses. Many of the standard objections to those subversive writers, from Mandeville to the French materialists, who insisted on the physiological basis of feeling, including aesthetic and moral feelings, dwelt on the element of 'grossness' which they introduced into the world of rationality.

It is also important that the inhabitants of the rational world are male. This gendered exclusiveness is so deeply embedded that it becomes an integral part of the attack on irrationality and fanaticism, especially when these conditions are transposed from the theological and political to the social arena. What was fanatical in the former becomes faddish and whimsical in the latter; and such whimsicality is often characterised as 'effeminate'. The powerful association between fashion, especially fashion in clothes, and the fickleness of women, especially women who had escaped what Lawrence Stone called 'the companionate marriage' and who were, therefore, 'loose', was a key element in the complicated eighteenth-century debates centred around the vice of the city and the virtue of the country.[21] That debate took another turn when such fickleness was translated into an intellectual defect, characteristic of women and even of a nation – the French – widely condemned in the later eighteenth century for a 'légèreté' of spirit that had an interest in fashion and a moral, largely sexual, instability as its characteristic accompaniments or symptoms. The reaction to the role of women, as hostesses of the French salons and, subsequently (also, by implication, consequently) as prominent members of the 'mob' in the early days of the French Revolution, reconfirmed this configuration of dangerous volatility as a threat to social order.[22]

Nevertheless, debates about the relation between reason and virtue modulated into debates about the relation between reason and happiness, as reason became increasingly identified with calculation and virtue and happiness became increasingly associated with sentiment. It was the benevolists who asserted that it was rational to be sentimental and the utilitarians who asserted that it was rational to be calculating. But the division between these attitudes was not essentially philosophical. Certainly by the 1790s, but probably as early as the Seven Years War, it had become political. The rational ideal of the Enlightenment only had force in alliance with a cosmopolitan and universalist view of human nature. Once that ideal began to give way to a newly assertive nationalism, predicated on notions of national character, its future was threatened. In Britain especially, reason was attacked as an abstract energy, dangerously detached from historical experience, and the rational man or woman was regarded as a virtuoso, an experimenter, whose highly mutable designs for social and political life were driven by an intellectual pride that ruthlessly pursued the project of its own perfection, irrespective of the cost to intuitive human feeling. An ideology of solid sense was developed to combat the smiling lunacies of the Man of Reason or the sodden effusions of the Man of Feeling. We meet versions of them in Henry Fielding, in Goldsmith, and in Henry Mackenzie, but it is the novelists of the nineties, radicals like Bage and Thomas Holcroft, counter-revolutionaries like More and Isaac d'Israeli – who brought them to comic and alarming extremes.

In their writings the system of benevolence became a system founded upon 'sincerity'. But for all the emphasis upon 'sincerity', Rousseau's work and, even more, Rousseau's reputation, had made the ethic of feeling suspect. From a Burkean point of view, we could say that there is 'Feeling' and there are feelings. The first is a radical and theoretical formulation; the second is an embedded historical reality. Moreover, the notion that benevolence is rational as well as sincere created a number of problems and conflicts that are singularly embodied in the writings and career of William Godwin. His chief work *Political Justice* (1793) brings the principles of rational benevolence to a point that would have made even Shaftesbury or Hutcheson quiver a little. For Godwin argues that the impulses arising from personal, 'natural' (and therefore untutored) feelings must concede to decisions based on a rational estimate of the consequences of any action for the human race in general. This raised the ire of readers who regarded Godwin as an exponent of an 'unfeeling' philosophy. He recommended as a principle of action what Burke, for instance, had condemned in Rousseau – the promotion of global benevolence by someone who had forgotten that charity begins at home with those who are nearest and should be dearest. It is Godwin who also brings the issue of the relationship between disinterested benevolence and what he calls the 'domestic affections' to light in a tragic (and characteristically ridiculous) way by his reaction to the death of his wife, Mary Wollstonecraft.[23] The sexism of the philosophy of rational benevolence is made manifest precisely in that division between intimate affection and disinterested judgement which, according to Godwin, his marriage had taught him to temper.[24] We should remember that Godwin himself saw in the society of Houyhnhnmland a rational ideal; those horses were benevolist thoroughbreds. who had won the race to happiness. It took almost a century for someone to out-Gulliver Gulliver. As a radical and an alleged sympathiser with France, Godwin, like many of his contemporaries, especially those who were made honorary French citizens, were regarded as foreign sympathisers, not only with France, but also with that revolutionary philosophy that was repeatedly characterised as inhuman, unBritish, given to the destruction of natural home-bred feeling.

The radicals and so-called English Jacobins were victims of the new ideology of national character that had replaced the Enlightenment ideal during the propaganda war that broke out with the Revolution. That ideology drew heavily on the debates that had dominated travel-writing throughout the preceding century. Burke's *Reflections on the Revolution in France* (1790) is an exemplary demonstration of this. Burke addresses two critical issues in this regard. One concerns the status of revolutionary France, both as a territory and as a political construct, in contrast to the France of the *ancien régime*. Burke consistently attacks the misrepresentation of France as it was before the revolution:

> From its general aspect one would conclude that it had been for some time past under the special direction of the learned academicians of Laputa and Balnibarbi.[25]

The aim is to make France appear shameful in the eyes of foreigners, paint 'their nobility and their clergy, as objects of horror' and to present it as an Oriental despotism, that European stereotype of political terror:

> To hear some men speak of the late monarchy of France, you would imagine that they were talking of Persia bleeding under the ferocious sword of Tahmas Kouli Khân, or at least describing the barbarous anarchic despotism of Turkey . . . Was this the case of France?[26]

The French, in Burke's view, had transformed France into a despotism worse than anything in Asia, in classical antiquity or in modern Europe. This was the effect of the Revolution which, for him, began on the day the King and Queen of France were led from Versailles to Paris by a triumphant mob.

> Excuse me, therefore, if I have dwelt too long on the atrocious spectacle of the 6th of October, 1789, or have given too much scope to the reflections which have arisen in my mind on occasion of the most important of all revolutions, which may be dated from that day – I mean a revolution in sentiments, manners and moral opinions. As things now stand, with everything respectable destroyed without us, and an attempt to destroy within us every principle of respect, one is almost forced to apologize for harbouring the common feelings of men.[27]

This passage is part of that section of the *Reflections* devoted to the plight of the French royal family and in particular to that of Marie Antoinette. It precedes the account of the English national character, its 'sullen resistance to innovation' and 'cold sluggishness',[28] its resistance to giving power or attention to men of letters and intellectuals,

> The whole has emananted from the simplicity of our national character and from a sort of plainness and directness of understanding, which for a long time characterised those men who have successively obtained authority among us. This disposition still remains, at least in the great body of the people.[29]

Burke professes surprise that the French, so narrowly separated from England, should know so little of that national character as to mistake the exultations of Dr Price whose speech *Discourse on the Love of Our Country* (1789) initially provoked Burke to write the *Reflections* – and his friends at the distress of the French king and queen for the response of the English people as a whole. To feel as Price does is to be foreign to the English spirit. More than that, it is to be foreign to nature. Hence the importance of the apostrophe to Marie Antoinette and to the contrast between the natural sympathy felt for her by Burke and the artificial sympathy he would feel were he to see such a scene on stage, in a tragedy. The imagery of stripping, nakedness and ruthless ingratitude that dominates his account of the assault on the French queen, and its association with tragic drama, evokes Shakespeare's *King Lear*, a play that operates for a time as the shadow text of the *Reflections*. In fact, *King Lear* is converted into *Queen Lear* through the agency of the French queen. The insult offered to her is an insult to European sentiment. The welcome given to this by Dr Price is an insult to the English national character. That

> mixed system of opinion and sentiment [which] had its origin in the antient chivalry', and which has now failed in France, is what has given its character to modern Europe. It is this which has distinguished it under all its forms of government, and distinguished it to its advantage, from the states of Asia and possibly from those states which flourished in the most brilliant periods of the antique world.[30]

The geometrical, arithmetical and metaphysical basis of the transformation of French territory into symmetrical administrative units, of the French people into gradations of qualification for the franchise and of the French finances into a new taxation system is intrinsically false and has the effect of turning the old France of history into a new and foreign France of theory. This conversion has its roots in a failure of sentiment and manners, the loss of the natural affections and their replacement by barbarous, ideologically directed hatred.

Burke forges an alliance between what is natural and what is national. Equally, he insists on the contrasting kinship between universal principles that derive from the Enlightenment and that are characterised by a high degree of abstraction and artificially induced feeling. Ultimately, the Enlightenment's conception of civic virtue is transmuted by him into a concept that is foreign to human nature. It has taken root in France; it has irrevocably altered the world for the worse. It dates from the 6th October, 1789. Its master discourse is that of methodical quantitative reasoning, as opposed to the ancient and traditional discourse of sensibility. In this light, the distinction between home and abroad, native and foreign, takes on a new force. Virtue has undertaken the most dangerous of all journeys, into the country of theory, in the territory that once was France.

5. PHILOSOPHES AND REGICIDES
THE GREAT CONSPIRACY[1]

. . . qui celebre elucubrasti opus ad evertenda, et profliganda novorum Galliae Philosophorum commenta.

Pius VI to Edmund Burke, 7 September 1793[2]

Burke's assertion that the French Revolution was the product of a long-fomented conspiracy in Europe, dominated by French philosophes, German Illuminati, freemasons and atheists, and specifically directed at Throne and Altar, has been dismissed as a melodramatic exaggeration.[3] This it is, although it was then persuasive to many, especially in the popular versions of the thesis promoted by the Abbé Barruel, his English translator Robert Clifford, John Robison and a host of pamphleteers, journals and newspapers, some of the latter manipulated by William Pitt to exploit the element of panic aroused by the very notion of a conspiracy.[4] Several sources contributed to Burke's conviction: the emigrés he received at his home in Beaconsfield from 1790 forward;[5] the publication in 1792 of Voltaire's correspondence with Jean d'Alembert and Frederick the Great of Prussia, prominently featuring Voltaire's war-cry, 'Écrasez l'infâme'; his reading in 1794 of Barruel's earlier version of the conspiracy thesis in his *History of the Clergy during the Franch Revolution*.[6] But these, by his own account, merely confirmed his suspicions about the leading conspirators – Jean d'Alembert, Baron d'Holbach, Diderot, Voltaire, Claude-Adrien Helvétius, Rousseau, the Marquis de Condorcet among them – that were then alarmed into conviction when he heard the discussions in the salons of the Rue Royale on the famous visit of 1773, and had seen the young dauphiness, Marie Antoinette, at a levée.

The effect of that visit is audible in his speech against atheism, in support of a Bill for the relief of Dissenters, which he made in the House of Commons on his return from Paris in that year;[7] in the Marie Antoinette passage in the 'Reflections', and in the concerted assault in that work on 'The literary cabal' [that] 'had some years ago formed something like a regular plan for the destruction of the Christian religion.'[8] By 1797, the last year of his life, in a passage from a letter to Barruel cited in Clifford's 'Application' to Great Britain and Ireland of Barruel's European intrigue, he retrospectively intensified the conviction born that sixteen or seventeen years since:

> . . . I have known myself, personally, five of your principal conspirators: and I can undertake to say from my own certain knowledge, that so far back as the

> year 1773, they were busy in the plot you have so well described, and in the manner and on the principle you have so truly represented. – To this I can speak as a witness. [9]

A university professor of mathematics from Edinburgh, John Robison, joined Clifford and Barruel with his *Proofs of a Conspiracy against all the Religions and Governments of Europe*, which had four editions in 1797–98, and was dedicated to Burke's close friend, William Windham. Robison's pamphlet was the same story retold, with some variation on the names of the chief French conspirators; both he and Barruel were regarded as confirming one another.[10] In these years, 1797 and 1798, the threat of revolution or insurrection in Ireland and England was a serious one and the conspiracy thesis was used to provoke popular hostility against any such allegedly anti-Christian revolt against established authority. It is clear that Burke's involvement in this body of potent anti-revolutionary propaganda is deliberate. But his support for the conspiracy theory is not merely a strategic ploy. In the accounts of the various masonic and Illuminist cults and rituals, he saw what seemed to him to be the characteristic structure of the French Revolution – the diabolic inversion of mystery, its hallowed language vulgarised into the jargon of the occult. Here was an imitation, sinister and blasphemous, of the religion it aimed to overthrow, a phantasmagoric representation of the real which had become actual. Thus the derision cast – at least since the 1820s – on the idea of such an international intrigue, although less vehement than it once was, is incompatible with a serious analysis of Burke's estimate of the causes of the Revolution.

This conspiracy thesis, like others of the genre, does attribute to individuals and groups a power and an influence that are more convincingly attributed to what Tocqueville would call 'inexorable processes'. Yet we gain a better sense of what Burke believed those processes to be if we understand how he used the figure of conspiracy as a way of understanding their concerted power. Such a figurative understanding is allied with, not opposed to or in contradiction of belief in the actuality of the conspiracy. It was always part of Burke's political credo that processes could not be understood apart from the people who helped to enact or embody them. The charges laid against individuals indicate the existence of widespread infamy and of concerted criminal action; but this tendency 'to think of political crises as if they were primarily problems of legal enforcement', as Christopher Reid puts it, [11] nourishes the belief in conspiracy and makes it the expression of historical process which, nevertheless, might not have emerged without the conspiracy and which therefore has nothing inevitable about it. Indeed, to believe in the inevitability of a historical process rather than in the chosen responsibilities of persons, acting individually or as a group, would have been a surrender to the appeal of abstraction which was, in Burke's view, perhaps the most seductive of the songs the sirens of revolution sang to the disenfranchised intellectuals and moneyed interests of Europe. Clearly, the appeal and appearance of 'abstraction' itself needs an explanation. It is for Burke the spirit of that mode of reasoning which he considered to be peculiarly modern, but he accounts for its widespread attraction by claiming that particular groups, weakened by 'libertinism' and 'infidelity', were susceptible to it and that this was a mark of corruption in them or in the age. This is plainly not an explanation but it is a polemical account of a process that Burke helped to popularise as one.

However, the existence and success of a conspiracy did provide an explanation of sorts for the completeness and swiftness of the rupture between the revolutionary world and the preceding *régime*. Burke had at least this in common with the revolutionaries – he too wanted to say that theirs was indeed a new world that owed little or nothing to the one it had abolished. It had produced a new species of human, a new political formation, 'a new power of a new species',[12] a new way of thinking, a new lexicon, a new (and wholly degraded) sexuality, and it was determined to effect this change not only in France but right across Europe, altering completely the idea of a European community of nations and culture which Burke claimed had been given its existing form by the triumph of French diplomacy at the Peace of Westphalia in 1648. Now it was the French revolutionaries who were dismantling that system as a matter of policy, planned long in advance and executed with a terrifying speed.[13]

There was never any secret about the names of the conspirators or of their works, even though some of the more daring among them (like d'Holbach) used pseudonyms, and there were deliberately falsified attributions and title pages with fake places of publication. That in itself was nothing new. But from mid-century throughout Europe the names of the philosophes formed a litany that could vary a good deal but always included Voltaire and Rousseau, followed by Diderot, Helvétius, d'Alembert and a host of others. The incantation of these names intensified throughout the revolutionary decade and was blended in with those of the revolutionaries themselves, particularly le Comte de Mirabeau, Jean-Paul Marat, Georges Danton and Maximilien Robespierre; and in the early decades of the new century, the publication of various memoirs or collections of letters and histories of the preceding era reintroduced the philosophes again to new generations that had learned over and over again that the subversion of the old European order was largely the work of Voltaire, Rousseau and the Encyclopaedistes.

The men of letters and the new moneyed classes were widely understood to be in alliance, formal or informal, against the established political and moral order. The intensified power of literature and philosophy to corrupt morals, especially sexual morals, was widely claimed after the Revolution to have been a sinister and premonitory development. La Mettrie, Diderot and Rousseau were regarded as the most notorious of those who, in assaulting sexual conventions, had given to French libertine literature a philosophical status that was to reach a scandalous culmination in the works of the Marquis de Sade. The appeal of this new macedoine of discourses was especially shocking to reviewers in the London journals and magazines and to pamphleteers and historians who regularly buttressed the conspiracy story with accounts of the 'rise' of 'libertinism' and 'infidelity' in Voltairian France.[14] It is obvious too that from the earliest days of the Revolution Burke shared their sense of shock, although no one was his equal in exploiting the linkages between sexual, financial and political licence, on the one hand, and an organised system of atheism and anti-Christian propaganda, on the other. The symbolic person whose fate cast these connections in both a tragic and criminal light was the Queen of France, Marie Antoinette.

Mother and Daughter; Queen to King

In part Burke's portrayal of Marie Antoinette was a response to the pornographic scandals that had been published about her and about the French Court,[15] but it is also true that his defence of sexual propriety and associated protocols of dress (the elaborate splendours of court dress, diplomatic and military uniforms, and Burke's own political-physical horror of nakedness and of radical fundamentalism) are integral to his repudiation of the new philosophy and its salacious forms of appeal. Once the Regicide has been accepted by Britain as the legitimate government of France and its new ambassador is received with ceremony, however much that may be a caricature of the traditional reception, then, he declares,

> Morals, as they were: – decorum, the great outguard of sex, and the proud sentiment of honour, which makes virtue more respectable, where it is, and conceals human frailty, where virtue may not be, will be banished from this land of propriety, modesty, and reserve.[16]

However, such moments depend for much of their effect on the inversion of the standard attacks of French pamphleteers on court corruption. They concentrated on financial speculation and the wasting of public funds as well as on sexual debauchery; these were also the themes of Burke's attacks on the revolutionary government. The damaging affair of Marie Antoinette and the diamond necklace in 1785–86 exemplified this sexual-financial relationship,[17] which Burke then exploited – as he did with every aspect of the queen's career and reputation – by accusing the revolutionaries and not the court of degrading sexual relationships in general and of undermining trust in the financial institutions of the state.[18] This accusation is repeated in all the anti-French writings of Burke's last seven years, 1790–97. It extends to include his wider attack on the misrepresentation of monarchy as a system of government, on the misrepresentation of the French monarchy as an institution and on the misrepresentation of the queen and king as persons, she as a modern

Messalina of the court and he as the financial head that was represented on the old coinage and devalued, erased (beheaded), when it was replaced. The execution of the king and queen inevitably heightened the tone and enriched the appeal of his defence of them and of all they had stood for. [19] The degradation of sex, the depreciation of money and the dismemberment of the body (individual and corporate), were inescapable features, in Burke's view, of the bloody experiment of the Revolution. Thereafter, he regularly derided any attempt on the part of England or the European powers to make peace with or come to terms with the Regicides of France by imaging it as, for instance, a sexual dalliance with a monster: war, no more than the making of a constitution, is not

> . . . a matter of experiment. As if you could take it up or lay it down as an idle frolick! As if the dire goddess that presides over it, with her murderous spear in her hand, and her gorgon at her breast, was a coquette to be flirted with![20]

In suing for peace, England, traditionally self-described as 'manly', is transmuted into a version of the Marie Antoinette, or the Madame du Barry of the pamphlet literature and in turn the old libertine France, traditionally 'feminine', becomes the formidable military Athena-Marianne of 1795.

Burke is fond of dramatising transpositions especially of a gendered nature, that summarise a revolution in behaviour. In the *Fourth Letter on a Regicide Peace* (1795), there is a complicated sequence, the second great set piece on Marie Antoinette (after the more famous one in the *Reflections*), in which the execution of the queen is re-enacted within two sequences, one belonging to the past and to her mother, the great (and warlike) Maria Theresa, who went to war on Prussia, and one belonging to the present, in which the Prussian and Austrian and eventually the English nations are represented by stand-in ambassadors, come to pay court to the assassins who have staged a grand display of their power and pomp in order to insult Europe and, with that, all that the murdered queen represented and all that the real Europe (not its surrogate version) should defend – or should have defended.

The 'Austrian coach' of the stand-in ambassador Carletti is driven over stones still wet with the blood of the former 'Austrian' princess towards the formal meeting with the government of assassins 'reeking with the blood of the Daughter of Maria Theresia'. (The idiomatic phrase for the destruction of ceremony and ritual, 'to drive a coach-and-four' is plainly audible here.) This repeats the journey of Marie Antoinette, 'whom they sent half dead in a dung cart to a cruel execution'; and the ambassador, 'this Renegado from the faith and from all honour and humanity' drives the coach over

> . . . that blood, which dropped every step through her tumbrel, all the way she was drawn from the horrid prison, in which they had finished all the cruelty and horrors, not executed in the face of the sun!

The execution was terrible, but what was not 'executed' publicly was worse. As in the *Reflections*, a sexual assault, a moral death, is intimated, worse than the open abuse. In her long Calvary to the guillotine, Marie Antoinette is again drawn from the darkness of dungeons, of inner chambers, where the conspiracy against her as a private person has festered, to the world of exhibition and spectacle, where the grim consequence of that conspiracy has to be endured. Moreover, in another reference to his earlier apostrophe to the queen in the *Reflections*, Burke inverts the linked experiences of the mother and daughter. Maria Theresa had been given the acclamation of the drawn swords of her subjects in her proposed war against France (actually against Prussia in 1741, but France is the rhetorically necessary country here); Marie Antoinette had been given no such protection in October 1789, save the imagined ten thousand swords of Burke's lament for her vulnerability. Maria Theresa's subjects had sworn, in Latin, echoing the Roman praetorian guard whom the revolutionaries liked to invoke as historical ancestors, to die for her – except that it is 'pro Rege nostro', 'for our King'. Burke knew that Maria Theresa, according to the Pragmatic Sanction, would be legally regarded as co-regent with her husband, Francis I. But he used the distinction between king and queen, forgoing for the occasion titles of empress and emperor and regent and co-regent, to enhance the transposition from female to male, from queen to king. This great queen, he announces, 'lived and died a King'. Kingship is a condition of authority and decisiveness gendered as male and associated with all those who must learn again to 'feel as Men and as Kings' or cease to exist as either. The 'manliness' of Maria Theresa and the 'femininity' of her daughter and the epicene quality of 'this miserable fop', the ambassador-philosophe, encapsulate for Burke the successive stages of the miltary-sexual decline and 'fallen dignity of the rest of Europe'. The Osric-like philosophe and the 'grim assassins' who insult him as readily as he, in the name of Austria and its royal household, takes the insult, are natural allies – sexual degenerates and butchers.[21]

At the heart of the First and Fourth of the *Letters on a Regicide Peace*, but central also to the other two *Letters*, is a determined attempt to link the idea and the image of a degraded condition with a dismembered body. Marie Antoinette is clearly the choice emblem for this interconnection, although others make their way through the characteristically name-crowded pages to act in supporting roles or as figures in a sub-plot that shadows the main plot. The political dismemberment of 'the great Christian commonwealth' of Europe[22] is the dominant theme but it is constantly articulated as a sequence in which sexual delinquency, prostitution, divorce, bloodshed, dismemberment, cannibalism and the swallowing of old Europe by the new follow one another in ostensibly logical provocation. The triad of 'Regicide, Jacobinism, Atheism', established by deliberate policy and accompanied by their 'correspondent system of manners', indicate the Jacobin Republic's determination to achieve 'total departure' from 'this civilized world'.[23]

The density of Burke's text is the index of his shock and anger at the energy and comprehensiveness of the scheme to amass and pervert all that had been civilised to the new barbarism. Exhibitions, pageants, theatrical parades, heroes and heroines, villains and monarchs, military commanders and tradespeople, and the mantra-like listings of names and of crimes, of nations and territories, wars and catastrophes, past glories and present-day debauch, select classical authors and the swarms of contemporary pamphleteers, famous quotations and infamous sayings, seem by their sheer weight to stifle the arguments they seek to display. Yet the rhythmic counterpointing of good and evil incarnated in contemporary figures gives the intricate argument a pace like that of a news report from the frontline of a great battle between civilizations. One obvious example in the *Third Letter* is the contrast drawn between the marquis de Lafayette, the head of the National Guard in the traumatic October days of 1789, now a prisoner in an Austrian jail, and Sir William Sidney Smith, a British naval commander, also a prisoner in a Parisian jail. Burke (in common with many others, then and since) could see nothing distinguished about Lafayette, 'unless his leading on (or his following) the allied army of Amazonian and male cannibal Parisians to Versailles, on the famous fifth of October, 1789, is to make his glory.' Those in Britain who plead for the release of this man from the prison of the Austrian emperor, the head of the household to which Marie Antoinette belonged, should remember, says Burke, the noble Sir Sidney Smith, taken prisoner while serving his country, and how the appeals for his release have been dismissed by 'the Regicide enemy'. What really distinguishes Sir Sidney's case, however, is the place of his imprisonment,

> . . . in the tower of the Temple, the last prison of Louis the Sixteenth, and the last but one of Maria Antoinetta of Austria; the prison of Louis the Seventeenth; the prison of Elizabeth of Bourbon.[24]

There he stays, amidst the ghosts of the slaughtered royal family, while Lafayette who should have protected them, is pleaded for; there he stays while Lord Malmesbury, the British ambassador to France, attends the opera and sees there not a face he would previously have known in Paris; instead 'a set of abandoned wretches, squandering in insolent riot the spoils of their bleeding country'. The connection with Marie Antoinette is what makes these men function as part of the general argument about British foreign policy and the distinction between those French sympathisers in Britain, 'men who may become more attached to the country of their principles, than to the country of their birth', and true patriots like Sir Sidney.[25]

A Foggy Day in London Town

Burke's unfinished *Fourth Letter on a Regicide Peace*, begun in 1795, is part of his campaign against the British Government's attempts to open peace negotiations with France. It opens with an elaborate and laboured conceit based on the fact that Lord Auckland's pamphlet setting out the official position had been published anonymously in the last week of October of that year. The fogs of October become an image of the incoherence of the government policy, of the internal contradictions of Auckland's pamphlet and make a startling contrast with the clear and systematic policy designed and pursued by the revolutionary government against 'the commonwealth of Christian Europe'. The month of October recalls for Burke October 1789, the terrible month when the monarchy endured its first premonitory humiliation: further, had the pamphlet appeared a week earlier it could have recalled the September massacres of 1792, carried out by the 'septembrists' or 'Septembrizers' (as he called them in the *First Letter*);[26] but now it has achieved its own notoriety since this is the week and the month which henceforward will be remembered as the time when the 'usurpation' at Paris was recognised by the British Government as 'France', announced by this government writer, now referred to variously throughout as 'the Octobrist', the 'October speculator', the 'October politician', 'the Politician of September or of October', 'this Physician of October'.[27] Burke is referring both to the new revolutionary calendar and to the new style of referring to months and *journées* in Paris as marking phases of development in the Revolution, indicating thereby a new and horrifying tempo of events that had made everything so fleeting and unpredictable and yet, by doing so, changed everything forever. So the various names that attach the author to the month of October are reinforced by the constant references to the 'fourth week of October, 1795', part of the pamphlet's title but also for Burke a symptom of its surrender to the new rhythm of revolutionary time that was so foreign to the slow evolution of the historical processes by which old Europe had been formed and to which the sensibility of its inhabitants had been attuned. Every indication of time and date is exploited to mark 'the end of civilised time'.[28]

The author's admission that his pamphlet could be outrun by events, even as he wrote, gives Burke the opportunity, perhaps too eagerly seized, to contrast modern with ancient authors, durability with ephemerality, the boast of the moderns to be transitory in their fame, and in their opinions and principles. Georgian satire's well-established attack on volatile fashion, as opposed to stolid and plain traditionalism, is remoulded by Burke into a critique of what he recognised to be a new configuration of temporality, in part created by and in part creating journalism and pamphlet literature – an insight reiterated by Thomas Carlyle among others.[29] Parading himself as taking the part of 'us simple country folk' against those who would indulge in 'the sportive variability of these weekly, daily, or hourly speculators', he attacks the pamphlet's disingenuous claim to provisionality and the long-term consequences of the policy it advocates in seeking peace with 'the present usurpation in France.'[30]

The dislocation of traditional seasonal patterns is affirmed again in Burke's account of how the House of Commons is, in effect, putting on a Christmas play by prosecuting a loyalist pamphleteer for misdescribing the power of the Crown in the British constitution while, outside the realm of such theatre, the regicides, indifferent to such constitutional fastidiousness, seek to destroy both Christmas and the constitution.[31] The season, the month, the day of the publication and of its translation into French, point up its own hapless view of its timing, of its failure to be timely. Burke compares it demeaningly to a popular almanac that fulfils the basic requirements of the modest genre it belongs to by, for instance, warning against the consequences of not taking precautions against the October fogs.[32] In the *Third Letter* of 1797 he returns to the unseasonable nature of the pamphlet and the subsequent Speech from the Throne when he compares them to a kingfisher building its halcyon nest as if a May breeze rather than an October storm were blowing on the ocean. All of these manoeuvres were in accord with what he called 'This Diplomatick Revolution', carried out by the Directory and aided by the British Embassy in Paris.[33]

The Ambassadors

The *First Letter on a Regicide Peace* (1796) has a similar sequence in which 'the fall of human greatness' is represented by 'the crowned heads of Europe waiting as patient suitors in the anti-chamber of Regicide'. The 'sanguinary tyrant' and 'bloody ruffian' who receives their homage is Lazare Carnot, who had voted for the execution of the king, and who, as he looks upon the ambassadors, 'is measuring them with his eye, and fitting to their size the slider of his Guillotine'.[34] But these ambassadors will emerge from this experience as 'sad and serious conspirators' because they will return home to spread the contagion of degradation and loss of self-esteem and national esteem they have undergone. Thus the masquerade of obeisance to the butchers of the Revolution extends the effect of the 'conspiracy' that has rotted Europe.

However, in the 'Austrian coach' sequence, Great Britain was not there; or, rather, like Prussia and Austria, it was speciously represented, without its consent, by James Monroe, the American ambassador to France who was deemed suitable because of the alleged hatred of President Washington for Britain. Again Burke wants to say how unprecedented and savage this procedure is, how diplomatic ritual and language have been mutilated in this pseudo-show, where, instead of the badge of office, the ambassadors received, not the traditional 'gold boxes, and miniature pictures set in diamonds', but 'boxes of epigrammatic lozenges'. Verbal insult, expertly delivered, replaces the emblems of office. Yet the whole episode has as its theme the system of fake representation that the Revolution had inaugurated and the degree to which this was a caricature of the old system. The absurd dress of the French government ministers, an extraordinary display of *nouveau-riche* vulgarity, is both a cover for and an exposure of their role in 'this monstrous Tragi-comedy' now unfolding.[35] Burke hopes he will never see Great Britain, 'in any rags and *coversluts* of Infamy . . . at such an exhibition'. Dress is a disguise for crime and conspiracy; it is a mockery of what once was; it covers the body of ambassadors who are being stripped naked and measured for death by the eyes of the butchers. It is stage dress. Those wearing it are actors, stand-ins for the real, and the whole effect would be comic were it not for the tragic reality that lies at the heart of the masquerade, the last trace of traditional monarchical society which is, appropriately, the royal blood of the dead queen on the cobble stones of the Place de la Révolution, formerly Place Louis XV.

Consistently, Burke had argued that the mark of the new world was most glaringly visible in its system and theory of representation. It supplanted that which was real with that which was fake. Its imitation of the real had been so successful that the distinction between the real and the represented had been elided. The parody of European ambassadors presenting their credentials to the French government is not to be understood as merely that. For while Burke may argue, as he repeatedly does, that this is not the real Europe and not the real France – the insistent theme of his 1793 publication, *Remarks on the Policy of the Allies*[36] – nevertheless these surrogate representations of them, absurd and sinister at once, have become actual. In recognising and treating with the Directory, the British government is conceding to the new universe of representation. The revolutionary government does not represent France, says Burke. The new France does not represent the real France; nor is Europe any longer a representation of what it once and really was.

And yet these misrepresentations or non-representations must be dealt with. They constitute an insult to the Old World, but they are the New World. They are present, the Old World is absent. Churches have given way to theatres as the sites of legitimating ritual and protocol for the political world.[37] The transitional agency from one to the other, constitutive of the new, not ancillary to it, is violence. The real world has been violently executed and a mock imitation of it has appeared in its place. The trace of the real is the still-wet blood of the queen and, Burke insists, that blood will remain wet while human beings remember how to feel in the face of tragedy; once they lose that capacity, the blood will dry and fade. Indifference to public atrocity will become the basis of the political world of revolutionary modernity. Even the most spectacular butchery, the dismemberment of the Princess de Lamballes, the dismemberment of Europe, the pornography of the sexually assaulted, mutilated and humiliated body, especially of the female body, will not elicit the outrage they merit. The 'cannibal Republic' will swallow the past, bulimic France will swallow country after country in Europe,[38] the Revolution will swallow its own offspring and yet, in this Goya-like darkness, Great Britain remains, in Burke's view, a country that has become morally and politically inert, 'a nation gamboling in an ocean of superfluity' that is 'undone by want'.[39] Economic prosperity and moral poverty in combination did not provide the political spirit, that sense of 'responsibility to conscience and to glory'[40] that was needed to face down an enemy that, in threatening all of Europe, also threatened Great Britain.

Persistently, the real is degraded into theatre and the theatrical scene itself is such a mixture of tragic, comic and farcical elements that it indicates the degree of chaos that now afflicts all basic categories. In one nightmare sequence, Burke envisages the reception that is to be afforded the new Regicide ambassador, perhaps the notorious executioner Antoine-Joseph Santerre or the inexorably cruel Jean-Lambert Tallien. The parade of notables echoes the processional roll-call passages from Virgil, Milton and, more directly, Pope's mock-epic version in the Lord Mayor's procession in *The Dunciad* IV. But its internal reference is even more effective, because preceding it by some forty pages is a satiric account of the ceremonies attendant upon the Directory's first taking office and, preceding that, in 1790, upon Burke's 'old acquaintance', the recently executed Anarchasis Cloots, leading 'a body of Ambassadors, whom he conducted, as from all the nations of the World, to the bar of what was called the Constituent Assembly'. The theatrical costumes of all these ambassadors are derided, but in the case of Cloots, the 'Ambassador of the Human Race', the ambassadors whom he introduces are representatives of the oppressed sovereignty of the various nations who declaim against their several kings. This is inversion and abstraction together. Even the fanatic Cloots, says Burke, 'could not have imagined that this Opera procession should have been the prototype of the real appearance of the Representatives of all the Sovereigns of Europe' at diplomatick ceremonies or at Feasts such as that in the Temple of Reason (formerly Notre Dame) in 1793, when a 'prostitute of the street' will 'be adored as a Goddess', and at last we 'shall have a French Ambassador without a suspicion of Popery' – something that will have the dubious merit of appeasing the fanatical Protestants of Ireland, if no one else.[41]

This is the triumph of the conspiracy. The reception of the ambassadors to the French Republic by the nations of Europe and of the ambassadors to those nations – particularly Britain – from the French Republic brings to a culmination the plot laid long before to destroy Throne and Altar in Europe. As opposed to the shambolic policies of Britain and the European powers, the French have been from the outset, determined, clear-sighted, acting in accord with a fiendish design. In the 'First Letter', we are told that

> Nothing in the Revolution, no, not a phrase or a gesture, not to the fashion of a hat or a shoe, was left to accident. All has been the result of design; all has been matter of institution. No mechanical means could be devised in favour of this incredible system of wickedness and vice, that has not been employed. The noblest passions, the love of glory, the love of country, have been debauched into means of it's preservation and it's propagation.[42]

The reception of the ambassadors is the culmination of the conspiracy's success. The revolutionary world is now accepted by Europe. Everything that had been ceremonial and decent has been inverted, but the grotesque parody of the manners of the Old World have become the means of establishing its fearsome replacement. The world of revolution has been parasitic upon the world of tradition. But the history of the parent world has now become the history of its parasite.

'A Silent Revolution'

There were three forms of conspiracy. First was the secret organised conspiracy that began with the men of letters, the philosophes and their moneyed friends, and that included various other groups – freemasons and Illuminati – throughout Europe. Second, there was the revolutionary conspiracy that culminated in the Directory and was in effect an extension of the first literary-philosophical conspiracy into a political policy. Third, there was the silent conspiracy of forces that by itself effected a revolution. Burke describes it at length in the *Second Letter*, in a re-emphasis of the account given years earlier both in the *Reflections* and in *Thoughts on French Affairs* (1791), as well as in the more recent *Letter to William Elliot* (1795):

> A silent revolution in the moral world preceded the political, and prepared it . . . Their causes no longer lurked in the recesses of cabinets, or in the private conspiracies of the factious. They were no longer to be controlled by the force and influence of grandees . . . The chain of subordination, even in cabal and sedition, was broken in it's most important links. It was no longer the great and the populace. Other interests were formed, other dependencies, other connexions, other communications. The middle classes had swelled far beyond their former proportion. Like whatever is the most effectively rich and great in society, these classes became the seat of all active politicks; and the preponderating weight to decide on them. There were all the energies by which fortune is acquired; there the consequence of their success. There were all the talents which assert their pretensions, and are impatient of the place which settled society prescribes to them. Those descriptions had got between the great and the populace; and the influence on the lower classes was with them. The spirit of ambition had taken possession of this class as violently as ever it had done of any other. They felt the importance of this situation. The correspondence of the monied and the mercantile world, the literary intercourse of academies; but above all, the press, of which they had in a manner, entire possession, made a kind of electrick communication every where. The press, in reality, has made every Government, in it's spirit, almost democratick. Without the great, the first movements in this revolution could not, perhaps, have been given. But the spirit of ambition, now for the first time connected with the spirit of speculation, was not to be restrained at will. There was no longer any means of arresting a principle in it's course.[43]

Louis did not see that revolution that was taking place; but the one he did see and supported, the American Revolution, was fatal to him and his throne. For in helping to found one republic in America, he also helped to found a second one in France. Despite having 'the whole Atlantick for a ditch', and the outworks of England and the rampart of European monarchies to defend him, he was overwhelmed by the republican idea. How then, Burke asks, can the French Republic not be recognised as a far more dangerous threat to all of Europe than the American republic 'of simple husbandmen or fishermen' had already been to France? The adaptation of the American Revolution as the real one of the modern period – suitably frugal and Protestant in contrast to the French debauch – was soon integrated into British counter-revolutionary nationalism by John Wilson Croker and Robert Southey in particular.

Ambition and energy and wealth, with the accompanying occupation of a strategic social position, are identifying features of the forces transforming the moral and political worlds, but crucially, it is the combination of these with one another and of all of them with the spirit of speculation that is ultimately catastrophic. Burke clearly gains all he can from the various meanings and nuances of the word speculation, especially as a term in philosophy and in finance,[44] with the implication of gambling and of embezzlement (peculation); and beyond that with the Latin words *speculare* (to see) and *peculium* (private property) which shadow his provocative use of it and its companion (speculator[s]). The moneyed class and the philosophes are both kinds of speculator; it is their co-operation that gives to the word its novel vertigo and that enables them to envisage an inverted image of the Old World, with a new system of education, a new church (of atheism), a new European world of community and, most fundamental of all, a new system of human relationships and of customary practices. All of these are founded on the deepest of all inversions – that is, of relationship understood as divorce. Clearly he refers here to marriage, but divorce is also the principle underlying the new church of atheism, when it becomes schism, and the inversion of the European law of vicinage between nations, when it becomes threat, and when it attacks all the 'system of manners' attached to the old order, seeking to break 'the secret, unseen, but irrefragable bond of habitual intercourse'.[45] Everything new is related both by virtue of its divorce from all that preceded it and by virtue of the fact that the divorce takes the form of inversion; but in addition, divorce from all that is fundamentally human and its inversion into ferocious and insensate cruelty becomes the form of relationship itself. Relationship between people and between nations in this new world is predicated on the idea of divorce. Indeed, divorce is *the* form of relationship for such a world, entirely dependent in its negativity on what preceded it. Yet this, Burke avers, has become the fashion and is to be sanctioned by those titled women – this makes it worse, of course, – who are unwittingly aiding in a revolution that will overturn their world;

> . . . Duchesses, Countesses and Lady Marys, choaking the way and overturning each other in a struggle, who should be first to pay her court to the *Citoyenne*, the spouse of the twenty-first husband, he the husband of the thirty-first wife, and to hail her in the rank of honourable matrons before the four days of marriage is expired![46]

The secularisation of marriage leads to the loss of the sacred bonds of feeling between parents (especially mothers) and children and thence to all social bonds of affection and respect, including finally the bonds of respect between the living and the dead. Thence, in a reversion to barbarism, the revolutionaries indulge in cannibalism and the human body once more becomes the ultimate site of the atrocious theories and conspiracies of the revolutionary leaders.

Rousseau

The Grand Guignol of the *Letters* and of the *Letter to a Noble Lord* (1796) is enhanced by Burke's deliberate contrast between spectacular ruin and the systematic design which has created it. He insists on this at every point. The downfall of traditional society is the consequence of a conspiracy that preceded the Revolution and of a policy executed during it, both of which have been characterised by determination, clarity and diabolic energy. His repeated tirades against the instrumental reason and the quantitative modes of measurement that he associated with the geometers, arithmeticians and even geographers (who replaced time with space) of the Enlightenment, most especially Voltaire and Helvétius, reveal that he could readily see a coherence between such systematic and false reasoning, atheism and libertinism. All depended upon a simplification of complex processes, an impoverishment of practices that were taken to be irrational because they were non-rational and, inevitably, on a prideful self-reliance that was the essence of the secular spirit.

Burke invoked Montesquieu as the political philosopher who most effectively rebuked the institutionalised sciolism of the philosophes. But it was Rousseau and the nature and scope of his influence who brought the idea of a conspiracy to another and more menacing level of intensity.[47] For Rousseau, Burke realised, was a cult figure, the first of a new kind of star personality whose public reputation was in part founded on the public exposure of his personal life in his *Confessions*, which, along with his famous didactic novel *Julie; ou, La Nouvelle Hélöise*, had presented to the world a model of the new hero without virtues, and had made identification with the heroines and heroes of his fiction a mode of affirming and extending the political belief in equality.[48] Jean-Jacques had become the performative version of Rousseau in a new kind of political theatre which Burke was hard-put to describe but which he recognised to have an extraordinary appeal. It catered to the taste for the marvellous, it was a deliberate exploitation of eccentricity, it was exhibitionism in pursuit of celebrity – although Burke's word for that was 'vanity'.

In the several pages devoted to Rousseau in *Letter to a Member of the National Assembly* (1791) Burke makes a serious attempt to understand his appeal and to estimate the disastrous effect of having such a writer adopted by the Assembly in Paris as the great moral teacher of the new France. 'Influence' is too weak a word for Rousseau's effect on the Assembly.

> Every body knows that there is a great dispute among their leaders, which of them is the best resemblance to Rousseau. In truth, they all resemble him. His blood they transfuse into their minds and into their manners. Him they study; him they meditate; him they turn over in all the time they can spare from the laborious mischief of the day, or the debauches of the night. Rousseau is their canon of holy writ; in his life he is their canon of *Polycletus;* he is their standard figure of perfection. To this man and this writer, as a pattern to authors and to Frenchmen, the founderies of Paris are now running for statues . . . Rousseau is a moralist, or he is nothing. It is impossible, therefore, . . . to mistake their design in choosing the author, with whom they have begun to recommend a course of studies.[49]

The derangement and delinquency of Rousseau in part explain the nature of his assault on domestic pieties, fidelity and chastity; nevertheless, his life and work were part of a planned attempt to destroy such habits and virtues. Even more plainly, his adoption by the Assembly is indisputably part of a design. The aim and effect of the design is to replace the real with its degradation and, in making that degradation appealing through a mix of specious and real sentiment (itself a symptom of design), to corrupt representation itself. Representation, as Burke speaks of it in the revolutionary years, depends greatly on those forms of idealisation that are founded in love. Therefore, the corruption of love is necessary to the success of the revolutionary design, and women especially, in whom so much of the idealisation processs is invested and, in every sense, embodied, are traduced and humiliated, with their governing roles as mothers and wives, daughters and virgins, queens and princesses inverted.

From an entirely opposed view, Mary Wollstonecraft, who admired much in Rousseau, also objected to the 'sensibility that led him to degrade woman by making her the slave of love' and to 'his ferocious flight back to the night of sensual ignorance' that marked his lack of faith in the future perfectibility of humankind.[50] But for Burke this reversion is the heart of the matter and sexual degradation its most glaring feature. It was for this that Rousseau was adopted by the revolutionary generation. For a total revolution in the socio-political world, the traditional basis of human relationships, sexual and familial, had to be replaced. Rousseau, in his view, provided the alternative basis; that was what made him so dangerous. In Wollstonecraft's view, it was, on the contrary, Rousseau's failure to provide such an alternative that made him so disappointingly reactionary at times. Her view of 'Frenchmen' was quite close on occasion to Burke's view of Rousseau; 'constitutionally attached to novelty and ingenious speculations', they were sure to be attracted by 'just and simple' ideas but too rash to effect them gradually.[51] But the standard national characteristics of the French, frequently invoked to explain the violence of the Revolution, were also transposable to anyone who affected an excess of 'sensibility', or 'imagination', fake 'compassion' and a desire to be conspicuous in the world by whatever means – all of these, in Wollstonecraft's eyes, the failings of Burke, just as in Burke's eyes they were the failings of Rousseau.

> Full of yourself, you make as much noise to convince the world that you despise the revolution, as Rousseau did to persuade his contemporaries to let him live in obscurity.[52]

However, Wollstonecraft's version of the Burke–Rousseau parallel, published in 1790, did not inhibit Burke's assault of the following year on the Rousseau who had become a cult figure for Europeans of all classes and nations even before he had become a revolutionary icon.

Thus, his Rousseau becomes a statue and a standard, a pattern and a model. His teachings are a substitute for true morality, his virtue 'new-invented', his goal 'a new sort of glory', his inversion of 'openness and candour' no more than 'abuse and perversion'. The politicians or 'practical philosophers' of the Assembly, 'systematic in everything', have conspired to replace the paradigm figures of teacher and of father with this surrogate, 'a lover of his kind, but a hater of his kindred'.[53] Taste is corrupted; gallantry and the whole system of what Burke called 'chivalry' is replaced by 'an unfashioned, indelicate, sour, gloomy, ferocious medley of pedantry and lewdness; of metaphysical speculations, blended with the coarsest sensuality'.[54] Equality appears now in the shape of a debauch, in which 'the first females of the first families in France may become an easy prey to dancing-masters, fidlers, pattern-drawers, friseurs, and valets de chambre . . .' The assault on Marie Antoinette is now extended to all the women of her class and status and the system of representation is comparably subverted by the commemoration of Rousseau as the model of wisdom, a new Socrates, a new father-figure who abandoned his real children and popularised instead the benevolence which is central to the '*ethics of vanity*' and to the whole attempt at 'a regeneration of the moral constitution of man.'[55]

Representations

Burke's text is laden with the names of individuals, groups and organisations, not to mention countries, regions, cities and states, to an extraordinary degree. This accords with his general view that the detail and the circumstances of any political issue should be known and that individuals and communities are embedded in histories that at least in part explain their behaviour. It is on this ground that he can hazard general accounts of the large scale developments in world history, especially in relation to Britain and France and the very different forms of global domination that each represented. Although the scandalous violence of the British factions in Ireland and India was such that it brought the very idea of colonisation into question, British government at home had for him the inestimable virtue that it fused religion and politics in a mutually dependent relationship. Sectarianism was clearly one by-product of this, and the example of Ireland a permanent reminder of the harm it could do. But the fury of religious extremism, of the sort Burke had witnessed in the anti-Catholic Gordon Riots in London in 1780, was precisely what he believed the established Anglican state was designed to placate, rather than encourage. Perhaps, as Sir Brooke Boothby hinted at the time, the violence he saw then made him anxious to avoid violence at any cost and therefore less ready than he might have been to countenance the behaviour of the Parisian mob.[56] But it was for Burke a fundamental difference between the French (or any other) absolutist state and the British state that in the latter religion consecrated political responsibility into duty. Freedom was thus prevented from ever breaking out into that dangerous kind of frenzy or effervescence that had once threatened domestic stability in England and was now creating chaos in France. This is the argument for church establishment in the *Reflections*. Where there is no 'state religious establishment' then popular sovereignty is without restraint. An 'unnatural inverted domination' ensues, in which the people exact from their representatives 'an abject submission to their occasional will'.[57] Once again, the central question is representation, once again the most menacing threat is that of inversion, whereby the representative merely becomes an instrument:

> When the people have emptied themselves of all the lust of selfish will, which without religion it is impossible they ever should, when they are conscious that they exercise, and exercise perhaps in an higher link of the order of delegation, the power, which to be legitimate must be according to that eternal immutable law, in which will and reason are the same, they will be more careful how they place power in base and incapable hands. In their nomination to office, they will not appoint to the exercise of authority, as to a pitiful job, but as to an holy function . . .[58]

The implied rejection of Rousseau's theories of popular sovereignty and the general will is clear enough but the larger point is that political authority is sacred, not secular, and the choice of representatives is therefore one that needs the support of religion. The point of a religious establishment is to identify the dual function of representation. A representative stands in for the people, but also it is necessary 'that all who administer in the government of men, in which they stand in the person of God himself, should have high and worthy notions of their function and destination'. In effect, Burke endeavours to give to the system of limited or 'virtual representation' a sanction that is ultimately divine but is also best realised by the British system of church establishment. He struggles with the various ways in which a representative – an ambassador, an elected member of parliament, a monarch – can stand in for the people, be in their place and yet not displace or replace them.

In one sense, it is comparatively easy to argue against those like Rousseau or Paine, who seem to demand a form of representation that involves unanimity. This can be said to be impractical and a metaphysical delusion. John Quincy Adams, writing under the pseudonym 'Agricola', derided this in Rousseau and in Paine.

> Rousseau contends that the social compact is formed by a personal association of individuals, which must be unanimously assented to, and which cannot possibly be made by a representative body . . . this is neither practicable, nor even metaphysically true . . .[59]

But while Burke goes along with this line of argument at various times, he sees that the logic of a Rousseauistic or Painite position leads to the abandonment of government altogether or to the avowal that government is no more than a necessary evil. For their theories of representation are actually anti-representational theories. No representation can be identical with its object. Representation is always imperfect precisely because it is a substitute, a surrogate, a stand-in, to use Burke's own phrase. What Burke wants to find is a way of defending the system of representation that recognises the element of substitution and that glories in it, that claims this is of the very structure of the divine system and that all attempts to elide the distance between that which is represented and that which is doing the representation are impious as well as foolish. It is only *because* there is a distinction between the object of representation and the representing agency that the system works. What the revolutionaries deemed to be its weakness, its irredeemable imperfection, was its strength.

Rousseau's lethal concept of the general will effectively destroyed that distinction, so central to the traditional political and aesthetic practices of the European commonwealth of nations. Stripped of its historical development and accretions, the concept was abstractly reconfigured so that the will of the People and of the Legislator became identical one with the other. It was through the exercise of this will that the People emerged into existence. Burke was perfectly right in saying that Rousseau's ambition was to alter human nature; Rousseau had said so himself in the *Social Contract*.[60] In addition, Burke believed that the actions of Robespierre or of the Directory, in using every possible means, cultural and political, to coerce this new vision of the person and of the people into existence, were in accord with Rousseau's irreconcilable doctrines of radical individual freedom and complete collective conformity.[61] They were powerful and yet grotesque because their craving to replace the old with the new produced nothing more than a caricature of the old. It was the recognition, diplomatic and other, of this caricature by Britain and by the European powers, that made him despair. They seemed not to know what it was they were ratifying. The incoherence of their policy towards France, if policy it could be called, certainly contrasted with the design of the revolutionaries towards them. To oppose the Jacobin energy effectively, he argued in *Remarks on the Policy of the Allies* (1793), Britain needed a policy of 'adventure' not 'caution'.[62] This ferocious energy, without any anchorage in property, frequently associated with frenzy and enthusiasm, is just as often linked to deliberate and implacable policy.

The rhetoric of all the anti-French writings combines the imageries of crazed destruction and of ruthless planning without any sense of dislocation; in fact, by thematising them as the interwoven elements of one continuous process, it intensifies the central paradox that lies at the heart of the analysis that depends on one version or another of the conspiracy thesis – that is, the paradox that all the conspiracies that seemed so addicted to design and system and so allergic to custom and precedent were finally achieving their aim of replacing the order of the Old World by exploding the gases (chaos) of the New. Chaos had been the aim or the almost unavoidable outcome of the conspiracies – of people or of circumstance – which had been characterized in their development by intricate plot and symmetries of purpose.

Thus, in the 'Reflections' and increasingly in *A Letter to a Member of the National Assembly*, *The Policy of the Allies*, *Letter to a Noble Lord* and culminatingly in the four *Letters on a Regicide Peace*, Burke uses the idea of a conspiracy in order to embody in persons and in personages his analysis of a catastrophic series of developments in contemporary Europe. Rousseau was a person but as Jean-Jacques became a personage. Marie Antoinette was a person but as Queen of France became a personage. There are many such figures in Burke's writings, many actual persons who become cultural and political icons, and part of his persuasiveness lies in his analysis of the processes whereby one becomes the other. In a more general sense, he certainly exploits the distinction between real historical events and theatrical representations but he often modifies the contrast in order, for instance, to distinguish between a representation and its caricature. This allows him to cast derision upon the Directory's attempts to mimick the dress and protocols of the *ancien régime*; but it also allows him to point up the sinister and cynical policy involved in doing so to deceive the allied powers. Such a policy, so apparently dependent upon representation, is in fact the instrument of an ideology and a regime, or of a series of regimes dating from 1790, that is entirely opposed to representation, whether that be understood in its traditional monarchical or republican forms. (He professed on occasion to admire the 'true republican spirit' which restrained authority by moral force).[63] Burke wants to argue that an extreme, 'a perfect democracy'[64] is really the most opposed of all forms of government to representation because it is based on the desire to extinguish the 'gap' between representing and represented agents. It seeks instead to remould the very idea of what constitutes a people. To achieve that, it needs to deploy coercion and violence strategically against those very forms of relationship, sexual and familial, religious and reverential, upon which the old idea of representation and the old version of society depended. This planned, sustained, brilliantly executed campaign had been so successful that it had persuaded governments and élites in Europe that it was the fulfilment of a destiny. Modernity had indeed arrived, Burke realised; but it could and should have been prevented. Its outcome he would not live to see:

> I shall not live to behold the unravelling of the intricate plot, which saddens and perplexes the awful drama of Providence, now acting on the moral theatre of the world.[65]

6. FACTIONS AND FICTIONS
BURKE, COLONIALISM AND REVOLUTION

I

It is a commonplace of the commentary on Burke that his life and work are characterised by a conflict or disjuncture the identification of which, it is believed, may provide the key to his political thought. He has been variously described as an Irish Catholic adventurer in the very Protestant eighteenth-century British state; as a Jacobite among Hanoverian Whigs; as an Irish Protestant defender of Catholic rights and subverter of the Anglo-Irish political system of which he was a product and beneficiary; as a man who failed to apply to Ireland the principles he applied to the Thirteen Colonies of America; as a long-time defender of revolution against oppression who finally defended oppression and reaction against liberty and revolution; as the aesthetician of a feminised sensibility that is used to support a patriarchal system; as a *novus homo* hired by the aristocracy to defend it against his own class; as, in short, a writer and politician in whom a powerful latent conflict erupted in public contradiction and betrayal.[1] For all that, Burke has been eagerly adopted by many groupings and factions to support political positions that need to disarticulate elements of his thought in order to give a semblance of coherence to the whole of their own.[2]

It is neither necessary nor illuminating to dwell on the possibility that there is a dynamic contradiction or suppressed loyalty in Burke's writings that might explain his supposed inconsistencies or allow some of his readers to forgive what they feel to be the extremity of his opinions or the excessive excitements of his rhetoric. Instead, by looking at Burke's positions on Ireland, America, India and France, and the relation of all of these to England or to Britain, it can be affirmed that a clear and consistent political philosophy emerges, even though it is beset by problems that it cannot fully answer or resolve. It is also evident that Burke's readings of the Irish, the American or the Indian situations have in common with his analysis of the French Revolution a vision so intense and tragic that all competing theories of progress and modernisation had thereafter to combat the charge that they lacked the depth and monumentality of the Burkean defence of 'tradition'. Tradition in this context refers to the artefacts of civilisation, its buildings, laws, customs and practices; but most of all, with Burke, it refers to modes of feeling that are the more precious for always being anachronistic, for being out-of-time and therefore enduring, rather than in time and therefore merely fashionable or transient. Above all, such feelings, while they would seem at times to run merely from the moist to the lachrymose, were most traditional when they included within them a sense of the tragic dimension of human experience.

Burke's development of this vision is, I suggest, consistent with all the political positions that he takes throughout his career; indeed, each of these positions helps towards the refinement and extension of that vision, in part because it is rooted in a belief in the sovereignty and the fragility of customary practice in preserving what is best in political systems.[3] For him this is immensely preferable to all of those forms of reflection that inevitably, in conceptualising lived experience, render it foreign to itself and reduce it, or turn it into an abstraction. Abstraction is a condition that politics must, as far as possible, avoid; one of the characteristics of colonial and of revolutionary political systems is that they nurture abstraction – a version of what the world might or should be – at the expense of the historically actualised world. In doing so, they create a spectral universe. When that happens, the inversion is so complete that everything that had previously defined the human and circumstantial world loses its weight and force. A parallel universe is formed, the ghostly replica of the real world. In this virtual reality, traditional feelings have become homogenised into a universalising conception of 'feeling' and have, as a consequence, lost their complexity and depth. This is the world of a utopian, placeless modernity.

Abstraction is the product of an extraordinary and perverted energy that manifests itself in symmetrically organised systems of power that are hostile to the native disorderliness and intricacies of human communities and their histories. This energy is encouraged by situations in which a monopoly of power is concentrated in the hands of a faction, sect or cabal. Politically, such energy tends to characterise a new *arriviste* class, since established societies have an inertial force that gives them durability and checks or even stifles volatile and subversive movements. Obvious examples of such an aspirant and urgent class would be the French Jacobins, Irish Protestants, East India Company men in India. Their rapacity, which is both economic and intellectual, knows no interest other than that of their own group; in providing for that, they destroy historical communities, arguing or implying that these are either defunct in themselves or hostile to progress and therefore unworthy of protection, attention or tolerance. Such groups or factions are, in Burke's view, at the heart of the French Revolution in its domestic and in its foreign incarnations; like the Reformation, the only comparable event in European history, it introduced '*other interests into all countries, than those which arose from their locality and natural circumstances*'; and as in post-Reformation Europe, 'that species of faction . . . broke the locality of publick affections, and united descriptions of citizens more with strangers than with their countrymen of different opinions'.[4] The invasion of an integrated native system by a foreign faction is Burke's basic figure for both Reformation and Revolution. But the foreign faction is, on inspection, really a native grouping that has inverted the normal hierarchies of feeling for the sake of asserting a set of fanatical opinions that operates both as an ideology and as a self-serving rationale.

II

Burke's political philosophy began to take shape first as a satire on Bolingbroke and Rousseau, *A Vindication of Natural Society* (1756), and then as an exploration in aesthetics, *A Philosophical Enquiry into the Origin of Our Ideas of the Sublime and the Beautiful* (1757; 2nd edn, 1759). Elements of both these works survive in his later writings and are in some instances crucial features of his mature thought. *A Vindication* anticipates, in an inverted form, much of what he will later say against the French revolutionary belief in the possibility of a secular society based on natural rights, productive of a 'perfect Liberty'.[5] It is a much more polished but much less influential performance than the *Sublime and the Beautiful*, where the treatment of the concept of the Sublime is so much more interesting than that of the Beautiful, largely because it is much less governed by a naive sensationalism.

The sublime is a fusion of religious and political elements that command awe and reverence in a manner recommended by Berkeley in his *Alciphron; or, The Minute Philosopher* (1732), but it is, in addition, productive of terror because of its intimacy with power; it is a 'modification of power', and 'power derives all its sublimity from the terror with which it is generally accompanied.'[6] Death is the 'king of terrors', pain its 'emissary'. However, 'when danger or pain press too nearly, they are incapable of giving any delight, and are simply terrible; but at certain distances, and with certain modifications, they may be, and they are delightful, as we every day experience'.[7] The pleasure we take in the distress of others has its gradations; more intense when it has to do with historical actuality, less so when it has to do with fable.[8] Such pleasure or delight is, oddly, the source of sympathy. The operation of sympathy is, in addition, more effectively produced by the spectacle of catastrophe and tragedy than by success and triumph because, in Aristotelian manner, tragedy stimulates both pity and terror, both of which have pleasure as a crucial component: '. . . for terror is a passion which always produces delight when it does not press too close, and pity is a passion accompanied with pleasure, because it arises from love and social affection'.[9]

Sympathy is a product of the interaction of pity and terror that occurs only when a certain distance from or modification of the tragic experience is achieved. Without that distance there is merely the paralysis of fear or terror. But Burke wants to make a further distinction. He rejects the notion that representation of a shocking reality produces pleasure because it is merely a fiction and because of 'the contemplation of our own freedom from the evils which we see represented'.[10] Instead, he wants to claim that sympathy is pre-rational.

'. . . as our Creator has designed we should be united by the bond of sympathy, he has strengthened that bond by a proportionable delight; and there most where our sympathy is most wanted, in the distresses of others . . . there is no spectacle we so eagerly pursue, as that of some uncommon and grievous calamity: so that whether the misfortune is before our eyes or whether they are turned back to it in history, it always touches with delight. This is not an unmixed delight, but blended with no small uneasiness. The delight we have in such things, hinders us from shunning scenes of misery; and the pain we feel, prompts us to relieve ourselves in relieving those who suffer; and all this antecedent to any reasoning, by an instinct that works us to its own purposes, without our concurrence.[11]

Burke sees the Creator as having so designed our nature that we spontaneously act in a social and sympathetic manner when we most need to; such spontaneity is beyond rational analysis and yet an utterly undeniable reality. There is, in addition, the imitation of others, which 'forms our manners, our opinions, our lives' and which we perform 'without any intervention of the reasoning faculty, but solely from our natural constitution',[12] and, finally, ambition, which drives us to be different in some respect from others and, in doing so, to enable human beings to progress[13] and to have contact with all that is sublime. These act with sympathy to create the world of the social. As in the sympathetic experience, 'a sort of substitution' takes place, whereby we put ourselves in the place of another or in some sense define ourselves in relation to others. Art is of great social importance because it is based on the principle of substitution, whereby the arts can 'transfuse their passions from one breast to another';[14] but when the subject of art is something grand ('such as we should run to see if real'[15]), the power of the poem or painting rests there rather than in the power of imitation itself.

The discussion of the sublime and the beautiful, when it is governed by Burke's conception of the social and by his related and equally important, although more cursory, treatment of words (in Part V), reveals a further, intramural distinction between the real and the fictive which is later to become more prominent in his political writings. Although many words are 'by themselves unoperative', they can become potent when spoken in a particular way or because they have already been 'heated originally by the breath of others';[16] dramatic poetry is imitative, but descriptive poetry (like sympathy) 'operates chiefly by *substitution*; by the means of sounds, which by custom have the effect of realities'.[17] Representation is always in some sense misrepresentation for Burke. No stage drama can or should be expected to compete with an actual event, like a public execution; 'in a moment the emptiness of the theatre would demonstrate the comparative weakness of the imitative arts, and proclaim the triumph of the real sympathy'. For no matter how perfect a tragedy may be, 'it never approaches to what it represents'.[18] Yet the distinction, although adhered to consistently, is not always easy to maintain, since words themselves are a sort of substitute for things and many people have experience only of those substitutes, not of the things which they represent.[19] Their passions are aroused by words, the more so by words which are 'strong' rather than 'clear'. Polished languages, such as French, have great clarity but are deficient in strength, whereas unpolished languages (like 'the oriental tongues') have 'a great force and energy of expression'.[20] It is in the light of these very late remarks in the treatise that we should interpret the earlier and much-quoted sentence from Part II, Section IV: 'In reality a great clearness helps but little towards affecting the passions, as it is in some sort an enemy to all enthusiasms whatsoever.'[21]

Thus, the real world and the represented world are clearly different from one another and the real world is the senior of the two. On the other hand, in a literary work (not in a painting), the clarity (but not the strength) of a representation is in inverse proportion to its effectiveness. It is human nature to be moved by the spectacle of tragedy as a literary form; it is human nature to be even more powerfully affected by a tragic situation, like the fall from greatness of a once-honoured person or persons, that has actually happened or is actually happening.[22]

This is the heart of the Burkean aesthetic. It is profoundly non-romantic. According to it, no representation can or should compete with the actual. Fables, romances and tragedies have their place, but history and actuality always take precedence over them. Representations are substitutes, not deceits. But the possibility of deceit lies primarily in the observer or spectator and it is not difficult to recognise its most egregious form – the preferring of the substitute over the real. Burke is careful in identifying this deceit. True feeling can be evoked by a representation as it also can and should be by an actuality. But when true feeling is elicited by a representation *rather than* by an actual event or sequence of events, then the natural constitution of the human world (and of the divine order of which the human world is part) is inverted. Once feeling flees to the world of representation and abandons the world of actuality, it has become a substitute version of itself. Those in whom that process takes place have yielded their humanity for a surrogate version of it. They have become victims of a delusion. In sacrificing feeling for what actually is for that which is merely represented they run the risk of sacrificing feeling altogether.

This is ultimately what happens to the revolutionary. He or she begins by losing contact with the world as such; goes on to give priority to the world of representation as such; and then finishes by giving ultimate priority to the world of his or her own representations. What is represented in such a case is not, in Burke's view, *the* world but *a* world, one peculiar to the sensibility or the imaginings of an individual. The distinction between the real and the imagined, so clear to Burke in his aesthetic theory, and so crucial for it and for his political philosophy, becomes blurred if not invisible in such circumstances. Egocentricity has replaced sympathy; but it is an egocentricity that craves acclaim from others even though it has no genuine feeling for others. When such an egocentric is commended for the uniqueness and the eccentricity of his or her imaginings, then the world of common forms has been deserted – but not lost. The terrible ambition of the Revolution, going that fatal step further than the Enlightenment, was to desert that world so thoroughly that it would indeed become lost or, at best, recoverable only in memory. The wholly rational and the wholly irrational, as convergent on one another for Burke as for Swift, would finally meet in the writer who would claim that a universal human nature would become visible in himself, not in spite of but because of his eccentricities and of all that had gone to making him radically unique. When uniqueness becomes a criterion of representativeness, then we are truly in the topsy-turvy world of modern literature and modern politics, in the world, as Burke saw it, of Jean-Jacques Rousseau and of Robespierre, in which normal feelings and expectations had been brutally inverted and perverted.[23]

III

It was in Ireland that Burke first saw how a selfish ruling faction could, by passing the Penal Laws 'against the majority of the people', create 'a national calamity' and, in their delinquency, act against 'the principle of a superior Law, which it is not in the power of any community, or of the whole race of man to alter – I mean the will of Him who gave us our nature, and in giving impressed an invariable Law upon it'.[24] No authority, classical or Christian, could be found to justify the position 'that any body of men have a right to make what Laws they please; or that Laws can derive any authority from their institution, merely and independent of the quality of the subject matter'.[25] Even the revocation of the Edict of Nantes against the Huguenots of France was less brazen, punitive and disastrous in its consequences; the Penal system against the Catholics of Ireland differed 'from any scheme of religious persecution now existing in any other country in Europe, or which has prevailed in any time or nation with which history has made us acquainted'.[26] Burke's memories of Protestant bigotry in Ireland, particularly of the judicial murder of Fr. Nicholas Sheehy in 1766, informed his suspicion and hatred of what he called 'faction' and its damaging relation to judicial process and the sovereignty of government. Factions exercised power but never authority; their chief weapon was terror, their preferred means a system of exclusions and punishments, their preferred disguise the law and that species of 'liberty which, by their political chemistry, was to be extracted out of a system of oppression.'[27]

Burke's assaults upon this faction were to be intermittently provoked by the impact on Ireland of the American and French revolutions and the various attempts to remove some of the penal disabilities on Catholics and thereby reduce the danger of their hostility to the British state. But it was an uphill struggle. The Protestant faction insisted that the oppression of the Catholics was a condition of its own survival. In so doing, it detached itself from the spirit of the British constitution and, even more, detached itself from the basic feelings that supported any political system. They saw themselves as Protestants, connected to their co-religionists abroad and not as Irish people, connected to their compatriots at home: this anticipated the linking of revolutionary factions in various countries in a specious brotherhood that denied and even derided domestic, home-bred loyalties:

> But to transfer humanity from its natural basis, our legitimate and home-bred connections; to lose all feeling for those who have grown up by our sides, in our eyes, of the benefit of whose cares and labours we have partaken from our birth: and meretriciously to hunt abroad after foreign affections; is such a disarrangement of the whole system of our duties, that I do not know whether benevolence so displaced is not almost the same thing as destroyed, or what effect bigotry could have produced that is more fatal to society. This no one can help observing, who has seen our doors kindly and bountifully thrown open to foreign sufferers for conscience, whilst through the same ports were issuing fugitives of our own, driven from their Country for a cause which to an indifferent person would seem to be exactly similar, while we stood by, without any sense of impropriety of this extraordinary scene, accusing, and practising injustice.[28]

Thus, danger threatens when a faction within a state acts as a substitute for or alternative to it and puts its own selfish interests in place of the state's concerns and responsibilities. Although the sinister system of the '*Double Cabinet* ' or 'king's friends', famously described in the Rockingham Whig pamphlet *Thoughts on the Cause of the Present Discontents* (1770), is one example of such a faction,[29] the Irish Protestant Ascendancy (as it came to be called in the 1780s)[30] and the East India Company were far more glaring and ruinous. Even though the king's inner circle of advisers may have been, in Burke's view, responsible for the loss of the Thirteen Colonies, they were, nevertheless, not acting as substitutes for the state. The Irish and the Indian groups were. Only the French Jacobins ultimately exceeded them in the malignity of their influence. In revolutionary France the new or foreign element within an old and established native system had overturned that system so completely that the distinction between the real (the historically venerable) and the substitute (the callow, experimental present) was inverted at the least and at worst entirely extinguished. In Ireland and India that catastrophe threatened also. The only fundamental mark of distinction between radical revolutionary ideology and these forms of subordinate colonial rule seemed to consist in the global missionary appeal of the French experiment. It was part of Burke's anxiety to distinguish the revolutionary and the colonial systems more clearly. But it was difficult to do so when the existing forms were so misshapen by the ceaseless action of the various factions that had operated in Ireland, America and India as a kind of secret or alternative government to the real one that lay in London, nestled in the heart of the British constitution and its true guardians, the Rockingham Whigs.

IV

Although he inveighed a great deal against a theory of empire – as in his 'Letter to the Sheriffs of Bristol' (1777) – and insisted instead upon the necessity of 'the principles of Colony Government'[31] to which practice would closely adhere, Burke's constant assertions of the need for such adherence is itself a theory which he often implicitly admitted was rarely embodied in any political system other than the domestic British one. America, Ireland and India were the main theatres for the imperial project and in no one of them had Parliament managed to make government by Britain conform 'to the character and circumstances of the several people who compose this mighty and strangely diversified mass', even though, as Burke said, he 'never was wild enough to conceive, that the one method would serve for the whole'.[32] But he flinched from the possibility that the colonial relation was of itself incompatible with any set of principles that could be said to be in accord with universal justice. Clearly, if the colonial relationship as such was in conflict with the 'eternal laws of justice'[33] which Hastings had clearly violated, then it was untenable. Burke's preferred, perhaps his only imaginable alternative was that in Ireland, India and America, but particularly in the first two of these, the failure was to be attributed to the agents who represented (or misrepresented) the British system.[34] Their practice was at odds with the principles of the constitution and what he called the 'national character'[35] of Britain. In 'The Rohilla War Speech' (1786), he was clear about the scale of the issues involved; when 'A Great Empire [was] liable to abuse of Subordinate Authority' and when there are no correctives to this comparable with those available in the Roman Empire, 'The question is about the fundamental principles of the English Government, the expectations of India and a Rule to future Governors.'[36] Hastings had exercised a ruthless system of despotism that denied 'the law of nature and nations', 'the collected experience of ages, the wisdom of antiquity, and the practice of the purest times', and therefore 'ought to be found defective in the radical duty of his station'.[37]

As ever, the characteristic procedure of Hastings and his agents was that of inversion; they inverted the natural order of things and then justified their behaviour on that basis. In his 'Speech on Fox's India Bill' (1783), Burke pointed out that the British invasion of India differed from all previous invasions in that it never 'made the conquered country their own'. Instead, the initial rapacious fury was sustained, but under the hypocritical disguise of 'protection'. Previous invaders had blended in with the existing Indian civilisation. But the reverse was the case with the English invasion. 'Our conquest there, after twenty years, is as crude as it was the first day.'[38]

Nineteen years later he was saying the same of the condition of Ireland. There too, although in an even more sustained manner than in India, the 'policy of a conqueror' had been adopted 'as a *permanent* rule' for the country's future government. Even the Romans had 'coalited' with the Gauls, the people they were most averse to; but over a still longer period than that, 'the Protestants settled in Ireland, considered themselves in no other light than that of a colonial garrison, to keep the natives in subjection to the other state of Great Britain'.[39]

Hastings particularly exasperated Burke by claiming that he was only following the custom of the country in his corrupt practices. This was, in effect, an inversion of Burke's own arguments in favour of the preservation of local custom. It was important for him to sustain the accusation that, in India and in Ireland, natural and normal moral and political practices were inverted and that this inversion was defended by specious and self-serving arguments which themselves were characterised by such inversion. Thus he took care to refute Hastings on this score on several occasions in his speech on the Opening of Impeachment in February 1788: moulded by an inexhaustible rapacity, Hastings's policies tried to disguise corruption as a principle of government.[40] A corrupt faction that exercised a monopoly of trade was bad enough, but was so much worse when it took upon itself the functions, the dignity, certainly the reputation of a state. This too was an inversion, more scandalously obvious in India than in Ireland, although common to both. The East India Company's status vacillated between what it seemed to be and what it was – 'merely a Company formed for the extension of the British commerce but in reality a delegation of the whole power and sovereignty of this kingdom sent into the East'. Or it reversed the usual sequence; not trade following the flag, but the flag following trade. It 'began in commerce and ended in Empire'.[41] In addition, it was a political body that had no people; all its members were officers, there was no rank and file:

> . . . there is something peculiar in the service of the East India Company, and different from that of any other nation that has ever transferred its power from one Country to another. The East India Company is not the British Nation . . . The Company in India does not exist as a Nation. Nobody can go there that does not go in its Service. Therefore the English Nation in India is nothing but a seminary for the succession of Officers. They are a Nation of place-men. They are a Republic, a Commonwealth without a people. They are a State wholly made up of magistrates. The consequence of which is that there is no people to control, to watch, to balance against the power of office. The power of office, so far as the English nation is concerned, is the sole power in the Country. There is no corrective upon it whatever. The consequence of which is that, being a Kingdom of Magistrates, the *Esprit du Corps* is strong in it – the spirit of the body by which they consider themselves as having a common interest, and a common interest separated both from the Country that sent them out and from the Country in which they are; and where there is no control by persons who understand their language, who understand their manners, or can apply their conduct to the Laws of the Country. Such control does not exist in India. Therefore confederacy is easy, and had been general among them; and therefore your Lordships are not to expect that that should happen in such a body which

> never happened in the world in any body or Corporation, that they should ever be a proper check and control upon themselves; it is not in the nature of things. There is a monopoly with an *Esprit du corps* at home, called the India Company; there is an *Esprit du corps* abroad; and both these systems are united into one body, animated with the same spirit, that is with the corporate spirit, which never was a spirit which corrected itself in any time or circumstance in the world, and which is such a thing as has not happened . . . in any one time or circumstance in the World, except in this.[42]

To justify treating the country they lived in as a foreign territory to be conquered, these ruling cliques had to produce 'the perversion of history'.[43] They had to, like the writers of 'those miserable performances that go about under the names of Histories of Ireland', depict the state of the country as one of continual rebellion rather than as one of 'the most unparalleled oppression'.[44] Or, like Hastings and his minions, they had to portray India as a lawless and barbarous place or as an 'oriental despotism' when, in fact, it was quite the opposite; 'Oriental Governments know nothing of this arbitary power'; a 'Mahometan Government' is 'a Government by law'; the Koran and the Institutes of Tamerlane, to name no others, form the basis for a complex, organised society under the rule of law.[45] The French Jacobins similarly slandered the old regime, depicting it too as a fierce despotism when it was in fact lenient to a fault and only in need of gradual reform.[46] All three factions are guilty of great crimes; the confiscations of Irish land,[47] Hastings's general confiscation of land in Bengal,[48] the Jacobin confiscation of the lands of the French Church,[49] with all the attendant violence and hypocrisy. Yet, had they prudence or maturity, they might have drawn or have let time draw 'a secret veil'[50] over the origins of their power, whether those be in the Battle of the Boyne, or of Plassey or in the September massacres.

But no awe or reverence can attach to systems that refuse to seek in silence and mystery even a hand-me-down version of the Sublime. The rulers of Ireland, India and France are too unsophisticated for that. The 'plebeian oligarchy' of the Protestant Irish is not fit to rule except by 'a power unlimited' based on a 'universal exclusion' of the Catholics, not only from 'the *state,* but from *the British constitution*'.[51] As for the East Indians, they are 'Animated with all the avarice of age, and all the impetuosity of youth, . . . [they] roll in one after another; wave after wave' and leave India as though it had been dominated by nothing 'better than the orang-outang or the tiger'[52]; the French Revolution 'is carried on by men of no rank, of no consideration, of wild savage minds, full of levity, arrogance and presumption, without morals, without probity, without prudence, and led by the 'ignoble oligarchy', the 'base oligarchy' of the 'Reflections'.[53] Such factions insist on reminding their victims of the violence and injustice that attended their own origins; their lack of political prudence reveals them to be very inept beneficiaries of the legacy of the Glorious Revolution of 1688. If a revolution must be made, as in 1688, it should be 'a revolution that ought to have precluded other revolutions' but, given the greed of the East Indians, it 'unfortunately became fruitful of them'.[54] Much of the latter part of the 'Letter to Richard Burke' of February 1792 is devoted to the impolitic behaviour of those Anglo-Irish who, even after 1782 ('I trust the last Revolution in Ireland'[55]), continued to pick at their scabbed origins.

The contradictions of the Irish Volunteer movement's demand for legislative independence were absurd enough in themselves, given the brutal history of those who were seeking through such independence to give a semblance of glamour, borrowed from the American Revolution, to sectarian prejudice in the form of a Protestant parliament for a Catholic people. More than that, any attempt at armed revolution on the part of the Irish Protestants or, indeed, anyone else (including the Irish Catholics), merely drew attention to the violent origins of the existing political system and thereby threatened its security. For there was no title of right that could be founded on an abstract claim for justice. Abstract claims paradoxically awoke historical memories. If politics were to be conducted according to such reasoning, what political system would escape whipping? One of the origins of political violence lay in the constant affirmation or justification of violent origins.

> The language of tyranny has been invariable; the general good is inconsistent with my personal safety. Justice and liberty seem so alarming to these gentlemen that they are not ashamed even to slander their own titles; to calumniate and call in doubt their right to their own estates, and to consider themselves as novel disseizers, usurpers, and intruders, rather than lose a pretext for becoming oppressors of their fellow citizens, whom they (not I) choose to describe themselves as having robbed.
>
> Instead of putting themselves in this odious point of light, one would think they would wish to let Time draw his oblivious veil over the unpleasant modes by which lordships and demesnes have been acquired in theirs, and almost in all other countries upon earth.[56]

One of the obligations of the British state, as Burke saw it, was to intervene in Ireland and in India so that the violent origins of the political and commercial systems in those countries would not continue to receive justification and support by permitting the presiding factions to insist on their supremacy over the native inhabitants and by allowing their absurd claims of independence from that state upon which they were in fact wholly dependent for their survival.

Once more, a representation, an appearance, (that of independence) is designedly produced by a faction to take the place of the actual (dependence). Such inversion of the natural order is ruinous. Where the fictive element gains precedence over the actual, then the stabilising force of the actual is weakened and the spectral world of abstraction begins to succeed. In their strange and perverted ways, the ruling factions in Ireland and in India were the precursors of the party in modern revolutionary politics – contemptuous of the people whom they exploited, driven by a rapacity that disguised itself as an ideology of progress, fiercely protective of their political monopoly, systematic in their destructive zeal, heedless of custom, violators of Christian principles, they witlessly helped to destroy the Old World from which they had emerged. The British system, extended to become a colonial system, fell into contradiction; from that there emerged the incipient forms of the revolutionary modernity that eventually took over France and treated the *ancien régime* and its people as a foreign country that had to be conquered in the name of 'liberty' or some such abstraction. The Ireland of the Protestant Ascendancy, the India of Warren Hastings and his cohorts, and the France of the Jacobins were all historically actual places that had been cruelly transformed into ghostly versions of themselves. Indeed, the process was even more intricate than that. For the English or British nation in India or Ireland, as well as those countries themselves, underwent this change too.

V

In France, the dazzling, chimerical capacity of modernity exhibited itself first in the erasure of the old France by the Revolution and then by the appearance under the old name of France of a new country or polity that renounced, or seemed to renounce, all those principles – like the rights of man – by which it had initially justified its sanguinary abolition of the *ancien régime*. The 'Fourth Letter on a Regicide Peace' (1795) is especially eloquent on this process of asserted and abandoned principle, of past savagery and present protestations of civility, that airbrushing of historical events that produced a troubling and endless mutation between the real and the chimerical. The sense of unreality that attended the actual post-revolutionary world had reached such a pitch that the very name of France had become illegible to someone who had witnessed the events of the six years between the October days of 1789 and the Convention of the fourth week of October 1795. Abstraction was the operative energy in this process:

> In that week, for the first time, it changed its name of an usurped power, and took the simple name of *France*. The word France is slipped in just as if the government stood exactly as before that revolution . . . just as if we were in a common political war with an old recognized member of the commonwealth of Christian Europe . . . This shifting of persons could not be done without the hocus-pocus of *abstraction*. We have been in a grievous error; we thought we had been at war with *rebels* against the lawful government, but that we were friends and allies of what is properly France; friends and allies to the legal body politick of France. But by slight of hand the Jacobins are clean vanished, and it is France we have got under our cup. Blessings on his soul that first invented sleep, said Don Sancho Panza the wise! All those blessings, and ten thousand times more, on him who found out abstraction, personification, and impersonals. In certain cases they are the first of all soporoificks. Terribly

> alarmed we should be if things were proposed to us in the *concrete*; and if fraternity was held out to us with the individuals, who compose this France, by their proper names and descriptions: if we are told that it was very proper to enter into the closest bonds of amity and good correspondence with the devout, pacifick, and tender-hearted Syeyes, with the all-accomplished Rewbel, with the humane guillotinists of Bourdeaux, Tallien and Isabeau; with the meek butcher Legendre . . . the virtuous regicide brewer Santyerre . . . But plain truth would here be shocking and absurd; therefore comes in *abstraction* and personification. 'Make your Peace with France.' That word *France* sounds quite as well as any other, and it conveys no idea, but that of a very pleasant country and very hospitable inhabitants, Nothing absurd and shocking in amity and good correspondence with *France*. Permit me to say, that I am not yet well acquainted with this new-coined France, and, without a careful assay, I am not willing to receive it in currency in place of the old Louis d'or.'[57]

But it is the *Second Letter on a Regicide Peace* (1796), subtitled 'On the Genius and Character of the French Revolution as it Regards other Nations', that Burke states most bluntly what had happened to the country called France. 'My ideas and my principles led me, in this contest, to encounter France, not as a State, but as a Faction . . . That faction is the evil spirit that possesses the body of France; that informs its soul . . .[58] This is 'a general evil', centred in France and 'in the corruptions of our common nature'; it 'exists in every country in Europe'; its 'circumference is the world of Europe wherever the race of Europe may be settled'. Further, the Jacobins understood from the outset that they were involved in a '*civil war*' which they would 'persuade their adversaries . . . ought to be a *foreign* war'.

> It is a war between the partizans of the antient, civil, moral, and political order of Europe against a sect of fanatical and ambitious atheists which means to change them all. It is not France extending a foreign empire over other nations: it is a sect aiming at universal empire, and beginning with the conquest of France. The leaders of that sect secured the *centre of Europe;* and that secured, they knew, that whatever might be the event of battles and sieges, their *cause* was victorious.[59]

The hyperbole of time is one of Burke's most favoured rhetorical weapons in his characterisation of countries, conditions or events that he regards as unprecedented. To say, as he repeatedly does, that there never was before in human history anything like the systems that prevail in Ireland, India or France – not to mention lesser occasions and more provincial conditions – might on the face of it seem to weaken a position that requires us to see each of several situations as unique. Yet it actually enhances his persistent diagnosis of the ills of these countries and periods in contemporary history because it sits so well with the claim that a New World is, alas, emerging; that it is the inversion of the Old World; that it is brought into being by a process of abstraction and that, in its surreality, it is unprecedented. There never was a place like Ireland or India, because there never were before countries (or colonies) that (unlike the Thirteen Colonies of America) pursued a policy that made the British presence within them evaporate and, simultaneously, made the countries themselves disappear, leaving only a ruthless faction in their place. America at least maintained itself, indeed affirmed itself. In some respects, Britain betrayed itself there and, as a consequence, had to suffer the result of a separation that was essentially more like a civil war than a revolution. Burke is indeed sensitive on this point. He dismisses the analogies that French sympathisers make between America and France: 'they sanction their cry for peace with the Regicides of France by some of our propositions for peace with the English in America'.[60] The truer comparison with France was to be found in Ireland and India, not in America. What was happening in those countries was a far more intricate betrayal of what the British polity meant; it involved an inversion of what Britain really stood for, because in both places a faction ruled and in both places the effect of that rule was to deny traditional society and the rule of law and replace them with an ideology of the will. 'We may bite our chains if we will, but we shall be made to know ourselves, and be taught that man is born to be governed by law; and he that will substitute will in the place of it is an enemy to God.'[61]

VI

It was bad enough, in Burke's view, that Britain should have betrayed itself in America and been betrayed by factions in Ireland and in India; but that it should be betrayed or be seduced into betraying itself at home would be, of all catastrophes, the very worst. It had always been his opinion, since the publication of the 'Reflections on the Revolution in France' in 1790 that the war – undeclared until 1793 – between Britain and France was 'of a peculiar nature', because it was a war in which Britain was fighting a system, 'an armed doctrine' that of its nature had 'a faction of opinion, and of interest, and of enthusiasm, in every country. To us it is a colossus which bestrides our channel. It has one foot on a foreign shore, the other on British soil'.[62] Of all factions, the home-bred variety was the most lethal. His Irish and Indian crusades were based on the hope or conviction that the factions in those countries could be seen and even punished as aberrations which Britain should disavow as unworthy of its own practice and reputation. However, if the faction was English and if it repudiated everything that constituted the English and British tradition while welcoming everything that was French and novel, then a foreign element had entered into the native system and inverted it. 'The [English] Jacobins are worse than lost to their country. Their hearts are abroad.'[63] Their sympathy for the French Regicides was so complete that it ended in justification of their crimes.

Ultimately, what the French themselves are saying in 1795 is accepted and absorbed into the depraved moral discourse of the time by the English

Jacobins. Since Thermidor, say the apologists for France, the revolutionaries 'have renounced the Creeds of the Rights of Man, and declared Equality a Chimera . . . They have apostatified from their Apostacy.' On that account, *because* they have admitted to every conceivable crime, they are to be welcomed and accepted; this truly is, says Burke, 'new, and to use a phrase of their own, *revolutionary;* every thing supposes a total revolution in all the principles of reason, prudence, and moral feeling'.[64] He refuses to allow the plea for forgiveness on the basis that conditions in France were anarchic. France was not and is not in a state of anarchy; what the French have had for several years is, he argues, 'not an Anarchy, but a series of short-lived Tyrannies'.[65] Moreover, the tyrannies were and are so thoroughgoing that 'the people are absolutely slaves, in the fullest sense, in all affairs public and private, great and small'; '. . . every thing has been the effect of the studied machinations of the one revolutionary cabal, operating within itself upon itself. That cabal is all.'[66] The point of the French and English Jacobin propaganda is to effect a change in human feeling, 'to mollify us to the crimes and to the society of robbers and ruffians!' Burke's 'Reflections' posed the issue in stark terms. If people can be moved to tears by a tragedy on stage and yet remain dry-eyed when faced with the spectacle of the humiliation of Marie Antoinette and her husband, then feeling has been inverted and the revolutionary dispensation has arrived.[67] The denial of the actual and the substitution of it by a fiction, a deceit, a stridor of propagandising voices that share the aim of making what was once immoral, moral – that is the work of faction. If it is successful, human beings will forget how to repudiate criminal behaviour; finally, they will forget how to love others. 'They never will love where they ought to love, who do not hate where they ought to hate.'[68]

Some of the characteristic features of Burke's rhetoric, more pronounced in his later writings, but common to all of his work, enhance the reader's sense of the enormous stress that is generated by the effort of the new and abstract universe to disengage itself from the old historical world. There is, for instance, his constant recital of proper names of people, or groups of people, and of places, usually with their identifying epithets or accompaniments. This recital can make the text shimmer with rage or become operatically lyrical while sustaining a political point about the importance of nomenclature. Groups like the Protestant Irish, the members of the East India Company and the French Jacobins are consistently referred to as factions, juntos, synods, delinquents, cabals, banditti, robbers, assassins, regicides, in an effort to condemn them morally while refusing them a proper political or representative name and status. Even when they rechristen themselves, as Protestant Ascendancy or as French ambassadors or government ministers, Burke refuses to concede that the new name involves any change in status; it is merely an attempt to obscure or legitimise their scandalous aims.

The point of his insults is to remind the reader at all times that these are small factions – faction being the root term from which all the others ramify

– within a larger group that have assumed an illegitimate political authority. The most bigoted of the Protestant Irish are a 'small monopolizing Junto, composed of one of the smallest of their own internal factions';[69] they are 'that Synod of zealous protestant Lay Elders who govern Ireland on the pacific principles of polemick theology, and who now, from dread of the Pope, cannot take a cool bottle of claret, or enjoy an innocent parliamentary job with any tolerable quiet;'[70] they are 'the delinquents in India',[71] 'the flights of birds of prey and passage, with appetites continually renewing for a food that is continually wasting'.[72] Equally, the great moments of apostrophe, to Marie Antoinette or to Admiral Keppel or the listing with all their resonant titles, of the victims of the French revolutionaries as well as their executioners, who, in a typically inverted way, attempt to hide their true titles of butcher and assassin behind those of the revolutionary state, emphasise the fusion of a particular person with a historical tradition, and make their murders or trials tragic moments of an unprecedented and resonating kind.[73] Conversely, the great tirades, of which that against Rousseau is the most famous, emphasise precisely the opposite condition, one in which the central figure progressively disengages from the historical and turns instead into himself, seeking there, in the guise of originality, a counter-resource to that offered by history and thereby inverting the very concept and practice of feeling by disguising as benevolence a cruel and heartless narcissism.[74]

Such tirades are clearly set pieces, deriving from many sources in their form, polemical vigour and in their voice-over sequences of powerful, arresting images. Cicero, especially in his Verrine orations, is the most obvious persistent influence. But Burke is Ciceronian in another mode and to quite different effect. When he appeals to the complexity of human affairs, of political systems, of human institutions and of historical processes, he is creating a version of the political Sublime which is designed to elicit from his audiences the appropriate awe and reverence before the spectacle of power and vastness – cosmic grandeur confronting human littleness.[75] But the enormous inventories and catalogues, which have the tirades as their polemical other, co-exist with and often conclude in moments of great epigrammatic concision and compression. This is an aspect of the double effect Burke's writing often achieves. It announces both the incomprehensibility of the cosmic world over which God or Providence supervenes and the clarity of the issues that dominate the social and political worlds that derive from that larger universe. Human reason, although it has its necessary functions and powers, cannot negotiate between these worlds. Only human feeling can. When it is corrupted, all sense of that critical relation is lost. Mystery is reduced to mystification and feeling becomes the servant of the will.

Colonialism, when governed by a faction, is the precursor of revolution in which the faction assumes complete control over everything. In this reading, France was the first colony of revolution and from it the new virus went forth to colonise the European world, both in its domestic and in its colonial domains. Yet there never was, in Burke's experience, a colony that was not ruled by a faction. He saw and even articulated the continuity but wished to argue for the discontinuity between British colonialism and French Revolution. Both were forms of Empire but, strangely, in Ireland, India and France and then, potentially, everywhere, the imperial systems succeeded only at the expense of the traditional worlds they governed. Systematic exploitation destroyed traditional custom and practice. The Sublime gave way to the symmetrical. The capacity for tragic feeling was replaced by a capacity to tolerate atrocity. What Burke called 'the moral basis' of traditional politics disappeared. Although he resisted it and refused it, he recognised the prophetic power of those English Jacobins who predicted that 'in proportion as we recede from the ancient system of Europe, we approach to that connection which alone can remain to us, a close alliance with the new discovered moral and political world in France'.[76] And those Whig aristocrats, who supported the Revolution, blinded by Jacobin rhetoric, were co-operating in their own destruction. 'If a great storm blow on our coast, it will cast the whales on the strand as well as the periwinkles.'[77] History, corrupted by factions, had produced the fictional, delusive world of modernity into which all that was once solid would disappear.

7. BURKE AND TOCQUEVILLE
NEW WORLDS, NEW BEINGS

Revolutionaries

Burke and Tocqueville agreed in their analyses of some of the causes of the French Revolution, most particularly on the role of the 'men of letters' and the prestige and influence which they gained as the traditional political élites lost power. This new intellectual class became what Daniel Roche has called 'a substitute government, at once omnipotent and powerless',[1] the product of a state that was an unhappy mixture of modern and archaic elements, in which those who once had power lost legitimacy and those who gained legitimacy failed to win power. Burke famously contrasted this situation with that in England, where men of letters, particularly those who scoffed at traditional pieties and beliefs, were rewarded with little notice in their lifetimes and near-oblivion thereafter. For Burke, this new grouping had the further disadvantage that it substituted the real world with the world of its imaginings, and then was shocked (or would have been so) to see these imaginings realised in actual practice. After the first year of the Revolution this charge was routinely levelled against the philosophes. They had indulged in visionary dreams that had become nightmarishly real.[2] Theirs was a pathology that derived from a fundamentally corrupt position that began in the powerlessness of the literary clique and ended in Jacobin dictatorship. As with the colonial predators in India and the Protestant Ascendancy in Ireland, these new intellectuals and/or revolutionaries had come to regard themselves as the true representatives of the state and believed its interests were their own. Quarantined within the worlds they dominated, they became criminal or proto-criminal formations who practised violence and injustice and called it civilisation. They represented a threat to the French or British states that foolishly nurtured them by policy or allowed them to flourish by default. Of the three groups, the intellectuals were the most serious threat since they were the creators of the new modern spirit that was to topple France and threaten Europe; the colonists were unwitting conspirators in this process since they disgraced the name and retarded the development of the institutions – the famous 'British Constitution' – that made Britain the benign alternative to French modernity.

Tocqueville's reading of the *ancien régime* as itself being the first revolution (and 1789 the second) at first makes a glaring contrast with Burke's view of 1688, since Burke argued that the Glorious Revolution was as unrevolutionary as it was possible for a revolution to be. In France, the battle between the nobility and the centralisation of administrative power by the Crown, the replacement of society by the state, constituted a revolution which began with Louis XIV rather than with Louis XVI.[3] The absolutist state created a caste system in its readiness to exchange power for a commodified version of status without function; titles were sold like fake antiques and intellectual systems and opinions had the glamour of novelties traded in the salons and journals by writers innocent of the practicalities of political life. If the British *ancien régime*, ushered in by 1688 was, in Tocqueville's terms, wholly unlike the centralising French system, it did nevertheless mark a real advance in the achievement of liberty, if not of equality. Ireland, with its bad aristocracy and its peculiarly decayed version of society, was excepted from this benign analysis. In this respect, Tocqueville's views chimed with those of Burke, although there were important differences. Tocqueville did not contrast the emergent modern society with a venerable and traditional order that must by every rhetorical resource available be rendered sacrosanct and timeless. On the contrary, he claimed that the centralised administrative state had concealed its operations behind an increasingly venal façade of traditional codes. His famous disagreement with Burke's analysis of the Revolution is rooted in this. 'Burke does not realize that what stands before his eyes is the revolution which will abolish the old common law of Europe; he does not understand that this is its sole purpose.'[4] Burke, in other words, believed the French system could be reformed, that the intermediate bodies, such as the *parlements,* could be revived, that a monarchy and nobility of the kind espoused by Montesquieu could be restored. He did not realize that the Revolution was already complete. The *ancien régime* had not been replaced by the Revolution; it had been the Revolution.[5] The modern world had finally discarded the camouflage of the ancient European order Burke hastened to lament and defend.[6]

Besides the importance and political insulation of the men of letters and of the new moneyed interest, Tocqueville also followed Burke and others in emphasising the importance of Paris, the historical parallel with the Reformation, the emergence of an unprecedented form of ruthlessness, manifest in the men of the new generation and the connection between this and the anti-religious character of the Revolution. He followed in the steps of commentators like Portalis, who claimed that Rousseau was right to declare that the principal objects of a society were liberty and equality but that the consequences drawn from this by him and even more so by his followers had been catastrophic. Only in France, Portalis claimed, had writers become 'une véritable puissance dans l'État' ('a real power in the State') and had dared to claim that they, rather than the clergy, had the exclusive right to teach morality as a secular science.[7] Such commentary was in part indebted to Burke, but it is also characteristic of the varied French Restoration analyses that attributed to militant anti-Christian ideologies a particular ferocity of temperament that was unprecedented in European, even human, history. Burke's account of the arrival of this new species is resumed in that of Tocqueville and many of his liberal and conservative contemporaries; the French Revolution had created 'new beings who . . . have since formed a race which has perpetuated itself, and spread among all civilized parts of the earth . . . We found them in the world when we were born; they are still with us.'[8] These revolutionaries had completely overthrown the limitations, even the idea of limitation, that religion imposed. The existence of people with such radical and destructive beliefs made the possibility of a European alternative to American democracy a frightening prospect.

Americans

For in America, 'while the law permits the Americans to do what they please, religion prevents them from conceiving and forbids them to commit, what is rash or unjust'.[9] America was not a secular country. It had reorganised the spheres of religion and politics, but the autonomy granted to each did not rob religion of its presiding influence as a rebuke to human pride and as a system of belief that allowed the dream of an ultimate reconciliation of opposing forces within the social system to become an important feature of the country's ideology. Such a notion, says Tocqueville, energises citizens to achieve perfect equality, 'a chimera that draws men on and retires before them'. Hence the desire for equality 'always becomes more insatiable in proportion as equality is more complete'. Americans remain close to their famous dream, always 'near enough to see its charms, but too far off to enjoy them'; from this derives the melancholy that often haunts the inhabitants of democratic countries.[10] Yet while Tocqueville may have had serious reservations about the virtual melancholy, the increasing social uniformity and the dullness of the American system, he preferred these to the despotic opportunities offered by the European systems to which the idea of an ultimate social harmony was quixotic.

Tocqueville's almost mystical belief in the principle of equality as the dynamic of all modern history allows him to indicate those features in the European and the American political systems that were in or out of tune with it and therefore to make his analyses inevitably assume the form of some contrast or conflict between modern and archaic elements. This becomes in his work a governing style of argument that is certainly discernible in Burke but has for him no comparably moulding force. It also persuades Tocqueville to make the rather astonishing claim that America is the only country in the world that achieved democracy without a 'democratic' revolution; that it was, so to say, born to equality and therefore did not have to undergo the long European struggle with feudal and neo-feudal systems that inhibited the growth of equality there. 'The great advantage of the Americans is that they have arrived at a state of democracy without having to endure a democratic revolution, and that they are born equal instead of becoming so.'[11] At the time of the American Revolution, Burke saw it not as a global event but as an internal British quarrel which, if anything, highlighted the dangers of a foolish policy that gave to the forces of religious dissent a political victory in America they would never have won at home. But it was their distinguishingly British combination of Protestantism and liberty that made them, in Burke's eyes, formidable rebels.[12] For him, at that stage, settler colonies were extensions of the national ethos, although in America the dissenters' influence (and memories) intensified the colonists' aggravation with the authoritarian attitudes of the government in London.[13]

Tocqueville agreed with the Burkean analysis, although he extended it further to enhance the well-known connection presumed to exist between the commercial spirit, the '*spirit of religion*' and the '*spirit of liberty*'. The New England settlers sought 'with almost equal eagerness material wealth and moral satisfaction; heaven in the world beyond, and well-being and liberty in this one'; they were 'at the same time ardent sectarians and daring innovators'.[14] For Tocqueville what America had retained and the French had lost was the sense of limitation that accompanies religious belief. Thus, in the light of 1789 and after, the American Revolution was more and more frequently interpreted as an example of what a true revolution could be and its status was accordingly upgraded. Tocqueville's comments on it have sometimes the apocalyptic nature of his comments on the French Revolution. He wants to see America as the culmination of an inevitable evolution, while also saying that it is an unforeseeable and extraordinary innovation. 'In that land the great experiment of the attempt to construct society upon a new basis was to be made by civilized man; and it was there, for the first time, that theories hitherto unknown, or deemed impracticable, were to exhibit a spectacle for which the world had not been prepared by the history of the past.' Sometimes he forgets that he had claimed America had never had a feudal past. 'A democracy more perfect than antiquity had dared to dream of started in full size and panoply from the midst of an ancient feudal society.'[15]

But it was America's 'feudal' present, as represented by the slave-owning South, that was more threatening to the vision of America that emerges in the first volume of *Democracy*. There were indeed several Americas – one in New England, one in the South, one in the western States and the most elusive of all, the idea of America that Tocqueville formed in the course of his autopsy on the France that had died in the Revolution and had not yet been reborn into modernity. But feudality was not an entirely negative condition. It could be so when the political system was largely governed by a fake or bad aristocracy – like the Irish Protestant or that of the Southern States. Austerely seen, aristocracy was politically defunct; nostalgically reconceived, it became for Tocqueville a condition that had become historically unavailable, most especially to modern democracy and its levelling tendencies. All of Tocqueville's versions of America are seen against an aristocratic European background, almost always French, and almost always rich in the virtues that democracy lacks, other than the capacity to survive.[16] Precisely because there were several Americas in Tocqueville's analysis and because of the increasing intensity of the battle between federal and state government on the issue of slavery, he could foresee that the Union itself might not survive, even though it did not seem to him that the idea of democracy would fade with it. In his eyes, this structural tension duplicated the very French dispute that had been at the heart of the crisis of the *ancien régime* and remained unresolved, although Napoleonic administration had immensely intensified the centralising and despotic power that had been briefly challenged in 1789. It is clear that readers of Tocqueville, like Lord Acton, adopted this potentially tragic vision of a battle for Liberty fought out between local or intermediate and federal or centralising energies. In Acton's case this gave him a way of understanding and participating in the disputes between the Vatican and national Churches, between authoritarian fiat and the rights of the individual conscience. It is clear too that Acton interpreted the American Civil War in terms Tocqueville had supplied; hence he regarded the victory of the North as a triumph of centralising and equalising forces over liberty.

Thus, in one version at least, the United States became for Tocqueville a possible democratic future for Europe, the more purely realised because it had not had aristocratic Europe as its past.[17] Such a future would be brought about or characterised by the inescapable 'Equality of conditions' with democracy as the companion political system. His democracy has two modalities; the American democracy of the first volume is the empirically detailed and sociologically analysed realisation of one of these; the other is the type of democracy itself, the description of which belongs to the second volume. 'I confess that in America, I saw more than America; I sought there the image of democracy itself, with its inclinations, its character, its prejudices, and its passions, in order to learn what we have to hope or fear from its progress.'[18]

Here Tocqueville's acknowledged debt to Montesquieu, especially to his *Considérations sur les causes de la grandeur des Romains et de leur décadence* (1734), is heavy indeed. Also, between the traveller's report on an existing system and the political philosopher's typology of the political form of which that system is an instance there is often a vexed relationship. Is the report the basis for the type or is the type the structuring principle of the report? It is a question that could be asked of Voltaire's *Lettres philosophiques; ou, Lettres sur les anglais* (1734), and Mme de Staël's *De L' Allemagne* (1810) as much as of *Democracy in America* (1835–40). In each case, another country and culture – England, Germany, America – is offered as an example or model of what France had failed to become, or of what it should acquaint itself with to supply its own defects. The descriptions of these cultures are clearly politically determined by a programme or a vision of reform or renovation for France. This does not necessarily weaken them as surveys or analyses. Indeed the analysis of and sympathy for the foreign culture are often enhanced by the implied or explicit critique of the archaic France with which they are being compared. So even those who claimed that their countries were misrepresented by these travellers or visitors were in part missing the point.[19] In every case the author was attempting to describe what seemed to him or her a new and admirable social and political phenomenon that prefigured for all who understood it the future of the world.

It is not surprising that the mid-twentieth-century's revival of interest in both Burke and Tocqueville was governed for the most part by a political agenda that saw them as counterbalances to Marx, especially in relation to the idea of global revolution. They were both, in different but comparable ways, incorporated into the West's defence of its democratic traditions during the Cold War. Each provided a contrast between the American and French Revolutions; each provided a critique of that kind of revolution that was based on theory as opposed to one allegedly derived from history, and each claimed that those who acted from theoretic principle were liable to become fierce ideologues who would destroy the whole Christian Western tradition. The more clamantly right-wing Cold Warriors tended to draw on Burke, the more liberal or neo-liberal theorists, whose chief pretence was and is not to be theoretically inclined at all, drew on Tocqueville. The central point in the middle decades of the twentieth century was to make a distinction between the French and Russian Revolutions, by claiming the first for the West and assigning the second to the East; or to say that the violence attendant upon both was of the essence of revolution and that no revolution ever had achieved as much as reformism. This mode of interpretation persists, even after 1989 and the 'triumph' of global capitalism.[20]

The American system, as Tocqueville understood it, produces a particular kind of citizen. The dynamic interplay between political and civil associations, the peculiarly pragmatic and unheroic American understanding of the principle of self-interest produce a citizen who is virtuous in a new and specific way. Midway between 'extraordinary virtues' and 'gross depravity', able to reconcile material prosperity and 'eternal felicity', skilled in organisation and appreciative of public tranquillity and physical well-being, this is a citizenry that is as far above the general level of mankind as it is below the extraordinary levels that can be achieved by individuals from an aristocratic society.[21] There is a risk that the 'virtuous materialism' of the American democracy might 'enervate the soul and noiselessly unbend the springs of action';[22] but this is a possible defect of a very real virtue, although such virtue is not to be found in Montesquieu's version of the republican form of government. There is no element of abnegation of the self here. Tocqueville's new political democrat citizen is as moderate and peace-loving as the new being of the French Revolution is extreme and violent. This is the icon of the new democratic system of equality; a private citizen who at one time 'seems animated by the most selfish cupidity; at another by the most lively patriotism'. The 'passion for their own welfare and for their freedom' are mingled uniquely in the American character.[23]

Although Tocqueville regards uniformity as – alas – one of the constitutive features of democracy, it has at least the advantage of making generalisations about its citizens easier. Another way of putting it is that democratic debates appeal to humankind in general, rather than to particular nationalities or systems; 'the political debates of a democratic people . . . have a degree of breadth that frequently renders them attractive to mankind. All men are interested by them because they treat of *man* who is everywhere the same.'[24]

Indeed, this is for him one of the advantages of modern civilisation; it seems to herald the emergence of a social and political type which is in accord with a general view of human nature. Such a type has outgrown the eccentricities and glamours of the aristocratic (or other) eras.

> Among aristocratic nations every man is pretty nearly stationary in his own sphere, but men are astonishingly unlike each other; . . . nothing changes, but everything differs. In democracies, on the contrary, all men are alike . . . The aspect of American society is animated because men and things are always changing, but it is monotonous because all these changes are alike.[25]

It is therefore a historical inevitability that variety should disappear 'as the men of each country relinquish more and more the peculiar opinions and feelings of a caste, a profession, or a family' and thereby 'arrive at something nearer to the constitution of man, which is everywhere the same'.[26] Even uniformity has for him its variations. American uniformity is produced within a system that allows for a variety of civic and political organisations that deflect the full force of centralised government. For the American system sponsors local politics to bring people together who might otherwise fall into the excessive isolation that individualism can create; and the connection between the general affairs of the nation and the local politics of its constituent parts is maintained. In France, centralisation produced the uniformity of a political system in which individual selfishness was encouraged in order to make concerted action unlikely. The consequent forms of individualism or eccentricity might achieve exotic growth but they remained politically neutered, private achievements.

Tocqueville modified the relatively recent belief that commercial societies were necessarily freer than their less flexible and more statuesque predecessors. He goes so far as to say that when the commercial arts are cultivated in a society the possibility of tyranny is at least as strong as the possibility of freedom. He shared with Adam Ferguson the suspicion of those who sought from the state above all else the tranquillity that would allow them to enrich themselves and he lived to see that tyrannical possibility become a reality as the despotism of Napoleon III replaced the dull and greedy *régime* of Guizot and Louis-Phillipe.[27] The tyrannical risk was also there in a commercial culture like America, but was alleviated by the voluntary and official institutions that promoted participation in the political process. Social uniformity was distinct from political conformity. To keep that distinction alive, a particular kind of citizenry had to be created, neither glamorously eccentric nor politically obeisant. Therefore the modern individual of the American and democratic type is a generic model of the human, the more satisfactorily generic the more modern, the more uniform the more universalisable. To appeal to the American citizen or to the American nation is, in this light, to appeal to humankind. As Pierre Nora has pointed out, the nation thus becomes the recipient and the guarantor of such 'democratic eloquence'.[28]

Yet the premonitions of Max Weber's analysis of religion, bureaucracy, the rationalisation of society and the loss of charisma are unmistakable here. Weber's visit to America in 1904 provides an even more pointed comparison, since for him, as for Tocqueville, America was the exemplary instance of the forms of organisation and distress – especially ennui or melancholy – that characterised mass industrial democracy.[29]

The argument against uniformity and the tyranny as well as the dullness that it heralded had already been developed extensively by Burke. But with him it had been reinforced by something more than a defence of aristocratic society as aesthetically attractive. This he certainly emphasised but added to it the appeal of doomed and tragic figures like the French king and queen in whom an ethical and an aesthetic tradition were dazzlingly embodied. The pathos of that disappearing civilisation in Burke is the greater because of the ruinous and selfish dullness that is to succeed it. Tocqueville's ostensibly more objective analysis of the conformity and uniformity of the commercial-democratic society reduces this Burkean appeal but it also incorporates something of its note of regret for such an inevitable and disenchanting transition. Sainte-Beuve said that Tocqueville 'a le style triste'. This is certainly appropriate to his rueful estimate of the political possibilities that remained in 'evaporating aristocratic time and expanding democratic space'.[30]

Inexorable Process

Thus Tocqueville often surrenders to the belief that history is governed by inexorable processes among which the growth of equality of conditions in the modern era is a dominant instance. It is a more 'professional' approach than that of those historians of the Revolution who gave such prominence to individuals like Danton or Robespierre and made the division between history and fiction even more insecure than it had been.[31] It breeds sententiousness of a new kind, neither that of proverbial wisdom (traditional) nor that of commonplace wisdom (modern) but something that partakes of both. Yet this belief at times appears to diminish to little more than a rhetorical stratagem designed to lend to his narrative the prestige of a revelation. For he seems also to be given to the belief that every culture, most particularly the French and the Anglo-American, has characteristics that may either contravene or realise the goals of the inexorable processes he describes. As a consequence, they lose their inexorable character and become merely contingent. The historical status of the French Revolution is a case in point. If it arose from particular conditions within that country, and nevertheless spoke to humankind in general when preaching its basic doctrines, did that make it, or revolution in general, a necessary feature of the passsage (or of one of the passages) to modernity? Modernity, after all, is the (quasi-American) condition in which provincial and local characteristics are subsumed into a universal nature. Tocqueville vacillates at times between seeing the Revolution as an especially vivid moment in a continuous and inevitable process or as a rupture within it. Did the centralising tendency in French political life culminate in the Revolution (or in Napoleon) and was that part of its peculiarly French or of its specifically universal character?[32] The desire for equality had been so strong in France, he claims, that it forgot the need for liberty. But then it was, in those terms, a revolution specific to France, not necessary to the development of any universal idea of society.[33]

Especially after 1848 and Napoleon III's *coup d'état* of 1851, Tocqueville was not inclined to look charitably upon his fellow-countrymen and their failure to escape the rhythmic variation from revolution to dictatorship. In effect, he sought to analyse a peculiarly French disease that had inhibited the nation from achieving the kind of liberty that had been created in Britain, a country in which he was predictably popular, not least because of his readiness to accuse the French people of infamy in their ready submission to tyranny.[34] This was the obverse of their spirit of radical innovation, the will to begin history all over again – as represented by the new revolutionary calendar or by the shooting at the church clocks during even the 1830 Revolution. Having in part prophesied the June days of the 1848 Revolution, and supported the assault of General Cavaignac's army on the workers, Tocqueville returned to ask anew the questions that had dominated his career. The first concerned liberty. Could it be reconciled with equality? If France achieved the latter (or was on the way to doing so), why did it repeatedly abandon the former in its revolutionary (and now socialistic) fury? Was the system of administrative centralisation peculiarly inimical to liberty and why was it so peculiarly advanced in and attractive to France? His bitterness towards his countrymen found memorable expression in his *Souvenirs* (*Recollections*) written at this time; it was there also that his diagnosis and fear of centralization began to predominate over his previously assured faith in the irresistible progress of equality. These were ingredients central to his proposed work on the Revolution of which the *Ancien Régime* is the only completed part. It is in the *Souvenirs* that Tocqueville retrospectively lamented the final dismissal of the aristocracy from the French political scene in the Revolution of 1830 and the triumph of a bourgeoisie for which he has the traditional aristocrat's contempt. In the ensuing confrontation between the bourgeoisie and the workers he saw the rights of property threatened by democratic envy and socialist theories, while the chances of the survival of liberty were sadly reduced by the bourgeoisie's anxiety to be given, above all else, the public order and peace they needed in order to enrich themselves further.[35]

However, Tocqueville's France had at least two faces; it was fatally inclined to despotism or extremism and this made it unique; yet it was also 'the democratic country par excellence', and this made it universal.[36] The relationships between the genius of a people, the forms or types of government and the universal laws that history exhibited are never entirely clarified in his writings; any one of these can play a dominant role at a given time. Yet whatever the local contingencies or the peculiar characteristics of a culture or of a situation, there is no doubt that Tocqueville constantly sought and often announced what seemed to him to be universal truths or, at the least, the existence of universal laws that gave form and meaning to the diversity of human affairs. Such laws and their accompanying processes are implacable. To believe in these and to discern their development in human history is also to provide an explanation for the destruction or disappearance of those societies, cultures or classes that stand in the way of the spirit of progress. The *ancien régime* is the most famous of Tocqueville's victims in this regard. But there were others.

Ireland

Britain (or more properly the United Kingdom) clearly provided an alternative, especially after the various reforms of 1828–32 abolished (at least in principle) the confessional basis of the *ancien régime* state, extended the franchise (influenced in doing so by the July Revolution of 1830 in France) and therefore seemed to have taken another notable step towards the achievement of American-style equality of conditions. It seemed to Tocqueville that the reluctant granting of Catholic Emancipation in 1829 was an example of the manner in which an 'archaic' element of the British polity – Ireland – enforced a much-needed modernisation.[37] It was, as I have said, inevitable that his belief in the irresistible but uneven progress towards equality should determine that he would would discover in all societies a mix of modern and archaic elements. This was least the case with America, most the case with Ireland. For, as Burke (and many others) had pointed out, Ireland suffered from the most bigoted and destructive of all aristocracies. The joint venture of Tocqueville and Gustave de Beaumont to Ireland in 1835 produced both Tocqueville's *Journey in Ireland* and Beaumont's *Ireland: Social, Political and Religious* (1839) in which they both agreed that, in Beaumont's words, 'The Protestant aristocracy which in England is the very heart of all political powers, seems in Ireland to be their cancer.'[38] Tocqueville's version was that the aristocracy in England 'has for centuries given the English one of the best governments that exists in the world, the other, to the Irish, one of the most detestable that ever could be imagined'.[39]

However, under Daniel O'Connell the immiserated Catholics had formed into a political nation; this phenomenon attracted a great deal of attention in

France, particularly among French liberal Catholics like the abbé Hugues Lammenais and Charles, le comte de Montalembert. In fact Montalembert's essay in the journal *L' Avenir*, 'Du catholicisme en irlande', in January 1831, clearly signalled that the alliance between Catholicism and democracy in Ireland was a lesson to France, most especially as the Catholic faith there was of a strength and steadfastness long lost to the French. Tocqueville and Beaumont agreed; like Montalembert they admired the Irish Catholic combination of a political commitment to democractic change with loyalty to religious belief. This was where the French had gone wrong; in abandoning all religious belief and practices they had abandoned restraint. It was this Catholicism that made the O'Connellite movement so formidable. It was a force for and a principle of cohesion, made more effective by a clergy that had the support of their flock and further consolidated by the hatred and contempt shown them by the members of the Protestant establishment whose powers were fading but whose persisting animus latterly exhibited itself in the Orange Order and its provocative marches.[40] Disavowing the standard accusation of Catholicism's affinities with despotism, Tocqueville saw the Irish Catholics, both at home and as emigrants in America, inclined by their faith and by their experience to support the cause of democracy.

> About fifty years ago Ireland began to pour a Catholic population into the United States . . . These Catholics are faithful to the observances of their religion . . . Yet they constitute the most republican and the most democratic class in the United States . . . I think that the Catholic religion has erroneously been regarded as the natural enemy of democracy. Among the various sects of Christians, Catholicism seems to me, on the contrary, to be one of the most favorable to equality of condition among men . . . On doctrinal points the Catholic faith places all human capacities upon the same level; it subjects the wise and ignorant . . . it confounds all the distinctions of society at the foot of the same altar, even as they are confounded in the sight of God. If Catholicism predisposes the faithful to obedience, it certainly does not prepare them for inequality; but the contrary may be said of Protestantism, which generally tends to make men independent more than to render them equal. Catholicism is like an absolute monarchy; if the sovereign be removed, all the other classes of society are more equal than in republics.[41]

The Catholic religion had, then, this particularly strong cohesive force which lent stability to a political community otherwise dispossessed.

The various attempts to revive French Catholicism as a political and a religious counter to the secular radicalism of the Revolution drew heavily upon the notion that a traditional, communal religious faith would help preserve the culture of the Old World and at the same time greet (or at least accept) the political forms of the New. Irish Catholics, especially in their most recent political reincarnation of 1823 as the Catholic Association, and the achievement of Catholic Emancipation in 1829, seemed to offer an example of how this could be done. In Tocqueville's account, Catholicism favoured equality, Protestantism (although not in its Irish mutation) favoured liberty. The heart of his and of Beaumont's inquiry into the United Kingdom system was to see if it could make the transition to democracy without undergoing revolution. Catholic Emancipation and the Reform Act of 1832 seemed to indicate that it would. Those seriously disaffected and previously excluded from the political system had been given the first instalment of a promise that they would be integrated. National solidarity could thereby be sustained.

The French Liberal Catholic attempt to understand Ireland's role in the modernisation and democratisation of the British state was a serious effort to save both religion and the Revolution – to show that traditional attachments were necessary for the preservation of liberty and the extension of equality. Some twenty years later, a similar attempt was made by Cardinal Newman through the promotion of the idea of a Catholic University which would save the British Empire, or perhaps all English-speaking peoples, from the alienating and secularising effects of a militant liberalism of the kind associated with the British Whigs, the *Edinburgh Review* and utlitarianism. These views on the Irish Catholic question and on the wider issue of liberal democracy could be said to owe something to Burke's complicated arguments about the necessity of retaining the integrity of local cultures within an imperial framework. He had deployed these arguments with increasing ranges of intensity in relation to America (or to the Thirteen Colonies), Ireland and India. But the preservation of a culture's integrity is perhaps only as persuasive as is the notion of 'culture' that is operative within or through it. Further, there is not – at least there is not in Burke – any accompanying or consequent threat to the imperial framework. As is regularly the case with apologias for imperialism, the 'local' must be either nurtured or supplanted by the dominant culture, in the belief or under the pretence that the imperial culture represents 'universal' values. This is a position Burke does not wholly occupy, but neither does he ever desert it entirely. The violence and rapacity of the Irish Protestant Ascendancy and of the East India Company's employees stained (he believed) the reputation of Britain, although quite how the imperial venture could be sustained without these unlovely qualities seemed beyond the range of his consideration. Perhaps what he wanted was a system of softening and disguise, one whereby initial violence would ultimately be forgotten in the afterglow of imperial consummation. But insofar as Burke thought of imperialism as an improving or modernising project, he thought that it, as much as the process of nation-building, needed to learn the arts of reverence towards ancestry, antiquity, historical survival. The great antiquity of Irish or Indian civilisation should have been an educative influence on the British colonial system, elicting reverential awe rather than stimulating hatred or contempt; such ancient civilisations and their laws and practices constituted versions of the Political Sublime.[42]

Algeria

In response to revolutionary fears or threats, and in pursuance of national stability, European states in the nineteenth century extended the suffrage and reformulated national identity. Such identities were, as before, defined in relation to others within the European system. But the French Revolution and the reaction against it, especially the Burkean version of reaction, had created the not entirely commensurable notions of a universal language of rights and of a specific European civilisation of Christian nations, economically powerful and culturally sovereign. As Tzvetan Todorov has argued, it therefore became possible for those who, like Tocqueville or John Stuart Mill, regarded themselves as liberals, to hold to ethical positions on relationships between individual persons, but to abandon these or to regard them as inapplicable or quixotic if extended to relationships between nations.[43] So it was possible for Tocqueville to write eloquently about the institution of slavery and to call for its abolition, partly on the grounds that France, of all nations, should be in the vanguard of such a crusade; yet, at the same time, and without showing any awareness of contradiction, he could support French policies in Algeria which were of a piece with those of all European imperial powers – murderous, rapacious, and pursued in the name of the extension of civilisation to a barbarous people. In this case, the unfortunate barbarians were the Algerians. The July Revolution and the occupation of Algeria belonged to the same year. For the remainder of his life, Tocqueville believed and argued that colonial possessions would help give to France the sentiment of pride and unity it required, reducing the prospect of internal revolution by providing the nation with a universal mission that would knit all classes together in a common enterprise. The development of liberty in France would be stimulated by the arrival of colonialism in Algeria. State violence, deployed at home in the interests of stability, could be exported in the name of progress – often by the same soldiers, particularly Marshal Thomas Bugeaud, Cavaignac and General Christophe Lamoricière.[44]

Tocqueville's various recipes for the French colonisation of Algeria were devised to make the successful exploitation of the country politically advantageous to France first by increasing her prestige and second by making the place economically advantageous to the colonists. In his 1841 'Essay on Algeria' he distinguishes between domination (like the English in India) and colonisation, recommending that France should begin with the first and use that as a means to partial colonisation. [45] Domination is the less attractive because it leaves everything in the hands of military men. Bugeaud, he admits in the debate in the Chambre des Députés in 1846, has 'rendered a great service to his country on the soil of Africa . . . He is the first to have applied, everywhere at once, the type of war that in my eyes, as in his, is the only type of war practicable in Africa. He has practiced this system of war with an unequaled energy and vigor.'[46] It is a system Tocqueville initially distinguishes from the 'Turkish manner, that is to say, by killing everything we meet.' On the other hand, he finds that there are men in France, whom he respects, who 'find it wrong that we burn harvests, that we empty silos, and finally that we seize unarmed men, women and children'. These are unfortunate necessities, not required in Europe because there 'we wage war on governments and not on peoples'.[47] Still, Bugeaud's savage methods were ineffective because he resisted the establishment in Algeria of civil government, preferring only a military domination. Tocqueville saw the risk that military exploits prosecuted abroad in the name of the nation and its civilising mission to the world could win glamorous reputations for successful officers and glorify the military profession – a legitimate anxiety given what almost immediately happened in France and was to happen in the same decade in Britain after the brutal suppression of the Indian Mutiny. He feared that a French general who had made a reputation in Africa might return 'on the stage of public affairs. God save France from ever being led by officers from the African army!'[48] Yet Tocqueville supported precisely such a person, General Cavaignac, particularly during the June days of the 1848 Revolution when he displayed in Paris a 'system of war' that could have been called unimpeachably 'African'.

Thus, Tocqueville's policy is to develop a system of colonisation and war together; to teach the indigenous population that it will eventually gain advantages from this colonisation; to abolish slavery in the French colonies; and to avoid beginning the 'history of the conquest of America all over again'. For the bloodshed that accompanied that conquest would now 'be a thousand times less excusable', since now, 'in the middle of the nineteenth century', the French 'are far less fanatical, and we have the principles and the enlightenment the French Revolution spread throughout the world'.[49] The blend of nationalist and colonial, enlightened and barbarous elements in his attitudes are classically those of European liberalism. Tocqueville's distress at the genocide of the Indians in America and the slavery of the Africans imported into the New World sits oddly with his support for such exterminatory policies in Algeria. Yet the contradiction helps the more to isolate the problem he raised in relation to America and refused to consider in relation to France: was there an inevitable connection between modernity and crimes on this scale? Where these peoples victims of the inexorable forces of progress and was it therefore right to join with history and side with modernity in erasing such barriers to its final expansion? It seems that his answer has to be yes, but he could not give it directly, at least not where France was concerned. Like Burke, he sensed the alliance between modernity and colonialism was atrocious in its consequences but refused to consider if these were constitutive of modernity, implying instead that they were of one its mysteries or one of its by-products. Alternatively, the process could be assigned to the 'nationalism of the state-nation, which created the imperial state', as Philip Bobbitt puts it.[50]

There is no gainsaying Jurgen Habermas's argument that the broadening of the 'public sphere' into 'public opinion', effected by the extension of the franchise, undermined the liberal conception of what an enlightened public discourse might be. Once the plebeian element entered or, in Tocqueville's earlier and prescient terms in relation to America, once the 'tyranny of the majority' became a reality, the liberal support for democracy transmuted into a support for an aristocracy of talent which tried to disguise itself as democracy.[51] This was also true in colonial terms, although in a much more brutal sense. Colonies and empire were politically useful because they provided a national and nationalist solidarity that class division threatened. In place of class, there was formed an ideology of race. This ideology was crucial to, not antithetical to European liberalism. Their true opponents were socialists and Marxists, although even they had difficulty in disengaging themselves from the appeal of a racial ideology that supported the idea of universal progress and the fantasy of local superiority.[52]

Tocqueville was an aristocrat who envisioned the New World; Burke was a new man who re-envisioned the aristocratic world. Burke successfully provided an ideology of tradition for the new imperial power when it faced its most critical challenge; he defined the British system as the alternative to revolutionary doctrine and violence but was consistent enough to find that it was at best difficult to reconcile it with colonial or imperial violence. Tocqueville reread Burke's analysis of the Revolution. In effect, he demoted it from the bad eminence Burke assigned to it in world history and absorbed it into a process or movement that had found one mode of realisation in the United States and was implacably pursuing other modes in France and in Britain and Ireland. Yet it seemed to him, as to many other liberals, that it was possible to identify the national spirit of France or of Britain (or of Europe) with that inexorable process which could be aided in its realisation abroad by the development of colonial systems and at home by the arrival of a democratic polity that would somehow preserve for intelligence the senior role formerly accorded to blood. There were 'new beings' in the world; revolutionaries indeed but also the soldiers of the imperial autocracies of the European nation-states. For him, opposition to the first group led by a logic that might be thought to be inexorable to support for the second.

8. FREEDOM BETRAYED
ACTON AND BURKE

In late 1945, in a lecture at University College, Dublin, F.A. Hayek, the Austrian economist who was to become the leading spokesman for economic liberalism in the post-war world, praised Tocqueville and Acton as the heirs to the Whig tradition of liberal individualism most nobly represented by Adam Smith and Edmund Burke.[1] This was an early and important incorporation of Smith and Burke into the Manichaean view of history that prevailed during the Cold War. Acton would certainly have welcomed his inclusion in this company and perhaps even for this purpose. He greatly admired Smith and Tocqueville, although Smith seemed to him by far the greater and more influential thinker – the man whose work influenced the French Revolution, socialism and the liberal economics and freedoms of the Anglo-American world.[2] But Burke was, even more than Smith, the central figure in Acton's account of the conflict between freedom and reaction in the modern period. It might have seemed bitterly appropriate to him that America, of all places, should have adopted (and adapted) Burke in its defence of 'the free world'. For in his view, the principles of Freedom in the modern era had been established and articulated in the American Revolution and in Burke's defence of it only to be later betrayed by both – by Burke (in 1790) and by America, during the Civil War.

Twice – as far as is recorded – Acton expounded in conversation his vision of the great History of Freedom which he failed to write, that 'Madonna of the Future' as he called it, after the title of Henry James's story. The second occasion was on a moonlit evening in the summer of 1879 in Venice. Seated on a marble bench, listening to Acton, were Herbert and Mary Gladstone. She tells us that 'All through that memorable evening two figures tramped up and down the Piazzetta in front of us – the Crown Princess, afterwards Empress of Germany, and M. Renan.'[3] She records the 'thrilling experience', which lasted for more than an hour, not in her own words but in those of the historian James Bryce who recorded the first occasion Acton had spoken to him – some years earlier – on this topic, but for several minutes only. 'It was', wrote Bryce 'as if the whole landscape of history had been suddenly lit up by a burst of sunlight.'[4] The burst of sunlight so described illuminates nothing more than the legendary status of the unwritten masterpiece which might have ranked with another – the history of England that Edmund Burke, to Acton's regret, did not write. The regret was expressed in 1858, in a review of Thomas Macknight's *History of the Life and Times of Edmund Burke*, in which he described Burke as the 'chief ornament' of his times, as 'our greatest statesman' who 'would have been the first of our historians' had he, rather than Hume, written that history.[5]

It is a little strange that Acton, who is best known for the fact that he never wrote the History of Freedom for which he had been preparing for much of his working life, should also be among the most decisive of historians. He liked lists of the greatest, the best, the most important, the crucial, the central, the most distinctive. T.B. Macaulay had also a highly developed 'love of ranking and comparison', a form of connoisseurship that is often much cultivated by the parvenu or the outsider. It was also attractive to a mass audience for whom epic catalogues, transformed into the grand parades of famous names that Macaulay taught historians to indulge, were then transmogrified into celebrity leagues in newspapers and journals.[6] He was among the first of renowned public figures to agree to make a list of the hundred best books to a popular journal.[7] Many of his opinions read now as though they were the responses to a quiz. So they can easily be reformatted to ask, for instance, who 'was as certainly the greatest genius among women known to history as Shakespeare among men'? and the answer is George Eliot;[8] if we ask, who 'did more than any single man to make modern History the development of revolution'? the answer is Luther;[9] or who was 'the most consummate practical genius that, in modern times, has inherited a throne'? the answer is Frederic the Great of Prussia,[10] or who 'first described the evolution of dogma, and cast every system into the melting-pot of History'? the answer is the Jesuit, Father Petavius,[11] or who 'has . . . written a larger number of mostly excellent books than any man who ever lived'? the answer is Ranke;[12] or who 'are our two greatest writers'? the answer is Macaulay and Burke[13] or who were 'the greatest writers of the Whig Party'? the answer is Burke and Macaulay;[14] or who was 'pre-eminent in the very small number of great political writers'? the answer again is Burke.[15]

As with people, so with events. The Edict of Nantes, the American Revolution, the Puritan Revolution in England, the first six months of the French Revolution were for him key moments in the development of liberty in the modern world, almost matched in their force by setbacks like the defeat of the South in the American Civil War, or the expansion of the modern state, or the triumph of Ultramontanism in the Catholic Church. Nothing, however, equalled the achievement represented by the Boston Tea-Party, which first made 'the Law of Nature' or, 'more properly speaking, of Divine Right' pre-eminent. 'On that evening of 16th December 1773, it became, for the first time, the reigning force in History.'[16] The precisely dated turning-point, like Burke's 6 October 1789, is highly effective in its hinging of a new era of world history on the events of one day, although its annunciation of Liberty's arrival is the inverse of Burke's lamentation for its passing. As in Burke, the global scale of a pronouncement is often paradoxically enhanced by the particularity of time and place in which it is embedded, as a slow process is suddenly incarnated in a single action. In Acton's case, this effect is intensified by the relatively contingent nature of the pronouncement's occasion – a book review, a lecture, a letter, an index card – the standard forms of the bulk of Acton's writings. His dictum on power is endlessly cited; less often we read or hear, among many examples, versions of the following dicta:

> All governments in which one principle dominates, degenerate by its exaggeration.[17] (which sounds like, but is not, a translation from Montesquieu);

> The most certain test by which we judge whether a country is really free is the amount of security enjoyed by minorities.[18]

> Liberty is not a means to a higher political end. It is itself the highest political end.[19]

> Patriotism is in political life what faith is in religion, and it stands to the domestic feelings and to homesickness as faith to fanaticism and to superstition.[20]

> This law of the modern world, that power tends to expand indefinitely, and will transcend all barriers, abroad and at home, until met by superior forces, produces the rhythmic movement of History.[21]

> Private vengeance in a savage community is the commencement of civil law; in a civilised society it is the inauguration of barbarism.[22]

The danger of such assertions is that in their determined pursuit of authoritativeness, their contexts ultimately disappear. Their attraction is that they aspire to reveal universal laws which are not merely inert moral *sententiae* but are the expression of a dynamic truth, the clarification of which is the purpose of History, that ongoing Revelation for which Acton hoped to write at least one of the gospels. These declarations, however, cannot escape having an inertial as well as a dynamic quality, because they seek to touch the ceiling as well as stand on the floor. He wants the scope of a universal law, the weight of a proverbial truth, as well as the flash of a revelation, of a brilliant individual insight. Along with the lists of names of people and events and places, these declarations belong to a repertoire of definition and decision that promises to produce a definitive work. Acton's celebrity in part depends on the fact that the great book he did not write had a reputation that the written work might not have been able to sustain. But from the outlines of the book that are glimpsed in reviews and in lectures we can see it has a clear family resemblance to its Victorian cousins, books that pursued the emergence and triumph in history of a great governing principle, such as W.E.H. Lecky's *History of the Rise and Influence of Rationalism in Europe* (1865) or Thomas Buckle's two volume *Introduction to the History of Civilization in England* (1857–61). The writing of histories of what Quentin Skinner has called 'unit ideas' does seem to be a highly polemical and ultimately vacuous exercise; in Skinner's words, 'there is no history of the idea to be written'.[23] In Acton's case, however, he did not lose confidence in the unit idea of freedom itself as in the possibility of seeing it 'prevail' in his own time. Uneasily situated between historians of ideas and world-systems theorists, he chased his phantom idea through thousands of pages in the hope that what had been so sporadically visible behind him would at last appear, fully realised, before him.

The dual quality of Acton's epigrammatic statements further indicates how he was caught up in the debate between the idea of a deposit of faith which is fixed and unchangeable and the gradual exfoliation in time of its full richness and splendour. It was a part of his religious faith and of his historian's vision to believe in that which is to be realised, in a history that has already been written and has yet to be written. These are not antitheses or contrasts, elements in a dialectic, nor items in a series. The religious word and concept for this is Revelation, although Acton was hard-pressed to distinguish it at times from secular versions of the March of Mind or of Progress or of some adaptation of evolutionary theory. Newman's version of development, as expounded in the *Essay on Development* (1845), by which Acton was at first thrilled and impressed, was essentially a theological meditation on this issue. Ultimately, Acton, never adept theologically, read Newman's essay politically and decided that it was deceitful, little more than a masquerade for the retention of the status quo, a sanctioning of authority on the grounds of its ancestral continuities.[24] This aspect of his attack on Newman was replicated in his objections to Burke, who was by far the most potent modern source of the appeal to existing, 'traditional' authority in the face of revolution. It was Burke who more than any other writer transformed the existing state of things into the traditional, conferring upon it the glamour of the past of which it was an extension and a refusal of the future that would, in denying it, deny all precedent. That future Acton believed would be realised on earth, through the convulsive moments of a series of revolutions. Burke had the strange distinction of having introduced the Old World to modernity and then of having invented a potent argument against ever renewing the acquaintance.

It was the interaction of the political and moral spheres that, in Acton's view, produced that high degree of definition which gave shape and meaning to the complex historical world. Through it, general moral principles that govern the minutiae of political circumstances remain permanently available to us. Freedom (or Liberty or Conscience) was an Idea which it was the goal of History to precipitate through that interaction. Catastrophe was the consequence of a divorce between the political and the moral; anyone guilty of allowing or nurturing such a divorce – Machiavelli would be a spectacular example – robbed political life of its ethical character and history of its capacity for judgement. The merciless killing of another, or others, for party advantage or in the prosecution of an ideological dispute, – the St Bartholomew's Day massacre or the massacre at Glencoe, for instance – could be condoned in such a world; so too could the eternal companions of massacre, the lies and defences that surround it and that crowd the historical record. It was ultimately one of the duties of the historian to illuminate such events, where the evidence makes it possible to do so, in the light of a moral principle. To understand and articulate such a principle was an achievement of the moral intelligence; it was the public form of the act of discrimination involved in the action of the private conscience. When conscience remains the ground of historical evaluation, even when every concession to historical understanding of existing circumstances is made, and when it becomes predominantly so, then, according to Acton, the reign of Freedom beckons. Thus the good and the bad are identifiable and can be charted at different locations on a historical map that, no matter how detailed it may be, always has Jerusalem or Rome at its centre.

Thus, for every Actonian list of the best, there is a corresponding list of the worst. Murder is the benchmark. A work on the French Revolution by Morse Stephens excused or seemed to excuse murder on the grounds of political necessity. This was a notion, wrote Acton in his review of 1892, that would be 'fatal to history':

> Our judgement of men, and parties, and systems, is determined by the lowest point they touch. Murder, as the conventional low-water mark, is invaluable as our basis of measurement. It is the historian's interest that it shall never be tampered with. If we have no scientific zero to start from, it is idle to censure corruption, mendacity, or treason to one's country or one's party, and morality and history go asunder.[25]

Clear condemnation has its attractions but since people are capable of both criminal and of morally admirable behaviour, the same names have to appear on both lists. There are those who became corrupt, or who remained moral on some issues and immoral on others. Inevitably, great events and issues posed the severest tests. In such instances, those who surrendered Liberty to its enemies were evil both on account of the act or acts in themselves and also for the evil effects that lived after them. The most famous and significant traitor in this regard was Burke, followed, among Acton's contemporaries, by Newman and Ignaz von Döllinger. But as Burke was by far the most important of these, because of his sublime gifts, and because he had lived through the two Revolutions that founded the modern world, so his betrayal was the more luridly visible, the greater in its effects and the more troubling in its implications.

Acton's paean of praise to Burke in the letter of December 1880 to Mary Gladstone immediately precedes the less-known passage on George Eliot who had died just the week before. Eliot is the one exclusively literary figure who had for Acton a significance comparable to a historical and political figure like Burke.

> But when I speak of Shakespeare the news of last Wednesday comes back to me, and it seems as if the sun had gone out. You cannot think how much I owed her. Of eighteen or twenty writers by whom I am conscious that my mind has

> been formed, she was one. Of course I mean ways, not conclusions. In problems of thought and life which baffled Shakespeare disgracefully, her touch was unfailing. No writer ever lived who had anything like her power of manifold, but disinterested and impartially observant sympathy. If Sophocles or Cervantes had lived in the light of our culture, if Dante had prospered like Manzoni, George Eliot might have had a rival.[26]

The attraction of Eliot was obvious. She exemplified for Acton the idea of conscience, independent of religious belief, Christian ethics without Christian metaphysics. She was deeply influenced by German intellectual culture and yet she was quintessesentially English. Most of all, perhaps, he saw in Eliot a combination of impartial, even serene judgement with the capacity to empathise with people of the most varied background, formation and convictions.[27] In his review of J.W. Cross's *Life* of Eliot, in which Acton laid the ground for much of the subsequent commentary on her work, he claimed that she 'had become a consummate expert in the pathology of conscience'.[28] In effect, she combined the internal detail of psychology and circumstance with the external vision of an impartial judge. She was Acton's model of a great historian, less eccentric and versatile than Dickens, less morbid than George Sand, less self-advertising than Mme de Staël. Only Shakespeare and Burke were to be ranked with her. Shadowing her always was Acton himself, more blessed than she with faith, less able than she to metamorphose the history of human consciousness embodied in her novels (but not in her essays) into a history of Freedom, outlined in his essays but not embodied in his proposed opus. So he mockingly gave his monumental work the title of a short story that epitomised failure and inner emptiness, spoke brilliantly of it, and finally wrote some of his most memorable passages in condemning those who had, like Burke, realised and then betrayed its theme.

The Two Burkes

Since the publication of his *Reflections*, Burke has been regularly accused of having betrayed the 'liberal' causes he had formerly supported. The standard elements of the mixed responses to him in the last decade of his life and in the first half of the nineteenth century – the universality of a Shakespeare and the servile agility of a political dependant, a confounding contrast between his genius and his delinquency – were effectively combined in a brief but devastating passage by Thomas Moore in his *Life of Sheridan* (1825). There Moore speaks of Burke's 'want of moral identity', and claims that 'political deserters' are generally of little use to the new cause, but

> . . . Burke was mighty in either camp; and it would have taken *two* great men to effect what he, by this division of himself, achieved. His mind, indeed, lies parted asunder in his works, like some vast continent severed by a convulsion of nature, – each portion peopled by its own giant race of opinions, differing

> altogether in features and language, and committed in eternal hostility to each other.[29]

Acton accepted the view that there were two Burkes, but modified and refined it into a part of his wider argument about the development of Liberty through Revolution in the modern era. Gertrude Himmelfarb was the first fully to demonstrate (in 1949) that Acton admired the Burke who defended the American colonists and repudiated the Burke who attacked the French Revolution.[30] In his view, the American Revolution had made the French Revolution possible; in turn, the French Revolution, for all its bloodshed and tyranny, had created the modern world because it had lifted the weight of the dead from the breasts of the living, an achievement more remarkable in Europe than in the Thirteen Colonies. (This echoes what Tocqueville said in *Democracy in America.*) Burke's great achievement, in this account, was to transform the limited party prejudice of the Whig party into a principled defence of revolution in America and of Revolution as such.[31] This he signally failed to do in France and although in the last seven years of his life, when he returned to his best, Burke did defend the Irish Catholics against the intolerable oppressions of the Protestant Ascendancy, he had failed in the interval to apply to Ireland the principles that he had defended in the American crisis. Burke wavered in Acton's estimation between being one of the greatest of all political thinkers and a party hack. In the latter incarnation, he had 'gilded the old order of things and wavered as to toleration and the slave trade',[32] and he had, in the guise of principle, created for future generations a version of tradition, continuity and prejudice that had been used to block the progress of Liberty in Europe and in the world. Because of his immense gifts, Burke's world-historical role in advancing and then retarding the cause of Liberty was more exemplary than that of anyone else. He defended the status quo in a spirit of servitude and for political gain.

As early as his 1858 review of Macknight's *Life*, Acton had voiced his reservations about Burke's opposition to the French Revolution as stated in the *Reflections*.

> That work, on which his popular fame chiefly rests, does not fairly represent his genius. It was written in a style calculated to produce a great immediate effect, and was in this respect eminently successful. It would probably have been less effective if it had been more original and more profound. In these qualities Burke's subsequent writings are generally superior to it.[33]

This review provides a benign version of Burke's later career, when 'the leader of a party became a teacher of mankind' and developed 'the universal principles of political philosophy' which he 'so eloquently upheld at the close of his life, and which led to the secession of 1791'.[34] But it was this secession from Foxite Whig to what Burke termed the 'old Whigs' which Acton was to bring under increasingly hostile scrutiny. In December 1880, writing to Mary

Gladstone and comparing Burke unflatteringly to her father, Acton composed one of his best-known vignettes of Burke as a betrayer of the cause of Liberty:

> Those who deem that Burke was the first political genius until now, must at this point admit his inferiority. He loved to avoid the arbitration of principle. He was prolific of arguments that were admirable but not decisive. He dreaded two-edged weapons and maxims that faced both ways. Through his inconsistencies we can perceive that his mind stood in a brighter light than his language; but he refused to employ in America reasons which might be fitted to Ireland, lest he should become odious to the great families and impossible with the King. Half of his genius was spent in masking the secret that hampered it. Goldsmith's cruel line is literally true.[35]

Yet only two weeks later he wrote to her again to place Burke back upon his pedestal:

> You can hardly imagine what Burke is for all of us who think about politics, and are not wrapped in the blaze and whirlwind of Rousseau. Systems of scientific thought have been built up by famous scholars on the fragments that fell from his table. Great literary fortunes have been made by men who traded on the hundredth part of him. Brougham and Lowe lived by the vitality of his ideas. Mackintosh and Macaulay are only Burke trimmed and stripped of all that touched the skies. Montalembert, borrowing a hint from Döllinger, says that Burke and Shakespeare were the two greatest Englishmen.[36]

The two Burkes he saw were, on the one hand, the man of principle, who had achieved moral clarity in the American crisis and, on the other, the man of party who had made a fetish of historic continuity and had muffled his principles with the gag of circumstance, who taught reactionaries to call the defence of the established order an act of prudence and make of that a display of pious tenderness in the face of the sublime and awesome spectacle of the inherited, preciously fragile world. These versions of Burke come and go in Acton's writings.[37] America brought out the best in Burke, because it was the American Revolution that began the History of Liberty in its modern sense:

> . . . Burke at his best is England at its best. Through him and through American influence upon him, the sordid policy of the Walpolean Whigs became a philosophy, and a combination of expedients was changed into a system of general principles.[38]

But France brought out the worst in him. His sympathy and support for the emigré clergy and nobles who were co-operating to form an alliance of European states against revolutionary France were especially abhorrent, for it was this which turned the Revolution from its true path into slaughter, militarism, and despotism.[39] The emigrés, he said in 1900,

> . . . . were instructed and inflamed by the greatest writer in the world, who had been the best of Liberals and the purest of revolutionary statesmen, Edmund Burke. It was not as a reactionist, but as a Whig who had drunk success to Washington, who had dressed in blue and buff, who had rejoiced over the British surrender in Saratoga, who had drawn up the address to the Colonists, which is the best State paper in the language, that he told them that it was lawful to invade their own country, and to shed the blood of their country-men.[40]

Two Revolutions

Acton's analysis of the French Revolution's failure to realise the aspirations of 1789 owes a great deal to Tocqueville's long meditation on the incompatibility of liberty and equality in France and the uniqueness of the American democratic experiment in reconciling them:

> The deepest cause which made the French Revolution so disastrous to liberty was its theory of equality. Liberty was the watchword of the middle class, equality of the lower.[41]

In 1789, . . . the finest opportunity ever given to the world was thrown away. because the passion for equality made vain the hope of freedom.[42] Again, like Tocqueville, Acton recognises that the American Revolution differed from the English one that preceded and the French one that succeeded it because in the English case liberty had always been founded on inequality and in the French case liberty was sacrificed in the pursuit of equality.[43] But Acton's critique of Burke's initial reading of the French Revolution, as he expressed it in the writings of 1790–92, was far removed from Tocqueville's. Acton recognised how important the apotheosis of the 1688 Revolution in England was to Burke's case. This was at the heart of Burke's betrayal. For to defend 1688 was, in Acton's view, to defend prejudice and provincialism. It was an event of European significance, no doubt; but it had no foundation in political principle.[44] Burke tried to make it so, and the specious principle he affected to discern in 1688 was that of compromise, accommodation with the existing state of things. In 1863, Acton wrote that it was only England's 'consistent, stupid fidelity to that political system which originally belonged to all nations that traversed the ordeal of feudalism'.[45] Burke and Macaulay had 'spent their finest prose' on a 'eulogy of 1688 as the true Restoration'.[46] To cast an aura of glamour over this episode and to make of the distasteful and near-criminal politicians and writers who had effected or defended it a litany of the saints of modern liberty was a melancholy achievement.[47]

Burke provided reaction with two of its most widely adopted arguments against revolution – first, the argument for prejudice, custom and continuity, which included a spurious nostalgia for a lost or threatened world of basic human feeling and its accompanying forms of reverence and servility; second, the prudential argument for the presiding force of circumstance in any given political situation and its corresponding dismissal of principle, which it miscalled abstraction or theory. In this lay the originality of Acton's contribution. He opposed the argument for circumstance by claiming it involved a denial of principle; and he admitted the Burkean argument against abstraction only on the condition that it not be confused with his own argument for the supremacy of principle. In his 1892 review of Morse Stephens's book on the Revolution, he declared:

> If he [Stephens] holds the supposed opinion of Burke, and means that in politics a theorist is shallow of necessity, because politics are insoluble by theory, the idea has a right to pass unchallenged in these pages . . .[48]

But he goes on to list Harrington, Locke, Rousseau, Jefferson, John Stuart Mill and Sieyès as members of 'the little band of true theorists'. He is not dismissing theory from politics if that word is understood in the Burkean sense. What Burke had done was to rob the word of its moral capacity to discern and articulate principle by reducing it to an incapacity to take account of circumstance. This was really a way of divorcing politics from morality and yet to do so under the guise of uniting them in the face of a Revolution that would separate them.

Burke's argument from circumstance often infuriated Acton. When he looked for an explanation for Burke's use of it, he sometimes ascribed it to his formation as a member of the Whig party or to mere political servility; at other times, he looked for a deeper explanation. When he did so, the questions he asked addressed much that beset him in his own life. Burke's betrayal – even if it lasted only for two years, or even if it was of principles which he had enunciated only for a moment in the 1770s – was crucial, both because the political philosophy it created had become so widely influential and because it queried the very meaning of what a Liberal was. This inevitably led Acton towards the conclusion that, in sponsoring the Glorious Revolution, Burke was being Anglican; and that in defending America or Ireland he was revealing his Catholic allegiances. In other words, Liberty had not only different histories within the Christian sects, but had particular and different elective affinities with them. Burke, the Irish Protestant with Catholic sympathies, was a true liberal when he was most Catholic, and betrayed that position when he became most Anglican.

> A liberal wishes that which ought to be – above what is – Burke too historic – The most historically minded of English statesmen. To the detriment of his reasoning power – and of his moral sense. He looked for what ought to be in what is. Is that not essentially Anglican?[49]

From the index-card notes, it would appear that what Acton called 'the buried treasure' in Burke, what made him 'superior to others'[50] was his Catholicism – which he imagines as a then dangerous residual allegiance that

Burke had to suppress and evade at times and yet which enabled him to go beyond the intellectual range of his rather purblind party.[51] Clearly, Acton's decisive repudiation of Burke's Whig interpretation of 1688, later adopted by Macaulay, was strategically central to his ambition to replace the somewhat amateurish and polemically Protestant schools of English history for a more professional, Germanic and Catholic account. Even though he had little or no respect for Carlyle's history of the French Revolution, he commented that it had at least the merit of delivering 'our forefathers from thraldom to Burke'.[52] Therefore, the vaunted Burkean role of 1688 in English and, more especially, in world history had to be diminished so that the history of modern liberty could be more accurately written. The true Glorious Revolution was the American Revolution and its true inheritor was (for a time) the French Revolution:

> During the six months from January 1789 to the Fall of the Bastille in July, France travelled as far as England in the six hundred years between the Earl of Leicester and Lord Beaconsfield. Ten years after the American, the Rights of Man, which had been proclaimed at Philadelphia, were repeated in Versailles. The alliance had borne fruit on both sides of the Atlantic, and for France, the fruit was the triumph of American ideas over English.[53]

In attempting to halt this accelerated American–French sequence, Burke had become very English, Protestant, and provincial until, in the autumn of his days, he had either returned to his former loyalties or, possibly, purged himself of all that was merely local and contingent in his political philosophy and attained a Catholic universalism:

> In the writings of his last years (1792–97) whatever was Protestant or partial or revolutionary of 1688 in his political views disappeared, and what remained was a purely Catholic view of political principles and of history.[54]

Yet in his *Reflections*, he had given to the restricted philosophy of 1688 an appeal that conferred upon it a specious grandeur and had thereby struck a blow against Liberty and its originating triumph in America. Although in Acton's estimation Burke returned to his most fundamental principles in his *Appeal from the New to the Old Whigs* and in his later writings on Ireland, it was the *Reflections* that provided the arsenal for future reaction and that remained the most damnably influential of all of his writings.[55]

There is, therefore, a history of punctual revolutions which demonstrate the phases of the emancipation of the European and American worlds from the various forms of absolutism that had preceded the reign of conscience. 'The modern age,' he declared in his inaugural lecture as Regius Professor of Modern History at Cambridge in 1895, 'founded a new order of things, under a law of innovation, sapping the reign of continuity.' The generation of Columbus, Machiavelli, Erasmus, Luther and Copernicus, 'set forever the mark of progress upon the time that was to come'.[56] That was the first stage.

In the subsequent history, 1688 plays no more than a catalytic role in the sequence Acton described in 'The Puritan Revolution', one of the Cambridge lectures delivered in 1899–1900 and in 1900–01:

> The Commonwealth is the second stage on the road of revolution, which started from the Netherlands, and went on to America and France, and is the centre of the history of the modern world . . . It supplied the English Revolution, the one that succeeded, the American, the French, with its material. And its ideas became efficacious and masterful by denying their origin. For at first they were religious, not political theories. When they renounced their theological parentage, and were translated into the scientific terms of politics, they conquered and spread over the nations, as general truths, not as British exports.[57]

Yet even were a larger world role for 1688 to be conceded, it would heighten rather than reduce the weight of the accusation against Burke's 1790 caricature of revolution. For Burke's traditionalist politics were founded ultimately on the defence of prejudice. This made a virtue out of blind obedience to authority. He consciously repudiated the supremacy of right over authority and tried to make the latter unquestionable by calling it providential.[58]

There were clearly affinities between this assault on Burke and Acton's disagreement and final break with his teacher, Döllinger, specifically in the latter's published admiration of Archbishop Dupanloup in 1879 and generally in Döllinger's seeming preference for authority over liberty.[59] For Döllinger, claimed Acton, like Burke before him, was willing to excuse crime or immoral behaviour on the grounds of an idea of historical continuity which could easily be flexed into a rationale for moral relativism. Acton wanted to have as full a knowledge as possible of the circumstances of an age or of a sequence of actions; but he did not want such knowledge of itself to provide a basis for moral evaluation. Burke had provided this attitude with a political and philosophical panache that had previously been lacking (save perhaps in Bolingbroke[60]) in any anti-theoretical position. Döllinger and Newman in their different ways had practised it, although the influence of the German historians, especially Ranke, in this regard was probably more potent than Acton fully admitted, and could paradoxically be overtheorised into a Hegelian or neo-Hegelian defence of 'das weltgeschichte ist das weltgerichte' ('world history is world right'). At any rate, one of the risks of the philosophy of continuity, and of historicism, was that no view of an age external to itself could be admitted. This was to deny the existence, even perhaps the possibility, of a presiding authority in morality. It also took the impetus from historical sequence and made the historian's art of periodisation and therefore of the ultimate disclosure of history's meaning a chimera.[61]

Further, this was the very reverse of what the Americans, particularly the Pennsylvania Quakers, had done. Out of the fires of the religious fanaticisms of the seventeenth century they had plucked the brand of a rational, non-sectarian liberty. Again, a Tocquevillian analysis is adapted to strengthen the argument against Burke's late deformation of the history that he had earlier helped to create:

> It was principally through Franklin and the Quaker State that America influenced political opinion in Europe and that the fanaticism of one revolutionary epoch was converted into the rationalism of another. American independence was the beginning of a new era, not merely as a revival of Revolution, but because no other Revolution ever proceeded from so slight a cause, or was ever conducted with so much moderation . . . Ancient Europe opened its mind to two new ideas – that Revolution with very little provocation may be just; and that democracy in very large dimensions may be safe.[62]

But the American Revolution had obviously clear implications for Ireland, since they were both part of the same system that permitted the legislature in London to

> . . . make laws injurious to the subject for the benefit of English religion or English trade. If that principle was abandoned in America it could not well be maintained in Ireland, and the green flag might fly on Dublin Castle.[63]

Why then did Burke not apply to his native land the principles he applied to America? The most sustained answer Acton gave to this question was in his lecture on 'The Influence of America' in his French Revolution series:

> The most significant instance of the action of America on Europe is Edmund Burke. We think of him as a man who, in early life, rejected all generalities and abstract propositions, and who became the most strenuous and violent of conservatives. But there is an interval when, as the quarrel with the Colonies went on, Burke was as revolutionary as Washington. The inconsistency is not as flagrant as it seems. He had been brought forward by the party of measured propriety and imperative moderation, of compromise and unfinished thought, who claimed the right of taxing, but refused to employ it. When he urged the differences in every situation and every problem, and shrank from the common denominator and the underlying principle, he fell into step with his friends., As an Irishman, who had married into an Irish Catholic family, it was desirable that he should adopt no theories in America which would unsettle Ireland. He had learnt to teach government by party as an almost sacred dogma, and party forbids revolt as a breach of the laws of the game. His scruples and his protests, and his defiance of theory, were the policy and precaution of a man conscious of restraints, and not entirely free in the exertion of powers that lifted him far above his tamer surroundings. As the strife sharpened and the Americans made way, Burke was carried along, and developed views which he never utterly abandoned, but which are difficult to reconcile with much that he wrote when the Revolution had spread to France.[64]

Further, the system that allowed England to make such laws was a modern, not an ancient system. It was one of the early manifestations of the modern absolutist state which Acton came to believe was the creation of modern Liberalism and was, as such, the enemy of everything that a true Liberal would defend. Thus,

> Both the oppression of Ireland and the oppression of America was (sic) the work of the modern school, of men who executed one king and expelled another. It was the work of parliament, of the parliaments of Cromwell and of William III . . . It had become necessary to turn back the development of politics, to bind and limit and confine the State, which it was the pride of the moderns to exalt. It was a new phase of political history. . . .[65]

Ireland had suffered under 'the two worst features of the Hanoverian reigns', both of which played a critical role in Burke's thinking 'the long domination of the great families established under kings who were foreigners, and the renovation of the penal laws and of the oligarchy in Ireland'.[66] Even though Ireland had endured a great deal more than America, Acton's point was that the two polities were linked by their subjection to a specific and modern tyranny. It was the tyranny of the new idea of the State, the new absolutism, which America (and Burke) had challenged on the central point of principle. It did not matter, according to this view, that the British decided to impose or not to impose taxes; or that the Penal Laws against Catholics were or were not implemented to the full. It was the belief that the right to impose or not to impose belonged to the British state, that it was by grace and favour that the imposition was lightened or removed. That was tyranny. It was against that form of tyranny that America defined its idea of liberty and, with that, its idea of a republic of equals which would not risk having the caprice of a monarch magnified into a law of the state.

Yet Acton believed that the victory of the North in the American Civil War threatened the success because it undermined the originating principle of the American system. For him, the central issue was not slavery but states' rights. It is a Tocquevillian anxiety about the tyranny of the majority that dominates Acton's analysis, but intensified in his case by the conviction that a new democratic absolutism, the absolute sovereignty of the people, had now won a crucial victory that could make it as great a threat to liberty as the absolute monarchies that had once prevailed.[67] Besides the tyranny of the majority, democracy had another danger that was native to it – 'the absolute essential equality of all men in civil rights'. Since it was clearly in the interest of the Southern States to refuse majority rule in relation to the Union and to refuse the principle of equality in relation to slaves, Acton arrives at the conclusion that they were (or might have been) the saviours of democracy. 'The Decomposition of Democracy was arrested in the South by the indirect influency of slavery.'[68] In addition, the bad reputation of democracy in Europe was, in his opinion, further damaged by the American crisis. The extreme Tories hoped the 'war of Secession' had ruined it completely, while Liberals believed that the independence of the South might redeem it.[69] If only America had managed to give 'the light without the shade of political life' European anti-democratic sentiment and regimes would have been vanquished by its example. But that was not to be. The unqualified democracy that ancient Rome and modern France had failed to achieve and that America had undertook to realise, had not appeared.[70] As he made clear in a letter to the great Confederate general, Robert E. Lee, he considerd this a tragedy for civilisation:

> I deemed that you were fighting the battles of our liberty, our progress, and our civilization; and I mourn for the stake that was lost at Richmond more deeply than I rejoice over that which was saved at Waterloo.[71]

The absolutist tendency of democracy had always been a matter of concern to Acton. In a sense, when he claimed that it was the American Revolution that had made Rousseau the most influential of European writers,[72] he was drawing attention both to the dangerous elements in Rousseau's thought and to the dangers to Democracy that were implicit in its own doctrines – those of the sovereignty of the people and of the general will.[73] With the American Civil War, it seemed to him that the great American experiment had become a centralised, tyrannical, Rousseauistic democracy, more fearfully so than Tocqueville had predicted, and more ironically so than any Liberal could have imagined. After 1848 in Europe, the distinction between the Liberal, who supported Liberty, and Liberalism, which supported the endless extension of the powers of the state, had become clearer. The omnipotence of the state was also, for Acton, the triumph of secularism, and the denial of the necessity of striking the balance between Church and state, all the more urgent in his mind because of the battle in Italy between the forces of Italian nationalism and the papacy.[74] Like Newman, he considered Liberalism to be a wholly secular and aggressive doctrine of state dominance, some of the contradictions of which were most glaringly disclosed in its educational policies in Ireland, where the endowment of Protestant educational institutions was not thought incompatible with the refusal to endow Catholic institutions.

Nevertheless, for all his fears that a new form of state absolutism was emerging in nineteenth-century America, Acton remained consistent in his claim that American independence was a unique achievement and that it should continue to be read in the light of the early Burke of the 1770s and not in the twilight of the Burke who wrote the *Reflections*. This was part of his objection in 1889 to James Bryce's *The American Commonwealth*, which claimed continuity between Magna Carta, the Bill of Rights and the Revolution:

> I descry a bewildered Whig emerging from the third volume with reverent appreciation of ancestral wisdom, Burke's *Reflections,* and the eighteen Canons of Dort, and a growing belief in the function of ghosts to make laws for the quick.[75]

It was the attractions of continuity, after all, that in one of his index-card notes Acton claimed had prevented Burke from being 'an entire liberal', despite all his liberal positions on a variety of issues:

> What stood against it? His notion of history. The claims of the past. The authority of time. The will of the dead. Continuity. Others held this before, but with other parts of conservatism. Burke was conservative by that alone, and that alone devoured all the rest of his principles, and made the first of liberals, the first of Conservatives. That is the element of unity and consistency. He is not consistent; but the element that prevailed at last existed from the first.[76]

An appreciation of the attractions of continuity was necessary, according to Acton, if the relatively new phenomenon of European nationalism was to be understood. It was most visible in Burke's great disciple in Germany, Karl von Savigny, whose

> . . . theory of continuity has this significance in political science, that it supplied a basis for conservatism apart from absolutism and compatible with freedom. And, as he believed that law depends on national tradition and character, he became indirectly and through friends a founder of the theory of nationality.[77]

For continuity also allowed, even encouraged, the belief in the uniqueness of national traditions and that in itself could (but did not necessarily) lead to exclusivist claims that then provided yet another basis for modern absolutism. Acton's reading of the historical and philosophical alliance between nationalism and democracy in the nineteenth century emphasises, more than Montalembert's for instance, how dependent this was on liberalism and how sporadically strategic was liberalism's support for it. Continuity was the key term for nationalism as much as equality was for socialism. Both were threats to Liberty.[78] And America, once its saviour, was now a sorry example:

> The spurious liberty of the United States is twice cursed, for it deceives those whom it attracts and those whom it repels. By exhibiting the spectacle of a people claiming to be free, but whose love of freedom means hatred of inequality, jealousy of limitations to power, and reliance on the State as an instrument to mould as well as to control society, it calls on its admirers to hate aristocracy and teaches its adversaries to fear the people. The North has used the doctrines of Democracy to destroy self-government. The South applied the principle of conditional federation to cure the evils and to correct the errors of a false interpretation of Democracy.[79]

Nationality and Nationalism

The version of local attachment most often associated with Burke's version of patriotism was part of his response to the internationalism or cosmopolitanism of the Enlightenment and of the Revolution. A feature of much 'liberal' thought in the nineteenth century, best represented by John Stuart Mill and Tocqueville, is its determination to keep that local attachment alive but to attach it to a civilising project other than that of revolutionary internationalism, especially in its Marxist and socialist extensions. For them, the alternative was empire – the British in India, the French in Algeria. Acton follows a similar path but he, like Newman, has two alternative internationalisms – the empire and the Church. It was the bad eminence achieved by the state that they opposed and which they identified as one of the triumphs of modern liberalism, the Protestant roots of which had in their view become disengaged from religious belief. For both of them, this was an unavoidable historical process for Protestantism. Only Catholicism could produce a liberalism that would remain true to religious belief. But there was in the United Kingdom, the centre of empire, a Catholic question, centred on Ireland (although not exclusively so), in which religious belief had become attached to a nationalism, which in political as well as philosophical terms challenged the imperial enterprise's assurance and stability. In his classic essay 'Nationality' (1862), Acton argues that a critical distinction between the nation and the State is ethical in character. A modern state is 'a moral and political being', whereas a nation is an entity derived from and dependent on material and physical causes, national liberty has as its enemy the centralised state; but the influence of religion, in 'the emancipation of Poland or Ireland' has produced a modified version of the state and allowed for 'a new definition of patriotism'.

> The difference between nationality and the State is exhibited in the nature of patriotic attachment. Our connection with the race is merely natural or physical, whilst our duties to the political nation are ethical. One is a community of affections and instincts infinitely important and powerful in savage life, but pertaining more to the animal than to the civilised man; the other is an authority governing by laws, imposing obligations, and giving a moral sanction and character to the natural relations of society. Patriotism is in political life what faith is in religion, and it stands to the domestic feelings and to homesickness as faith to fanaticism and to superstition. It has one aspect derived from private life and nature, for it is an extension of the family affections, as the tribe is an extension of the family. But in its real political character, patriotism consists in the development of the instinct of self-preservation into a moral duty which may involve self-sacrifice.[80]

Much of the phrasing of the essay is reminiscent of Burke and it is no surprise to find him quoted on the distinction between the purely geographical France (the revolutionary one) and the 'moral essence' which constitutes it as a state.

However, Acton's accompanying claim in support of this ethical patriotism – that the person who surrenders everything either to the nation or to the state denies thereby 'that right is superior to authority' – is less persuasive because that is precisely what he charged Burke with having done in his defence of local and party interests during the French Revolution against the universal principles that he had earlier defended in America. This is a symptom of Acton's eagerness to recruit Burke when he needs him. It is wrong, he declares, to make 'the State and the nation commensurate with each other in theory' because this 'reduces practically to a subject condition all other nationalities that may be within the boundary'. But if the end of civil society is 'the establishment of liberty for the realisation of moral duties', then the British and Austrian Empires that include without oppressing various nationalities are the most perfect states.

As with democractic systems, Acton always opposes unity rather than union; centralisation rather than confederation; the retention of intermediate bodies rather than their abolition. This is language common to Montesquieu, Burke and Tocqueville. Yet in Acton's case, it is clear that he wants to argue for the federated empire or the federation of states within a democracy as the modern version of the period of the Church's 'undisputed supremacy' when all Western Europe 'obeyed the same laws, all literature was contained in one language, and the political unity of Christendom was personified in a single potentate, whilst its intellectual unity was represented in one university.'[81] It is a Catholic-medieval version of modernity, refashioned in the structures of the two empires, Austro-Hungarian and British, to which Acton had always given at least a modified intellectual allegiance. By the time of the Franco-Prussian War, 1870–71, he seems to have believed that German nationalism, in its literary and philosophical (especially Hegelian) forms, had helped to produce the anti-Catholic, illiberal Bismarckian state, the epitome of modern absolutism. Yet even in 1860, his view of the state, its relation to the Church and to nationality, was fully formed:

> In our conviction the true view of the origin and nature of the state, and the only one which must not inevitably succumb to the revolutionary logic, is that which recognises in the state the same divine origin and the same ends as in the Church, which holds that it belongs as much to the primitive essence of a nation as its language, and that it unites men together by a moral, not like family and society, by a natural and sensible bond . . . It was the business of modern history further to develop the system to which the medieval polity tended; and this it failed to do because of the inordinate growth . . . [not] of the power of the king only, but of the power of the state. State-absolutism, not royal absolutism, is the modern danger against which neither representative government nor democracy can defend us, and which revolution greatly aggravates.[82]

Two years later, he announced that the independence of Greece was 'the first breach opened in the system of the Holy Alliance', the 'first abandonment of the principle that the badness of a government is no reason for upsetting it', and that this 'was a victory gained, not by the right of resistance, or by toleration, or by law against an arbitrary despotism, but by the principle of nationality'.[83] The consequences were the more far-reaching because it was the European powers, with their sentimental attachment to the idea of Greece, that had won independence for the new kingdom. After Greece, came Belgium and Poland, although Poland's role was perhaps more central than any country's in the rise of nationalism, since it had been the partition of Poland, 'the most revolutionary act of the old absolutism', that had 'awakened the theory of nationality in Europe'. Burke is cited to prove the point.[84]

Acton's views on nationalism, as expressed in the early sixties, undergo no significant alteration in the next forty years. Perhaps he does come to emphasise more its effect as a counterbalance to centralisation, one that operates best within a federal system or an imperial system that has learned from Burke, or Dean Tucker or Adam Smith, the lesson that the extension of territory and influence does not need to be accompanied by corresponding force.[85] Within such a system, nationality acts as a mediating influence; it reduces the force of centralisation, it permits of diversity and preserves local loyalties and in turn its own parochial tendencies are reduced.[86] But when nationality becomes the sole principle of a political system it then becomes nationalism. The modern state system, which seemed to Acton to combine bureaucratic administration of an oppressive kind[87] with an ethnological rather than a historic sense of the union between its members was fatally given, in both respects, to absolutism.

IRELAND

Acton was for a relatively short time an ineffective MP for Carlow and fancied himself for a longer time to be a key adviser to Gladstone on Irish affairs, particularly on the issue of Home Rule, which Acton supported as a cause and perhaps helped to persuade Gladstone should be a crusade.[88] He thought Catholic Emancipation little more than a half-victory, but recognised that the linkage between religious emancipation and democratic freedom, so important in Poland and Belgium also and so popular among liberal Catholics like Montalembert in his attempt to renew Catholicism as a spiritual and political force in Europe, was critical in Ireland. He considered the disestablishment of the Anglican Church in Ireland in 1869 (it passed into law in 1871) as a triumph for freedom and as a necessary preliminary to the successful achievement of Home Rule.[89] Since 1688, the exclusion of Catholics within Britain had been a disabling heritage of the religious wars and a permanent limitation on the capacity of English political ideas to achieve universal appeal. But with the forging of the United Kingdom to include Ireland in a new species of federation, the exclusion of Catholics became even more unjust and politically untenable. The question of providing Catholics with education, in which Newman's Catholic University was to play so resonant and melancholy a role, made the sectarianism of the British state even more painfully obvious.

Acton was at one with Matthew Arnold and Newman on the anomalous and incoherent policy of what the short-lived journal the *Chronicle* (1867–68), called 'The Government of Endowed Orangeism',[90] whereby state support for the education of the Catholic majority was regarded as inconceivable while that for the Protestant minority, even the most bigoted sections of it, was deemed normal. The *Chronicle's* Irish contributors, especially Thomas O'Hagan, W.K. Sullivan and George Sigerson, pressed the Liberal party hard on questions of reform in Ireland.[91] What they did not wholly share with Acton was his view of the flawed nature of the British state in relation to religion. Irish education was the topic, but a larger question arose from it. Again as in Arnold, Prussia provided the contrast of a state that effectively achieved a separation between Church and State, despite (maybe even because of) the history of religious division within Germany as a whole.

> The Church is necessarily at all times an educational institution . . . For centuries it was never discovered that education was a function of the State, and the State never attempted to educate. But when modern absolutism arose, it laid claim to everything on behalf of the sovereign power. Commerce, industry, literature, religion, were all declared to be matters of State, and were appropriated and controlled accordingly. In the same way as all these things education belongs to the civil power, and on the same grounds with the rest it claims exemption. When the revolutionary theory of Government began to prevail, and Church and State found that they were educating for opposite ends and in a contradictory spirit, it became necessary for the State to remove the children entirely from the influence of religion. This spirit of hostility was not, however, universal, and it was quite possible, especially in these countries, to admit the claims of the modern State without serious danger. For there are two alternatives almost equally plausible, suited to different states of society. Either the school belongs to the Church, and preserves a confessional character, where people of different religions reside together, or else the particular religious tone is completely neutralised. This can only be done with the assistance of the State, and of a State which is not involved in religious quarrels. In Prussia this is possible, for religious equality is acknowledged in government. But in Ireland the State has failed to do that which was required of it to make the national system work well. It does not stand above sectarian differences: it has not stripped off a confessional character. Instead of controlling parties, it is still the instrument of a party. It cannot escape from the fatal union with the Established Church in Ireland. Whilst that institution subsists and blights the country, the Catholics cannot place entire confidence in the State. The independence of Church and State is not enough for freedom, so long as the Government acknowledges a specifically religious character.[92]

A government should no more be identified with a Church than a State with a race. For in such matters, toleration is necessary; its development (which

Acton dates in the modern era from the Edict of Nantes) is integral to 'the history of liberty, which is the marrow of all modern history'.[93] Ireland was a demonstration of the state absolutism that threatened when the neutrality of the secular power and the independence of the Church were absent.

Acton's reflections on the Irish situation were of a piece with his general theory of the proper relations between Church and State, and the fatality to Liberty of their union. It was especially important, in his view, to break that union in Ireland. 'All established churches', he said in one of his notes, 'have persecuted',

> and the establishment in Ireland has been the occasion of the most atrocious persecution that ever disgraced the Protestant religion in my country or in the world.[94]

If Ireland's justified demand for autonomy could be achieved through 'legal and constitutional means', then the victory would be for Liberty, not for nationalism as a principle. 'England's rule over Ireland rests upon robbery.'[95] It was the Ireland of the pre-emancipation era, though, that sometimes appealed to him – as to Montalembert – as the model for the Catholic Church in its struggle against the seductions of material and political power. Acton did not want to see the triumph of Italian nationalism nor did he wish to see the preservation of the papacy's temporal possessions, especially given the appalling political reputation they had earned. In effect, he increasingly envisaged the Church as becoming a more concentrated spiritual power in the world as a consequence of the loss of the papal territories and he seemed at times to go along with Montalembert's vision of Ireland as a country where Catholicism had become more intensely itself, more spiritually alive, in proportion to its material humiliations and persecutions.

Two essays of 1862, the *annus mirabilis* of Acton's youth, his review of Goldwin Smith's *Irish History* and his essay 'The Protestant Theory of Persecution', articulate his early view of the connections between nationality and religion. In the review, he in part follows Smith in saying that the Irish, although more cultivated than their conquerors, profited greatly from the conquest. To illustrate this, he takes issue with the nationalist argument that it is always wrong for a nation to belong to a foreign state. History shows otherwise, even though he readily admitted the initial grant of Ireland to Henry II by Pope Adrian had no justification.[96] Dominion and subjection are the law of civil progress. Thus, as the Roman Empire and the Roman Church subjected 'all countries to the authority of a single power' the arguments of nationalism are historically inadmissable. 'The political theory of nationality is in contradiction with the historic nation.' Religion, with the help of the secular power, promotes civilisation – the Normans in Ireland are a case in point. So 'the theory of nationality, unknown to Catholic ages, is inconsistent both with political reason and with Christianity'. However, in the Irish case in particular,

Acton needs to deal with the problem of persecution which, at this stage in his career, he can regard as an issue that can be in part excused and certainly almost wholly explained on the basis of its historical conditions. Both persecution and toleration, he argued, 'are true in principle', but toleration belongs to a more advanced stage of civilisation. A state characterised by religious homogeneity or unity, in making the necessary transition to religious liberty, sometimes persecutes for a time in order to avoid making religious disabilities a permanent feature of its constitution. This expresses itself in religious exclusion, as in Louis XIV's France or Emperor Nicholas's Russia. Ireland was different and worse.

> But the system applied to Ireland, which uses religious disabilities for the purpose of political oppression, stands alone in solitary infamy among the crimes and follies of the rulers of men.[97]

The cited support for this view is Burke and the whole argument does indeed owe a great deal not only to Burke's attack upon the system of the Penal Laws in Ireland, but also on Burke's lament for the destruction of local affection brought about by the Penal laws, whereby members of one's own religion were believed to be closer in kin than one's own countrymen of a different faith. Acton takes the Burkean argument one step further in the essay on Persecution and in the review of Smith, when he argues that Protestantism, whether or not it established itself as a national Church, is of its nature given to persecution (just the opposite of what Protestants say of Catholics) because, according to Reformation doctrine, it is a duty to persecute; the 'object was to avenge God, not to preserve order'.[98]

Thus, the achievement of toleration and the dismantling of the institutional apparatus of the persecuting Protestant system in Ireland were for him entirely congruent with one another. The long battles over emancipation, tithes, education and Church disestablishment in Ireland in the nineteenth century were part of that difficult transition that the United Kingdom had to make from being in effect a sectarian State that pretended to unity of religion – which the inclusion of Ireland in the federal system had rendered wholly false – to being a state in which Liberty prevailed. The political emancipation of Catholics, English and Irish, especially the latter, within the United Kingdom was for him an opportunity for the advance of Freedom in the world and within the British Empire. Acton was fond of drawing an analogy between the British Empire and the Roman Church of his own time and the ancient Roman Empire and the Church of the Middle Ages. Church and State were parallel, not convergent systems, but each needed the other for its healthy survival.

Although he does not comment at any length on the Fenian movement nor on the various forms of Irish nationalist 'unrest', it is plain that Acton would have been as out of sympathy with these as he was with the Orange

Order or the Protestant interest in Ireland. The latter was a system of intolerance for which any excusing historical conditions had disappeared; and the former was a symptom of that modern revolutionary disease – of which he thought it heralded the final phase – by which, as in revolutionary France, the historic nation was to be obliterated and replaced by an ethnological fiction. It is obvious that this version of Irish history and of the rise of the modern spirit owes much more to the Burke of the *Reflections* than Acton could have, in all consistency, admitted, although he is careful never to quote from that text. It is a unique inflection of Burke's vision of Ireland, although it does seem that, in the latter part of his career, Acton's animus against Burke's failure on Ireland seemed to intensify in step with the failure of Gladstonian liberalism to effect there the transformation that would have made it a monument to the achievement of Liberty within the British system that Acton wanted Ireland to be. There was also, of course, the growing and baneful influence in Irish Catholicism of the Ultramontane spirit. Although he did not say so in his public reply to Gladstone's *Vatican Decrees*, he was certainly in sympathy with Gladstone's anger at and suspicion of the Irish hierarchy's rejection of his Irish University Bill of 1873, for which Acton had made suggestions. Gladstone felt his attempt to complete the payment of the debt of justice to Ireland had been unfairly dismissed. Acton agreed and knew the source. It was Ultramontanism, now the senior force in Roman Catholicism's drive towards centralisation and despotism, in Ireland as elsewhere.[99] Rome Rule was already throwing its shadow over Home Rule.

The defeat of Home Rule in Ireland in 1886 and 1893 spelt the failure of the Acton-Gladstone grouping (with help from John Morley and James Bryce) to finally apply to Ireland the principles that had prevailed in the American Revolution. Yet some of its opponents – unionist ideologues like Lecky or Sir Henry Maine, A.V. Dicey or Fitzjames Stephen – also drew on Burke, the 'other' Burke who defended custom, habit, prejudice, precedent and opposed all radical change as unhistorical. Despite what Burke had said about the peculiar evils of the Anglo-Irish Ascendancy, and its fake pretensions to aristocratic status, this group, with Lecky to the fore, defended the idea of an aristocracy or an élite group and linked it to the absolute sovereigny of Parliament. The dispute was an outstanding example of the amenable nature of Burke's political philosophy, although it is an irony of a special kind that it should have been so exploited as a philosophy against revolution by those who defended a system in Ireland that Burke believed to have stimulated revolution. In this light, Home Rule was not Rome Rule, so much as it was revolution.

The Infallible Empires

Liberal Catholicism in Europe reached its apogee in the Malines Conference of 1863, where Montalembert made his famous speeches on toleration and on a free Church in a free State, and at the Munich Congress of 1864, opened by Döllinger. Acton reported on and endorsed the proceedings of both congresses. But that was the culmination of the increasingly chafed relationship between Catholic Liberalism in any of its national or European forms and the Vatican. It was replaced by a series of assertions of authority to which submission was required. Acton's painful struggle with the Church's increasing authoritarianism and anti-intellectualism, from the Dogma of the Immaculate Conception (1854), through to the Papal Brief *Tuas Libenter* of 1864 which made all conclusions of scholarship subject to the decisions of Pontifical Congregations, to the Encyclical *Quanta Cura* and the appended Syllabus of Errors (1864) and to the Declaration of Infallibility at the Vatican Council of 1870 is a history of disillusion often told. The appearance of the Syllabus, the defeat of the South in the American Civil War and his discontinuance of the *Home and Foreign Review* in the face of Vatican hostility all combined to make 1864 a watershed in his development. He spent the next four years on a tour of European archives and then was consumed in preparations for the leadership of the minority view against the Declaration of Infallibility at the General Council. But, despite his efforts, the Dogma of Papal Infallibility was defined on 19 July 1870 during a violent thunderstorm. The next day, war was declared between France and Prussia. A sea change had taken place.

Far more than the defeat of the Liberal party and its Irish policies in the election of 1868, more than the defeat of secession in America, this was a blow to any hope that the Idea of Freedom would increasingly reveal itself in contemporary history. Ultramontanism was, as much as nationalism or socialism, an enemy that perverted a truth into an error and that heralded the reign of mendacity and the abandonment of the moral vision in the light of which history could be read. The surrender of conscience to authority and the readiness to deny truth for the sake of solidarity with that authority was characteristic of that 'spurious Ultramontanism that ramified from de Maistre'.[100] Maistrean reaction to the French Revolution had produced, against the truths of science and of history, a form of religious absolutism that Acton claimed produced the very stereotype of Catholicism that Protestants had promulgated for so long, a stereotype that had as its central ingredient the 'repudiation of the liberty of conscience'.[101] Persecution may have had for the young Acton a peculiarly Protestant character, but the failure of his own Church to admit its own crimes in that regard seemed to the older man to make the spirit of Catholicism wither into a version of that *realpolitik* that had been invented as a word and concept in post-1848 Germany. Here with a vengeance was the divorce between morality and politics that Burke had decried and by which Acton himself became obsessed.

After the Council, Acton immersed himself in the problems of the relationship between the papacy and the Italian state – an exemplary instance of the Church and State issue – and betrayed an increasing anxiety about the intensifying centralisation of Church power in the Vatican. But the repercussions of 1870 became more painful and public. In Germany, Döllinger was excommunicated in 1871; finally, there came the open dispute generated by Gladstone's pamphlet of 1874, carefully published on Guy Fawkes Day, *The Vatican Decrees in their Bearing on Civil Allegiance.*[102]

In Acton's reply to Gladstone, in four letters to *The Times*, he effectively displays his pedantry and his increasing fascination with the crimes of the Catholic Church while almost dismissing Gladstone's strange and overheated argument that the decree of Infallibility had removed the grounds of civil obedience which Catholics had accepted as a condition of or at least as prior to being granted emancipation. In one sense, Acton is saying nothing has changed, except the oath binding Catholics to submission that had accompanied emancipation. But in another sense, his citing of several examples of criminal behaviour by the papacy was designed to provoke the very fears and anxieties he was ostensibly writing to assuage. [103] The reply of Newman is, by contrast, directly addressed to the questions of conscience, and its counterfeit, 'the right of self-will', to the history of Catholicism and 'official rule' in England and to the 'evolution of doctrine' in the Church which would contradict Gladstone's view that Infallibility had created something entirely new.[104] Acton regarded Newman's role in the whole debate as contemptible; Newman was, in his view, justifying Infallibility according to the doctrine always implicit in his writings since the early *Essay on Development*. Yet while he refused to sanction it, he also failed to deny it himself.

This fascination with crime and its concealment, with Ultramontane absolutism as a doctrine and with Vatican centralisation as its institutional form, lessens to some degree in the decade of the nineties but never again entirely disappears from Acton's writings. It is in part on that account that he reconsiders Burke's historical position, associating the conservative, anti-revolutionary Burke with Joseph de Maistre and therefore with all that flowed from that source. Yet it is rather astonishing that Acton never once turns his attention to Burke's most sustained crusade – that on India – and on the legion of crimes that he catalogued there in a detail far in excess of anything he devoted to the crimes of the French revolutionaries. Moreover, for Acton, as for many of his contemporaries, India was the most treasured and most challenging imperial possession. For one so insistent that the Whig tradition was best embodied in Burke and Macaulay, the latter's extraordinary apotheosis of Warren Hastings and his highly wrought account of the opening of the impeachment proceedings against him, led by Burke and Sheridan, must have been a potent example of the rhetorical resources and the picturesque, partisan versions of history so characteristic of both men. Yet, despite the prominence of this famous episode, the notion that colonialism in India was a crime to be expiated does not even reach a level at which it might be entertained by Acton, otherwise so alert to, even entranced by, the prospect of naming the great criminals of the past. It is late in his careeer, after the defeats in America, Rome, and Ireland, that he manifests any qualms about

England's colonial enterprises. In his 'Colonies' essays of 1862 he lists 'the establishment of the freedom of conscience' as one of the debts England owes to her colonies. In illustration, he cites connections between the American War of Independence and Irish Emancipation and the granting of religious liberty to Catholics in Canada as the prelude to relaxations in the Penal Laws in England and Ireland.[105] However, there is a profound distinction between 'our real colonies', the white settler countries, and India. The problem of 'reconciling liberty with the government of a dependency peopled by a variety of distinct and inferior races' is great but

> . . . what we must desire, for the sake of religion, is that the oriental career of our country should extend beyond the destruction of Eastern politics, even to the demolition of Eastern society.[106]

Thus, 'the future progress both of Christianity and of civilisation' would reach the point of producing in India a new society that might then be able 'to accept the teaching of a race more faithful than ours, who will then be able to make the Indians Catholics'.[107] Thus, 'the idea of the political union of mankind', always an ambition of the Church, is an idea 'brought nearer to fulfilment by colonisation than it could ever be by conquest', by means of the colonies of Spain and England.[108]

Like Mill and Tocqueville, Acton entirely gives himself over to the idea of the civilising mission of the higher races to the lower, even if this involves the extermination of the American India or the destruction of Asian societies. The world-historical plan involved will culminate for him, as for Newman, with the imperial triumph of the Catholic religion too. In his essay of 1858 on Montalembert, he claims that his French Liberal Catholic counterpart

> . . . has understood that this semi-Protestant country has the glorious mission of representing in Asia the civilisation of Christianity. The cause of religion will be more truly served by our victories in India than it ever was by the arms of the Crusaders. With the English dominion must stand or fall the hope of converting and civilising Asia; and our troops are fighting the battles of the Pope as much as of the Queen.[109]

It is perhaps kinder not to apply Acton's own criteria for moral condemnation to this very characteristic nineteenth-century liberal version of the Christian Empire, penned so soon after the Indian Mutiny, in the very year that the East India Company was finally abolished and India taken under the direct rule of the Crown, as Burke had advocated a lifetime before. In this instance, a study of Burke's Indian as well as his Irish writings might have produced a more anxious questioning of the form of freedom that colonies produced or, at the very least, a mention of the long catalogue of atrocity that India had endured under the British military-colonial state and was experiencing in heightened form as Acton wrote.

Macaulay, Acton and Mill form a liberal triad that sings in unison on the necessity of violence for the sake of Progress and modernisation in India. Yet a belief in the advantages of modernisation and a belief in Progress or in the historical necessity of colonial rule[110] do not in themselves require an endorsement (silent or vocal) of such violence, as the newspaper articles of Karl Marx and Friedrich Engels on India for the years 1857–58 readily illustrate.[111] For a man who was so well-versed in and admiring of Burke and who was to earn the title of 'the magistrate of history'[112] for his condemnation of murder and violence for political ends – as, for instance, in the French Revolution – Acton's incapacity to see colonialism in India as anything other than a civilising mission is, according to his own standards, morally gross and perfectly characteristic of the liberalism which he exemplifies and from which he often wanted to distinguish himself. Where he is most evidently a participant in 'liberalism' is in his colonial attitudes and in his view of the British Empire. The evangelical fervour of Liberals for the Empire, often articulated by Gladstone, and the readiness to use the idea of empire as a tonic for the revival of unity within the Liberal party,[113] intensified the odour of sanctimoniousness that pervaded the discussion of the enterprise. Yet, as Uday Singh Mehta has shown, Burke is fundamental to a critique of the continuity between liberalism and imperialism.[114] For all his close attention to Burke's importance, for good or ill, to the Whig party, Europe, Ireland, America and the cause of Freedom, Acton managed to ignore the bearing of his thought upon the ideologies of colonial and imperial domination. Even where there are claims in Burke's speeches or writings on India of Europe's superiority in the achievement of political liberty, Acton seemed unaware of them, even though they hinted towards what Frederick G. Whelan has called 'the kind of liberal justification for imperialism that was to be greatly elaborated in the following century'.[115]

It seems entirely appropriate that Acton's successor as Regius Professor at Cambridge should have been J.B. Bury, whose most famous work is *The Idea of Progress* (1924),[116] for that was an idea to the more intellectually insouciant forms of which Acton wanted to give an important inflection. His conception of the disclosure of Freedom within History was more complicated than complex and could quickly degenerate into a theory of Progress no more sophisticated or persuasive than that of Buckle, the populariser of that doctrine whom Acton so condescendingly reviewed in 1858.[117] For all his anxiety to establish a moral rule external to the Machiavellian world of the actual, that rule often turned out to be nothing more than the anticipation in a past event of its future reverberations. The future is always, in such a light, a fulfilment of what has gone before. Although Acton believed that the nineteenth-century's rediscovery of the Middle Ages (itself part of the reaction against the French Revolution) was at least comparable to the Renaissance rediscovery of the ancient world, he was remarkably free of the nostalgia for that feudal past which Burke and Scott had helped create.[118] It seems strange that, as a

Catholic, he remained disengaged from the High Church and Roman Catholic neo-medieval critique of modernity that includes figures such as Robert Southey, William Morris, A.W. Pugin, Hilaire Belloc, G.K. Chesterton, Ford Madox Ford and T.S. Eliot.The medieval revival, and the enrichments of history that he attributed to the German historians and to the historical novelists (especially Scott), clarified the role of the Church in the emergent history of freedom and even its connections with the dissenting sects of the Reformation and of America who had advanced that history so dramatically in the modern era. Scott's Stuart sympathies and Hanoverian endorsements provided an amiable coherence that the polemics of history-writing in English could or should have learned to emulate.

Yet Acton so readily saw the past as a preparation for the ineluctable future that he only differentiated himself from British Whigs by making his own Whiggism appear cosmopolitan in its range and universalist in its moral basis. As in his early career, although more urgently in his later years, he saw the divorce between a belief in moral universals and a belief in progressive development as the fatal characteristic of the modern era. He wrote that 'the doctrine of the justice of History' which he called 'the nursling of the nineteenth century' is no more than a Machiavellian removal of 'the ethical basis of judgments', that we dare not say 'that the code shifts with the longitude'. Yet his notion of progress often leads him to 'judgment by results'.[119] What he said of the role of the European civilisations in the colonies also reappeared at different times in his accounts of European history, whereby the great empires of Rome or even of the Tsars had to be allowed the impetus of inevitability at the expense of those not so given to co-operation with destiny. 'It is better', he once claimed, 'to suffer any wrong than impede with microscopic interests the majestic march of civilisation.' So Russia could no more give up Warsaw than Great Britain Dublin.[120]

European nationalisms seemed to provoke in him the coarser and more aggressive versions of the Idea of Progress which he could never entirely surrender, complicate it as he might. It is in the light of the threatened conflict with Germany that Acton finally seems to have lost his belief in that Progress to which he had been so long committed. He began to look at British policy in Europe and the colonies with a degree of candour that had not been evident for many years. In a late note, he says:

> In judging our national merits we must allow much for our national hypocrisy. Wherever we went, we were the best colonists in the world, but we exterminated the natives wherever we went. We despised conquests, but we annexed with the greed of Russia.[121]

Neither Empire, Roman nor British, could finally reveal to Acton a credible account of the History of Freedom. We can see from the immense range of his journalism, lectures, letters and preparatory writings what the great work would have looked like, but freedom's realisation in the late nineteenth century, which at one point seemed likely, disappeared as a possibility one after the other, at Richmond, Rome, and Westminster. His career became more splendidly laden with awards and recognition; audiences at Cambridge listened to the famous Catholic Regius Professor to whom it had denied a place decades before because he was a Catholic; his lectures on the French Revolution and on Modern History, and his brief generalship of the Cambridge Modern History Series filled the virtual space of his History of Freedom. It has become a minor legend, a dazzling conversation piece remembered only for its brilliance and not at all for its content. Perhaps Acton's liberalism gave intellectual distinction to Catholicism and to Gladstonian Liberalism, but he was unable ultimately to universalise the position he occupied in and for each of them. It is to him, not to Burke, that Goldsmith's famous lines more tellingly apply.

9. NEWMAN
CONVERTING THE EMPIRE

One of Newman's ambitions was to find in the history of civil society the spiritual dimension that would integrate it into Church history. He believed for a time that he had found a way to do this by helping to found the new Catholic University in Dublin. Ireland was to be assigned – not so much by as through him – the role of converting the British Empire to Catholicism and thereby rescuing Christianity from internecine factionalism and the world from infidelity. It was a bitterness to him that Edward Gibbon was the greatest English historian of the emergence of Christianity from the ruins of the Roman Empire; the anti-Christian animus of the last two chapters of the first volume of Gibbon's *Decline and Fall of the Roman Empire* (1776) was especially disturbing to Anglicans after the French Revolution, when the call to defend the religion of the English state was loud and peremptory. Burke had claimed that the French monarchy had been toppled by an anti-Christian conspiracy and that an unprecedentedly secular ideology threatened to dominate the old civilisation of Europe. Even before Burke published his 'Reflections' in 1790, Gibbon had come to very similar conclusions. In his view, revolution was to be resisted at all costs, even if that meant going along with Burke's spectacular defence of Church establishment in England.[1] This Church–State relation was always a preoccupation for Newman, and eventually became for him an agony. But Burke was exemplary; in him Newman found a history of civil society in Britain and in Europe and a history of Christian belief that intersected in the figure of Christ and in the great afterglow of the Incarnation which he called the Sublime. There was no such irradiation in Gibbon or in the Enlightenment or in the liberalism which Newman confidently regarded as their Scots-English inheritor.

There is a small irony in the fact that Gibbon for a time converted to Catholicism in his youth, in part, he alleged, because of the stupor that then afflicted Oxford, that Anglican seminary which had failed effectively to teach the state religion. The conversion was of transient importance compared to that of Newman or, say, Henry Edward Manning, two Oxford Anglicans, later cardinals, who transformed Roman Catholicism in the English-speaking world. And Oxford was many things to Newman; an Anglican fortress that had fallen to liberalism, the failed idea of a university, a beloved place. 'At Oxford,' said Lytton Strachey in *Eminent Victorians* (1918), 'he was doomed. He could not withstand the last enchantment of the Middle Ages. It was in vain that he plunged into the pages of Gibbon or communed for long hours with

Beethoven over his beloved violin.'[2] Equally, one could say that in Dublin too he was doomed, for the university project failed; yet in Dublin too he succeeded in theorising what a university might be and in finding for it within the British Empire a central role for those Irish Catholics whose exclusion from civil society Burke had always found to be a threat, a disgrace and a contradiction. By the time Newman came into his strength, Dissenters and Catholics had forced their admission into civil society and the question of Church establishment was forever altered both as a political and as a theological issue. Burke could hardly have approved, because this was a concession to the democratic spirit; but he could hardly have disapproved either, because it was a concession also to natural justice. Newman inherited this ambiguity.

An English-speaking Catholic University

The Classical and Mathematical Schools of the new Catholic University were opened on the Feast of St. Malachi, Friday, 3 November 1854 at University House, Stephen's Green, Dublin. It was a modest affair. All the Catholic archbishops were in Rome for the ceremonies surrounding the declaration of the Dogma of the Immaculate Conception. While in Rome, Archbishop Cullen, who had already unconscionably delayed Newman's formal appointment as Rector, seemed to be more concerned to bring to the attention of the Congregation of Propaganda the threat of Gallicanism in the Catholic seminary at Maynooth than to hasten the inauguration of the new Catholic University in Dublin. This tension between his Ultramontane vision and any form of independent national feeling, especially any tainted by secularism or anti-clericalism, like the Young Ireland movement, was to remain a contentious element in the history of Irish Catholic university education for the rest of the century.[3] Cullen stayed in Rome until 1855; in the meantime, Newman began the practical work of establishing the School of Philosophy and Letters, the School of Science and the Medical School.

Among the twenty students enrolled was the grandson and namesake of Daniel O'Connell, 'in consideration of whose name the authorities presented his descendant with an Exhibition, enabling him to reside at the University House, for four years free of expense'. Given his opinion of O'Connell,[4] this could hardly have pleased Newman. Nevertheless, on the following Sunday, he gave a soirée and, according to the report of the occasion, told the students that 'the Holy See had thought it was time . . . the Catholics of this country, and all speaking the English language, should have the means afforded them of that higher education which hitherto the Protestants had monopolized'. In a final flourish, he rather inappropriately quoted the famous speech before Agincourt from *Henry V*, assuring all those then present who lived to old age that they would regard themselves as one of 'We few, we happy few, we band of brothers', who had been there on the auspicious day.[5]

Under one of the titles from the Loreto Litany of the Virgin, 'Sedes Sapientiae, Ora Pro Nobis', ('Seat of Wisdom, Pray for Us'), Newman wrote essays for the new Catholic University's magazine, *The Catholic University Gazette*, published weekly between 1 June 1854 and 8 March 1855, and monthly thereafter until the end of 1856.[6] Most of these were published in book form in 1856, under the title *Office and Work of Universities*. In 1858, several were republished with other material, as *University Subjects: Discussed in Occasional Lectures and Essays,* dedicated to the Irish MP and convert to Catholicism, William Monsell. They were then renamed by Newman as *Rise and Progress of Universities* in 1872 and then incorporated into *Historical Sketches*, published in three volumes in 1872 and much reprinted thereafter.[7] The *Catholic University Gazette* essays are clearly an integral part of Newman's thinking about the founding of the new Catholic University in Dublin. He included two of them, 'English Catholic Literature' and 'A Form of Infidelity of the Day', in Part II of *The Idea of a University.*

Newman emphasises three elements in the great enterprise that was launched on that November afternoon of 1854. These were that the new university was to be Catholic, English-speaking and a specifically Irish experiment that nevertheless also had an English dimension.[8] Six days earlier, he had published the second part of an essay on the general theme of the historical wisdom of the papacy, in which he proclaimed this vision:

> I see an age of transition, the breaking up of the old and the coming in of the new; an old system shattered some sixty years ago, and a new state of things scarcely in its rudiments yet, to be settled perhaps some centuries after our time. And it is a special circumstance in these changes, that they extend beyond the past historical platform of human affairs; not only is Europe broken up, but other continents are thrown open, and the new organization of society aims at embracing the world. It is a day of colonists and emigrants; – and, what is another most pertinent consideration, the language they carry with them is English, which consequently, as time goes on, is certain, humanly speaking, to extend itself to every part of the world. It is already occupying the whole of North America, whence it threatens to descend upon the South; already is it the language of Australia, a country large enough in the course of centuries to rival Europe in its population; already it has become the speech of a hundred marts of commerce, scattered over the East, and, even where not the mother tongue, it is at least the medium of intercourse between nations. And, lastly, though the people who own that language is Protestant, a race preeminently Catholic has adopted, and has a share in its literature; and this Catholic race is, at this very time, of all tribes of the earth, the most fertile in emigrants both to the West and the South. These are the manifest facts of the day, which would be before our eyes, whether the Pope had anything to say to them or no. The English language and the Irish race are overrunning the world.
>
> When then I consider what an eye the Sovereign Pontiffs have for the future. . . . and what a flood of success . . . has lifted up the Ark of God from the beginning of this century; and then, that the Holy Father has definitely put His

> finger upon Ireland, and selected her soil as the seat of a great Catholic University, to spread religion, science, and learning, wherever the English language is spoken . . . I know and cannot doubt that a great work is begun.[9]

In the second number of the *Gazette*, under the title 'The Prima Facie Idea of a University', Newman reminds his audience that a university was a 'School of Universal learning', that this 'implies the assemblage of strangers from all parts in one spot'.[10] In the third number, he provides a compressed history of the historic university sites of Athens, Paris, Louvain and Oxford, the last of which, even in its present 'sorrowful degradation' still illustrates 'what should be the material dwelling place and appearance, the local circumstances, and the secular concomitants of a great University.' In his threnody for Oxford, Newman sympathises with those who wonder if Oxford will ever again be Catholic. 'But for me', he says, 'from the day I left its walls, I never, for good or bad, have had anticipation of its future; and never for a moment have I a wish to see again a place, which I had never ceased to love, and where I have lived for nearly thirty years.' Now in modern times, he looks elsewhere, for a more central site for a university than Oxford, in 'a land both young and old', to 'a people which has had a long night, and will have an inevitable day.'

> I am turning my eyes towards a hundred years to come, and I dimly see the island I am gazing on, become the road of passage and union between two hemispheres, and the centre of the world . . . and I see England taught by advancing years to exercise in its behalf that good sense which is her characteristic towards every one else. The capital of that prosperous and hopeful land is situate in a beautiful bay and near a romantic region; and in it I see a flourishing University, which for a while, when its first founders and servants were dead and gone, had successes far exceeding their anxieties. Thither, as to a sacred soil, the home of their fathers, and the fountain-head of their Christianity, students are flocking from East, West, and South, from America and Australia and India, from Egypt and Asia Minor, with the ease and rapidity of a locomotion not yet discovered, and last, though not least, from England, – all speaking one tongue, all owning one faith, all eager for one large true wisdom, and thence, when their stay is over, going back again to carry peace to men of good will over all the earth.[11]

In the ninth number of the *Gazette*, Newman begins to indicate how the new university will be specifically Irish and universal and how it will differ from the Oxford he had known, dominated by the struggle between teachers who believed in 'personal attachment' and 'the dry old red-tapists'. It had been in the 1830s, what he was determined Dublin would never be, 'an ice-bound, petrified, cast-iron University, and nothing else'.[12]

As he charts in these essays the historical movement from the Oxford that had been to the Dublin that would be, Newman also provides an account of the histories of England and Ireland, stressing their common and glorious early Christian heritage, and then, without at all supplying any historical account of their divergent fortunes, intimating that Ireland's time has now arrived and that it, via Catholicism, would become the centre of a new empire that would avail of the territories and modify, perhaps even convert, the spirit of the Protestant British Empire. The contrast between the national characters of the two countries – Greeks versus Romans, the central cliché of Arnold's later analysis of the Irish and the English – is one of the conventional stratagems in his argument, which nevertheless has the aim of conciliating in the future histories which had once been part of a common Christian civilisation in the past, with Ireland at its most refulgent in the sixth and seventh centuries, and England in the seventh and eighth:

> Distinct, nay antagonistic, in character and talent, the one nation and the other, Irish and English, the one more resembling the Greek, the other the Roman . . . they obliterated whatever there was of human infirmity in their mutual intercourse by the merit of their common achievements.[13]

The crucial difference is that

> . . . after all, the Irish, whose brilliancy of genius has sometimes been considered, like the Greek, to augur fickleness and change, have managed to persevere to this day in the science of the saints, long after their ancient rivals have lost the gift of faith.[14]

Newman's belief in, or perhaps his eager wish that the Irish, with their loyalty to the ancient faith, would provide for the deficiencies of British imperial civilisation was a counter to his conviction that England was of itself beyond redemption.[15]

An old battle as well as a new vision dominate the university discourses and their accompanying materials. Much of the animus directed against science and utilitarian education in the Third and Fourth Discourses of *The Idea of a University* derives from Newman's hostility to 'the new London University of the 1820s and from the controversy over the admission of Dissenters in 1834–35'.[16] Nor does that controversy entirely fade from the pages of the *Gazette*. Its May 1855 issue carries an essay, probably by the editor Robert Ornsby, which asks,

> The Establishment has tried and failed to withstand English liberalism in London: will the Catholic Church, by means of her own University, be more successful in Dublin?[17]

The cultivation of the intellect, the avoidance of the kind of vocational and specialist training offered by London, the suspicion of the kind of education to which political economy would be central – a blend of London and Scottish principles, espoused by the writers for the *Edinburgh Review*[18] – together form only one aspect of the educational ideal Newman proposed in and for Dublin. It is important that his hostility to an exclusively vocational education, which had political economy as one of its central disciplines, was formed in relation to what had been happening in England and specifically in the new University of London. The major educational experiment in Ireland that preceded his own was the founding and extension of the National Schools system, an attempt to replace the informal 'hedge-schools' with an official and uniform state system that would be non-sectarian, English-speaking and modernising. Attacked chiefly by Protestants and more sporadically by Catholics, it was an experiment that nevertheless had a very different resonance in the appalling conditions of pre-Famine Ireland. Newman's recognition of the need for more good secondary schools to supply his university was never matched by any comparable recognition of the need for a primary educational system worthy of the name. This could not be said of his former friend and teacher at Oxford, Richard Whately, who became Protestant Archbishop of Dublin (1831–63) and founded the Whately Chair of Political Economy at Trinity College, was a controversial Commissioner for Education and an outspoken opponent of the Tractarian Movement. In their opposing ways, both men developed an educational programme for a country neither of them understood.[19]

Universities and Colleges

The *Gazette* essays make it clear that Newman had begun to alter the emphasis in his thinking about university education from a direct assault on liberalism and utilitarianism, as represented by the new University of London and the Oxford that seemed to him to have been transformed between 1845 and 1850 'from a religious and theological to a liberal, secularist university',[20] to the envisioning of a new kind of university at Dublin that would be unprecedented in its nature and formation. He was not, as is often said, transposing an Oxford ideal to Dublin. Instead he was developing, through a critique of Oxford's failings, an idea of a university that would still be able to survive in the modern world of the British state and Empire, and of the Catholic Church, in its various Liberal (French and German) and Ultramontane versions. For instance, in his essays on colleges and their relation to a university, both of which focus on Oxford, both initially published in the *Gazette* in 1854, Newman persistently writes of the political and national function and status of Oxford: 'Never has learned institution been more directly political and national than the University of Oxford.'[21] Yet to the extent that it was successful in representing in its colleges the various interests of the nation, it was unsuccessful in incarnating the universal realm that the university represents. This change had begun in Oxford about the beginning of the fourteenth century, when 'the ancient University of Dublin, or Ireland' was set up; both processes were in response to

> . . . the mutual divergence and distinctive formation of languages and of national character, national histories, national pride, national antipathies, would all carry

> forward the course of events in the same direction; and the Collegiate system . . . cooperated in making a University a local institution, and in embodying it among the establishments of the nation.[22]

The history of the abortive attempts of the fourteenth and sixteenth centuries to found the ancient university of Dublin becomes, in Newman's hands, a shadowy anticipation of his own venture, with the history of Oxford's mutation from a university into an assemblage of colleges, from a universal to a national institution, as a commentary and a warning. Times have now changed. 'Ireland is no longer the conquered possession of a foreign king; it is, as in the primitive times, the centre of a great Catholic movement and of a world-wide missionary enterprise.'[23] Newman has it both ways. He gives the idea of a great Catholic University in Dublin the appearance of precedent and authority, while also arguing that this is an unprecedented experiment. It is part of the papal effort to revise the idea of university education in the world by its support for foundations in Louvain and Quebec; yet it is also unique among these, since this is a university that is starting out of nothing, no previous foundation, no earlier example. Precedented and unprecedented, it is an innovation in Irish and world history and a continuation of the Irish scholarly and religious tradition in the Western world. Above all, unlike Oxford, Dublin will be a university and, unlike Berlin or the Scottish universities, it will also be a college; it will be an intellectual centre and a society, a rare blend, since 'such a union, such salutary balance, is of difficult and rare attainment. At least the present day rather gives us instances of two antagonistic evils, of naked Universities and naked Colleges, than of their alliance and its benefits.'[24]

Oxford then is specifically not the model for Newman's idea of a university;[25] nor is anywhere else. Because Ireland was unique in being predominantly English-speaking and Catholic, and because it already had, in seminaries like Maynooth and All Hallows College,[26] examples of successful missionary endeavour, Newman regarded the new university as having a distinctly grander ambition than could be entertained even for a comparable institution like Louvain, a place with long associations with the Irish Catholic emigration of earlier centuries. The Synodal Meeting of the Archbishops and Bishops of Ireland of 18–20 May 1854 took Louvain as the model for the Catholic University in Dublin, when it finally confirmed Newman as Rector – although his appointment was by the Pope.[27] Yet the missionary, English-speaking aspect of the Irish venture remained central in Newman's writings over the next year. This is not to say that the new university was to him merely a seminary with a difference. He believed that there had been a decisive shift in papal policy; Maynooth, All Hallows and the new Seminario Pio in Rome[28] were all invigorated or inaugurated as missionary centres by the Pope in an effort to reChristianise Europe and the world. Ireland was regarded as an important Catholic territory in and through which the Church's educational project could be extended. In Ireland itself, the university was of course regarded as an institution that would preserve the Irish middle classes from the unbelief that had pervaded their European counterparts. A widely advertised book, from a Dr O'Brien of All Hallows College, *Lectures on the Church and the Country* (1854), declared that the new university had made the Catholic gentry 'safe' but that other educational or proto-educational organisations, like O'Brien's 'Young Men's Societies' were needed to look after the interests of the indefatigably loyal Catholic poor. The Catholic University Committee declared in 1851 that it was the action of secular universities that communicated to 'the higher classes on the Continent . . . the irreligion and infidelity that, by a necessary consequence, penetrated to the subordinate grades of society, until the masses of the population became tainted by the moral corruption'.[29] After the opening Mass and Benediction of June 1854, the reporter for the *Gazette* concluded:

> The poor seemed equally interested in the ceremony as the more educated class; and their prayers, it may be confidently expected, will have as great a share in the success of the undertaking, which only indirectly concerns them, as the donations and active exertions of those on whom it will visibly depend.[30]

There was no doubt that the new university was for the male middle classes of Catholic Ireland and that it had a dual role, within and beyond the country, to keep and extend the Church's teaching, to combat, in the University Committee's language, the substitution of 'a cold and prayerless rationalism for the reverent spirit of inquiry'[31] by which Irish Catholic youth had always been actuated.

The University in the Empire: Liberal Catholicism

There is nothing in Newman's thinking about class or gender, the benefits of tutorial teaching or even, in grander terms, the cultivation of the intellect that is wholly new or distinctive, although the combination of such attitudes seemed more so in the England of Lord Brougham and John Stuart Mill than it would have in Wilhelm von Humboldt's Germany. Still, his new university would not be like Oxford nor the Scottish universities, not like London nor like Berlin. It would be distinct from, although connected to, the Irish and European seminaries for the training of a national and of an international priesthood. It would be like and also unlike Louvain, in part because because the Dublin enterprise was a genuine innovation, taking place in a Catholic English-speaking country with a peasantry loyal to the faith and a middle class scarcely emergent from the local Protestant-British oppressions and still resistant although increasingly vulnerable to the secular appeal of the British and continental varieties of progressive 'rationalism' and 'infidelity'. But what is distinctive in Newman's vision of the new university is the proposed fusion within it of an intellectual and missionary role in the English-speaking imperial territories and in the United States. Even so, it still has no claim to uniqueness, for it is in part anticipated and in part emulated in this respect in the thinking of the French Liberal Catholic group, dominated by Montalembert, that emerged in Paris in the late 1820s, especially as that was influenced by its interpretation of Ireland and of the role it might play, after Catholic Emancipation, in the Catholic Church at large and in the British Empire. The importance of the emergent Irish Catholic community for its English counterpart had already been noticed by Fr John Milner, who had preceded Newman in his attempts to correct the anti-Catholic propaganda that had been reignited in the early years of the century in the arguments about Irish antiquities. However, it was Lord Acton rather than Newman who acknowledged Milner's importance.[32]

Although the relationship between Church and State was central both to the Tractarian Movement at Oxford and to French liberal Catholicism, as it initially developed in the pages of Lammenais's periodical *L'Avenir* of 1830–32, there were serious and ultimately irreconcilable differences between their various interpretations of how this might or should be understood. Newman's 1837 review of Lammenais's story of his collision with and condemnation by Rome, *Affaires de Rome* (1837) is a sardonic commentary on the position of the Anglican and Gallican Churches in relation to the British and French states. The Anglican Church might be better off than the Greek Church under the Turks on the grounds that 'our rulers were appointed, not by pagans, but only by schismatics, latitudinarians, profligates, socinians and infidels', yet could now console itself that the Gallican Church was 'in a captivity . . . far greater than ours'.[33] The papacy was another matter. Newman's sympathy for Lammenais's view that the 'temporal splendour of the Popedom has been the ruin of its spiritual empire' does not extend to Lammenais's appeal to 'Christian liberty', or to 'certain indefeasible rights of man' or to his defence of rebellion; 'what we . . . in our English theology', says Newman, 'should call the lawless and proud lusts of corrupt nature, he almost sanctifies as the instinctive aspirations of the heart after its unknown good'. Lammenais seems not merely naive; he is dangerously radical; perhaps to be one is a condition of being the other. He believes that

> the fact that things change and revolutions take place to be a command to take part in change and revolution. It is not wonderful that, with these principles, he cordially approves of what the Roman Church and Mr. O'Connell are doing in Ireland, sympathizes in their struggle, and holds them up for the edification of the Pope and Papal world.[34]

However, Lammenais's admiration for O'Connell was far exceeded by that of his friend and ally, Montalembert, who provided the first liberal Catholic analysis of the Irish situation in his three-part essay, 'Du catholicisme en irlande', published in *L'Avenir* in January 1831. This was the most extended continental commentary on the position of the Catholic Church in Ireland since the founding of O'Connell's Catholic Association. It was probably, as Thomas Wyse said, from about 1825–28 and in particular when the National Census began to reveal more clearly the disparity between Catholic and Protestant numbers and privilege, that French and American interest in Ireland awoke and developed into an influential element in the emancipation campaign.[35] The immense privileges attached to the minority Protestant Church in Ireland, and its established status, emphasised just how corrupting and tyrannical the state system could be when it dominated not only a Church but another nation, using the confessional allegiance as an instrument of political dominion. What attracted Lammenais and Montalembert to Ireland and to the O'Connellite campaign for emancipation was the exemplary relationship, as they saw it, between the Catholic Church and the forces of democracy. Here was a cause deserving of *L'Avenir's* motto, 'Dieu et la liberté'. Or, as Montalembert rephrased it, 'Liberté et pauvreté!', the cry of the priests of a truly living spirituality who, with their people, assumed throughout three hundred years of persecution and heretical dominance an enduring fidelity and chose to forgo material welfare for the sake of the true faith. The Irish hierarchy, with the exceptions of the famous J.K.L. Doyle of Kildare and Bishop Murray of Dublin (one of Newman's supporters in later days), are not so benignly viewed. They had threatened with excommunication any Catholics who joined in the rebellion of 1798, for fear of 'l'impiété française' and they now, claims Montalembert, aid the civil power (the police and army) in persuading their parishioners to co-operate peacefully with a system that, even under emancipation, humiliates them and disallows the bishops themselves to assume the proper titles of their dioceses.[36]

Ireland was an example to France and to the Church. The Church was not the hierarchy, nor the priests, but the whole people; and its career in the world was indissolubly bound up with the attainment of freedom and the disavowal of temporal and material possessions and of political power. Although Montalembert's early assault on the British-Protestant system, and most especially its record of spoliation and injustice in Ireland, was fierce, and although his admiration for O'Connell remained steadfast, he began, especially in the light of the political changes in France in 1848–51, to change his view of the historical role Ireland could play in relation to the Church in the modern world. Once he realised that the new Napoleonic despotism was stonily determined to control the Church in France, he forsook any reliance on particular political leaders, be they Charles X or Napoleon III, and sought instead to reorganise French Liberal Catholicism around the idea that despotism, not revolutionary systems, had always been the enslaver of the Church. The Church, therefore, was to look to the principles of 1789 for its law-given freedom, to seek no special role for itself within the political system and to accept all those other freedoms – of conscience, of the Press, of equality before the law, of association and of religious liberty – that were part of the heritage of the revolution that created the modern world. Increasingly, though, the central country in the establishment and preservation of specific liberties and of the idea of Liberty itself became, for Montalembert, England rather than France. The publication of *Des Intérêts catholiques au dix-neuvième siècle* (1851), translated into English in 1852, was a restatement of liberal Catholicism of which *L'Avenir* had been the first articulation. Its revision of the English–Irish issue is important to the movement's attempt to rediscover a historical basis for the conjoint career of Catholicism and Liberty in the latter part of the nineteenth century. In effect, Montalembert argued that, despite its barbarous anti-Catholic legislation, England, saved by Burke and Pitt from the revolutionary infection and participating in the general restoration of religious feeling in Europe of the previous decades, had developed 'wonderful institutions' that were of fundamental service to the cause of liberty. In a long panegyric on O'Connell, he declared that it was he

> . . . who, with Ireland at his back, knocked at the door of the English parliament in the name of his people, and the Catholics of the three kingdoms were admitted with him, and for ever. The conqueror of Napoleon delivered up his arms to the moral chief of a people unarmed, but rendered invincible by the force of right . . .[37]

Thus, the circle to be squared was the reconciliation of English Protestant liberty, now increasingly distinguished from French revolutionary 'liberté', with Catholic universalism. The Irish, the belated beneficiaries of that liberty, are proposed as the spiritual conquerors of the British Empire; and the movement in England towards Rome is what Montalembert imagines might spare or minimise the English humiliation:

> The Irish race, prolific as it is faithful, . . . carry with them the true faith henceforth enfranchised; and that immense British empire, extending over the five parts of the globe, and upon which, it may truly be said, that the sun never sets, becomes like the Roman empire of old, a vast nursery of Catholic episcopal sees and missions. And in order that England may not be humiliated by this victory, obtained by a foreign and subjugated race, God permits that there should be developed in the very bosom of the Anglican clergy an unforeseen and prodigious movement towards the tradition, the authority, the unity of Rome.[38]

This is remarkably similar to what Newman wrote in the *Gazette* in 1854. The differences are in part explained by the fact that Lammenais and Montalembert, like Jean-Baptiste-Henri Lacordaire, had 'inherited, and made the best of, the French Revolution' while Newman had inherited Toryism, 'the creed of Oxford', as he pointed out in his *Apologia*.[39] Prominent among the differences is Montalembert's (or Lammenais's) belief in Progress, which

Newman at least for a time also believed to be a characteristic of Catholicism;[40] it is very far removed from his own revised concept of development which posits for the Catholic tradition the persistence of a core spiritual and intellectual unity and coherence through a variety of adaptations and changes that expand but do not and cannot traduce it.[41]

However, Newman does share with Montalembert in particular the belief that there may be a destiny assigned to different nations and that the national character of a people has an important bearing upon the institutional modes by which it expresses itself historically. Montalembert's identification of Irish and Christian spirituality with poverty is conversely extended by Newman in his essay of 1839 on 'The Anglo-American Church'. The Anglican Church in America, he wrote then, was open to 'the influence of a refined and covert Socinianism', like that which threatened Anglicanism fifty years before. There is no specific threat of heresy,

> . . . but it is difficult to be in the neighbourhood of icebergs without being chilled, and the United States is, morally speaking, just in the latitude of ice and snow . . . We allude, not to their [the Americans'] national character, nor to their form of government, but to their *employments,* which in truth we share with them. A trading country is the *habitat* of Socinianism.[42]

Poverty creates a need for 'a deep religion'; traders, the commercial classes in general, 'despise enthusiasm, they abhor fanaticism, they persecute bigotry. They want only so much religion as will satisfy their natural perception of the propriety of being religious.' The consequence could be 'a sleek gentlemanlike religion'.[43] This is the antithesis of the Irish experience, as Newman later came to write of it while in Dublin and as Montalembert had been writing of it since 1830. However, the notion that the Irish Catholics had a profound spirituality, tested by persecution and poverty, was increasingly difficult to reconcile with the notion that England was also the home of liberty and that Irish Catholics should learn to appreciate that their former tormentor had become, by some alchemical or historical process that Montalembert never explained, an ally and support in their struggle for freedom. Montalembert's anglophilia grew to such serious proportions in the 1850s, especially with his *De l'Angleterre* (1854), that it seemed to Irish commentators to threaten the very basis of what many (including Montalembert) had believed to be the symbiotic relationship between Catholicism and Irish nationalism. Catholic universalism was one thing; but a universalism based on the territory of the British Empire and on the principles of English versions of freedom and civilisation was quite another.

George Henry Moore, the Irish politician and father of the novelist, George Moore, answered Montalembert with what he evidently took to be a conclusive repudiation of the English and their national-imperial system:

> It is only on the subject of their gross insular habits, their stupid insular prejudices, their narrow insular opinions, their exceptional insular institutions,

> and their absurd insular religion, that they are arrogant, tyrannical and cruel. They are firmly persuaded that a body of institutions, civil and religious, which are but the type and embodiment of their own habits, passions, prejudices, and superstitions, are fitted to meet all the exigencies of all the human race, and ought to be forced upon the convictions of every people in the world.[44]

From an Irish nationalist point of view, this was a necessary corrective. What Montalembert was plainly and Newman more covertly doing was to take the religious impetus out of the national movement for cultural and political independence and to attach it instead to a cosmopolitan (but not Ultramontane) Catholicism that had somehow been reconciled with British imperialism. The tension between national Churches and Ultramontanism had an intricate history in nineteenth-century Ireland but it was only with the declaration of papal infallibility in 1870 that the separation between the Roman spiritual empire and the British secular empire was fully and securely integrated into the ideology of Irish nationalism. It was the Roman Empire that gave institutional form to nationalism's spiritual destiny in the world and allowed it to claim an ancestral authority that contrasted with the medley of relativisms that allegedly characterised the increasingly confused and confusing world of secular rationality which the Church had condemned.

Protestant Predjudice and Conversion

The idea of ancient authority was at the heart of Newman's intellectual inquiry into the history and nature of Anglicanism and of its increasingly ambivalent relationship with liberalism. All through his writings, at every period, he dwells on the implications of the Protestant idea of private judgement and the Catholic idea of authority. The standard polemical contrast he makes is the analogous one of chaos as against clarity; chaos is often figured as the 'interminable division'[45] of the Protestant sects, which lead inevitably to scepticism, relativism and the eventual disappearance of the religious principle.[46] There is no fundamental difference in this regard between what he wrote as an Anglican in 1836 in the essay review, 'Apostolical Tradition'[47] or in *An Essay on the Development of Christian Doctrine* in 1845 and what he wrote in 1867 in his *Apologia* or in *A Grammar of Assent* in 1870, although the gradations of his concept of what constitutes certitude and his distinction between it and infallibility on the one hand and conviction, prejudice, inference on the other are more and more subtly shaded.[48]

Newman's subtlety is often taken to be a symptom of deceitfulness, the more nefarious for being so delicately achieved and the more vacuous for being so much a mere matter of stylistic felicity and timing.[49] The stark absence of these qualities in his most notable opponents, like the apostate Dominican Achilli and Charles Kingsley, merely enhanced the contemporary suspicion of Newman's sinuous distinctions. Yet he could hardly have been clearer in what he was saying to his different audiences in England and Ireland. The English were often deaf to what he was saying of their bigotry and superstition, for they attributed such things to papists and foreigners; and the Irish, or some of them, heard only the recommendation that the new university should aim to produce a version of the secular Oxford gentleman. G.H. Moore almost saw the point at issue when he attacked Montalembert's appeal to the Irish to convert the world to Catholicism and Liberty via British imperial civilisation, to which of course they should convert, reconcile or otherwise yield themselves. Moore's emphasis on the insular nature and the universal claims of British civilisation had been in fact long anticipated by the Oxford Movement as it confronted Catholicism on the one hand and liberalism on the other. It challenged, as Christopher Dawson wrote, 'the whole national tradition' that for two centuries 'had been bound with a fanatical hatred of foreign popery, of everything Popish because it was foreign and of everything foreign because it was Popish'.[50]

Newman's argument began here. He recognised the anti-Catholic spirit of the British political system, although he was even more appalled, if somewhat prematurely, by its threatened replacement of that by an anti-Christian one. The old papal dream of the conversion of England seemed to him to be connected to the conversion of the British Empire, or indeed of the English-speaking world, by the one Catholic nation in the United Kingdom. He certainly had, by 1854, a messianic vision of what the Catholic University and the Irish could eventually accomplish; they would convert the English-speaking world by exhibiting an alliance between secular and religious knowledge that would make the new university differ from any other modern example.[51] But the process of conversion had to begin at home, with the English in particular; and the cultural conversion necessary for the success of the Catholic venture in Ireland was the conversion of the English from their almost immeasurable prejudice against Catholicism (which included their prejudice against the Catholic Irish), which he saw as central to their national identity, itself predicated upon the corrupting dependence of the Protestant religion in England upon the state and, specifically, upon the sovereign. This prejudice flourished on a regular diet of popular superstition and legend, much of it of a grotesque and specifically Gothic nature.[52] It seems appropriate that the fifth of the nine lectures on *The Present Position of Catholics in England*, delivered in July 1851, should have been an attack on Achilli, who was providing lurid accounts of the Roman Inquisition to large audiences. This led to Achilli's libel case against Newman; and the dedication to the Dublin *Discourses* is to all of those who supported Newman throughout that 'great anxiety', which were 'Composed Under Its Pressure/ Finished on the Eve of its Termination'.[53] Achilli had, of course, been encouraged to take the case against Newman because of the tidal wave of anti-Catholic feeling which swept England in the wake of the papacy's restoration of the Catholic hierarchy, the 'Papal Aggression', in 1850.

English prejudice is integral to Newman's thinking about the relationship between religion and the state. Ultimately, prejudice itself and the conditions for its disappearance became of critical importance in his account of the process of conversion. It is obviously necessary for a convert to be able to say that certitude and belief can survive change and that conversion from one religion to another is by no means an event that would support any argument for the relativity of all beliefs. It is the easier to argue this by showing that conversion involves, at the least, the shedding of prejudices which are irrational in themselves and are also the product of a deliberate political and cultural policy.[54] In such an analysis, Newman had to make much of the beleaguered position of the English Catholics and it was natural that he should look to them to support his Irish venture. It was a shock to him that they did not and he made this an important contributory reason for its failure.[55] Neither the English Catholics nor the Irish Catholics realised that the university Newman was founding was for them both and that if it failed to be for both, then it would not succeed in being for either. Perhaps it had not occurred to him that anti-Irish sentiment in England was not an exclusively Protestant business.

However, Roman Catholics in England were comparable in Newman's eyes to the early Christians in Rome, a despised minority at the heart of a great pagan Empire. In his novel *Callista* (1855) the parallel is obvious. The legal, educational and cultural system was opposed to Christianity and 'the bigoted and ignorant majority, not only of the common people, but of the better classes, was steeped in a bitter prejudice, and an intense, though latent, hatred' of it.[56] The novel, finished during the early years in Ireland, is concerned with the martyrdom of the eponymous heroine as an event which resuscitated a Christian spirit that had been weakened by luxury and scepticism and thereby helped towards the conversion of the pagan Empire. Conversion was fundamental to Christianity from the outset. It is a natural hypothesis, he says somewhat sardonically, 'to consider that the society of Christians, which the Apostles left on earth, were of that religion to which the Apostles had converted them'.[57] Conversion is a change from what is mutable, diverse and sectarian to that which is authoritative and immutable; it is the dynamic of Christian history. The conversion of the Roman Empire is a model for the conversion of the British Empire; the multitudinous sects of the pagans and of the Protestants are similar, not only in their diversity but also in their logical culmination in the denial of the divine, and the Christian minority within the Old World anticipates the English Catholic minority within the contemporary world. Christian history stretches back for 1,800 years; it is from this that Protestantism is separated. England, claims Newman, has no ecclesiastical historian other than 'the unbeliever Gibbon'; this is a manifestation of its awareness that 'the Christianity of history is not Protestantism. If ever there were a safe truth, it is this. And Protestantism has ever felt it so . . . To be deep in history is to cease to be a Protestant.'[58]

In place of history and the real Apostolic Tradition, England has popular tradition, violently anti-Catholic, but enormously influential. By this sort of tradition

> . . . is meant, what has ever been held, as far as we know, though we do not know how it came to be held, and for that very reason think it true, because else it would not be held.[59]

Such tradition is fine as an initial mode of gaining knowledge about historical and other matters; but it lacks authority, is insusceptible of proof and, in the English case, is moreover, 'a single and solitary' tradition, unsupported by any other, and yet forms 'the sort of ground on which Protestants are so certain that the Catholic Church is simply a monster of iniquity'.[60] To shed such prejudice would be an advance, although one scarcely to be envisaged in a country where this popular tradition is the product 'of calculating heads, of kingcraft' and is in effect the basis for the establishment of the Church as a function of the state. Protestantism, unlike Catholicism, is dependent for its survival on establishment.

> Establishment is the very life of Protestantism; or, in other words, Protestantism comes in upon the nation, Protestantism is maintained, not in the way of reason and truth, not by appeals to facts, but by tradition, and by a compulsory tradition; and thus, in other words, is an establishment.[61]

The English character, unphilosophical, unhistorical, anti-intellectual[62] and insular has made this kind of political situation the easier to sustain; based on personal attachment to the monarch, 'English Protestantism is the religion of the throne'. Thus, 'to doubt its truth is to be disloyal towards its sovereign'; instead of saints and doctors, the Englishman has kings, for he likes 'somebody or something at which he can cry "huzzah" and throw up his hat'.[63]

Ireland is the living proof that Catholicism does not depend upon establishment. Rather the reverse. Persecuted for three hundred years, it was yet more vigorous than ever. In no country in the world, Newman claimed, had Protestantism thriven under persecution as had Catholicism in Ireland. The reason is that persecution binds such a community and consolidates its faith. Protestantism, with its principle of private judgement, could not survive such persecution nor could it survive at all without establishment, since such a principle, lacking the communally adherent qualities of the Catholic faith, produces disunion.[64] What religion lacks, however, the state supplies. Thus, in English eyes, a Catholic cannot be loyal to the British state and to Rome since Catholicism inevitably denies the monarch a sovereignty (spiritual and temporal) accorded the Pope. In Catholic eyes the obsequiousness of the English Church to the state is a true servitude readily accepted and ingeniously disguised or excused by those who take Catholics to be the epitome of enslavement. This issue was brought to a head by the Declaration of Papal

Infallibility and Gladstone's extraordinary essay, known as the *Vatican Decrees* (1874), responded to by Newman the following year. Gladstone regarded the Declaration of Infallibility as a victory for the Ultramontane party within the Church and as a denial of civil allegiance.[65] Newman argued that infallibility could not extend to matters that involved civil allegiance, nor could it contradict conscience.[66] This did not please Ultramontanes nor did it satisfy Catholic liberals like Lord Acton nor, of course, his teacher Döllinger, who was not impressed by Newman's response.[67]

The Doctrinal and the Aesthetic: Another Conversion

There was a brutal element in the response of Gladstone, Acton and Döllinger to Newman's ostensibly evasive and miminalist defence of infallibility; what was common to them all was the belief that the distinction between authority and authoritarianism was crucial and could be demonstrated from history, a discipline in which Acton and Döllinger thought Newman to be unqualified, even ignorant. The brutality seems to have been in part provoked by frustration; in the words of Kingsley's crude pamphlet of 1864, the question was *What, then, does Dr. Newman Mean?* As in his theory of the university, Newman believed that there was no necessary discrepancy between civil freedom, the dogmatic principle in religion and the position accorded by Catholics to Rome. For most other commentators, there was either an inescapable contradiction there or at least an ambiguity that implied an uncertain belief or even an intellectually dishonest surrender to it. Such an ambiguity, or such a claim for it, was not nearly so acceptable at the time in historical or theological as in literary circles, where the search for an alternative to traditional spiritual authority had long been both a stimulant and an oppression for many writers. Lord Acton's famous review essay of 1885 on George Eliot illuminates the issue in the well-known claim that 'It was the problem of her age to reconcile the practical ethics of unbelief and of belief, to save virtue and happiness when dogmas and authorities decay.' But in a less-known remark in that essay, he distinguished between the doctrinal (positivist) and the aesthetic elements in Eliot: 'If the doctrine, separate from the art, had no vitality, the art without the doctrine had no significance.'[68] The civic icon of the exquisitely cultivated gentleman and the religious icon of the believer are versions of the aesthetic and the doctrinal positions that Newman believed the Catholic University could bring into a new accord, or in one of his favoured images, constituted an 'assemblage' that could be 'bound up in a unity'.[69] It would be wrong to say that this would be either an aesthetic or a doctrinal achievement. As in Acton's account of Eliot's work, the two interact to produce something that neither could independently manage. It is always a problem with Newman's mode of argument that its doctrinal content is so often separated from its stylistic articulation. For those who do not share or who are unsympathetic to his religious convictions, Newman's urbanity has to be separated from his belief, whereas it is his belief that gives substance to his urbanity. Acton, who could see this in Eliot, seemed to miss it in Newman, despite their shared Catholicism (or perhaps because of the different understandings of Catholicism that both united and divided them).

Arnold was the first important interpreter of Newman, James Joyce the second to see that conversion was the process by which the doctrinal became the aesthetic and that this was the key to the understanding of Newman's idea of education. (This is the central trope of Joyce's *A Portrait of the Artist as a Young Man*). Both of them may be said, with some truth, to have endowed or burdened literature with what they saw as the ruined and ruinous authority Newman assigned to religion and to have recognised that to be emancipated from such authority was as much a jeopardy as a release. For both, the conversion of the doctrinal into the aesthetic was an abiding preoccupation bequeathed to them by both the distant and the recent religious and political histories of Ireland and England. The English–Irish connection encapsulated in its most paralysing form the attritional relation between modernity and tradition that was commonly understood as exemplary of Protestant and Catholic religious attitudes, of racial or national destinies, and of commitment to the future of science and reason or adherence to superstition and the past.

Arnold, of course, had different futures and different pasts to propose than those offered by liberalism or modernity. His debt to Newman in formulating these is deep and often acknowledged. In Arnold's view, Newman's bugbear, liberalism, 'broke the Oxford movement', but had itself 'lost the future' to a new force, Arnold's protean 'Culture'. He saluted Newman's movement for 'the keen desire for beauty and sweetness which it nourished, the deep aversion it manifested to the hardness and vulgarity of middle-class liberalism, the strong light it turned on the hideous and grotesque illusions of middle-class Protestantism'.[70] In addition, again drawing on Newman's critique of popular English Protestant belief and the residual anti-Catholic hostility of English liberalism, he ridiculed liberalism's claim to a principled opposition to the endowment of religions. This was hypocritical; it was both obeisant to and supportive of the religious fanaticism of Protestant England; the political effect had been, says Arnold in 1874, that because England 'will not allow a Catholic university with a charter from the Crown, so Ireland will have a Catholic university with a charter from the Pope.'[71] Although he defended Anglicanism and its history against Newman's version, and was careful to state his preference for Protestantism as a religion over Catholicism – sounding very much like the Anglican Newman in the process – Arnold supported the argument for Newman's Catholic University, on political grounds; further, he understood Newman's wish to create an integrated culture of the individual as against the narrow and purblind specialist of the modern kind. Yet, an important difference remained: Arnold assigned to literature, and especially national literatures, an even greater importance than Newman had claimed for it or for them.

Nothing in the *Idea of a University* now seems quite so dated (or was so curiously influential) as the first three lectures of Part II – 'Christianity and Letters', 'Literature' and 'English Catholic Literature'. The first and third of these lectures were first published in the *Gazette* in 1854 and were subsequently altered in various respects for the later volume.[72] Newman was by no means the first to broach the topic. It seems likely he owes an unacknowledged debt to James Duffy's *Irish Catholic Magazine* of 1847–48 and especially to Duffy's opening editorial, in which Duffy refers to the Oxford Movement.[73] However, Newman integrates these essay-lectures into his wider account of the Catholic (and Irish) University's ambitions, although, typically, he seems to be mildly allergic to the very idea that he promotes – that of a literature in English that could replace the achieved Protestant tradition. Even if England were to become Catholic. 'English Literature' would never be so, since it has its classics and 'we' (the Irish, presumably), 'are but a portion of the vast English-speaking world-wide race, and are but striving to create a current in the direction of Catholic truth.'[74] In brief, Newman claims that the senior form of civilisation is that derived from the Greeks and the Jews; that Christianity is its companion; that literature, classical and vernacular, is a powerful agent of national expression and, at its greatest, of human nature; and that 'English Classical Literature' is a Protestant formation beyond the powers of those 'who are desirous of Catholicizing the English language' to undo. On the other hand, Shakespeare was, more or less, a Catholic; and English literature, Protestant as it is, at least is not marked by the spirit of infidelity so marked in French and Italian literature. In addition, 'we have well nigh seen the end of English Classics'; the great writers have moulded the mind and speech of the nation, the spirit of patriotism has declined, the language will lose its 'distinctive character', become 'tame and spiritless' and will be 'corrupted by the admixture of foreign elements'. This early version of the decline and fall of the national literature into a pallid cosmopolitanism is developed much later by T.S. Eliot and F.R. Leavis, as is the discussion of the relationship between classics of literature and the nations they belong to. The 'dissociation of sensibility' is one of the founding theories both of modernism and of English cultural nationalism. Samuel Taylor Coleridge, most especially the Coleridge who turned to the Anglican Church to find in it a sanction for the anti-revolutionary British state, originated the idea; Newman, also fond, like Coleridge, of looking to the great Anglican divines of the seventeenth century for such a sanction, finally found in the fathers of the early Church the original authority for the nurturing of an evolving human culture of which national cultures would form a decisive but not a final phase.

Newman's argument for the special importance of literature is that, like religion, it is not dependent for its reception and understanding on a series of propositions verifiable on scientific grounds.[75] The culture of a nation is in his view heavily dependent upon its writers. Literature can reinforce religious feeling through its part in the creation of a national culture and identity that becomes associated with religious practices and structures of belief. Belief itself is not, however, dependent upon a specific culture, although it seems that, in the contemporary instances of England and France, unbelief might be. The forms of belief are engraven within a culture but can fade with that culture's decline. Newman believed in the permanent nature of English literature's Protestantism and in the impermanent nature of the culture it belonged to, while also believing in the possibility of a future literature in English that would be Catholic and to which the Irish would make an important contribution. Great writers like Shakespeare and Virgil belonged to their nations, but their greatness was in this: 'what they express is common to the whole race of man, and they alone are able to express it'.[76]

Arnold extended this account to the point where literature in effect takes the place in his thought that religion has in Newman's, where those who 'were thrown on letters' were thereby able 'to correct, in reading the Bible, some of the mistakes into which men of more metaphysical talents than literary experience have fallen'.[77] When Arnold speaks of conversion in the limited sense, he speaks of a process in which the human is passive and the activity is God's. (Wesleyanism is one of his examples.) But in the larger sense, exemplified by St Paul, conversion is a realisation of oneself, the incorporation into a given nature of all in which it is primarily deficient. Thus a severe nature would realise itself more fully by internalising all that was lacking in it – sweetness, gentleness and the like.[78] So too with culture and Christianity. The conversion to Culture includes all that was in Christianity but much else besides that Christianity, or at least the Christianity of the Churches, lacked. Doctrine contributes to Perfection, but Perfection is not simply religious doctrine converted into cultural terms. Perfection involves a degree of human agency, a specifically human rather than divine contribution of which art and science are the most dazzling achievements. The serenity of this condition, removed from the squabbling and discord of sects, is a symptom of its spiritual authority. It is Newman's vision of Catholicism, reinflected and transposed, a doctrinal conviction aestheticised, an aesthetic achievement dependent upon, yet not identical with its doctrinal heritage and substance.

Joyce

Unendowed by the state, denied a charter, dependent upon public subscriptions in post-Famine Ireland, the Catholic University's chances of survival were slim to begin with; an Act of Parliament replaced it in 1879 with the Royal University, which really began functioning in the year of Joyce's birth, 1882. The Royal (in a bitter irony) was modelled on London University – in effect was an examining body. The Catholic University became a college of the Royal and rechristened University College. It was entrusted in 1883 to the Jesuits.[79] Joyce entered as a student in 1898; in 1901 the new student magazine *St. Stephen's* refused his essay 'The Day of the Rabblement'. In a neat turn, the first article in the first number of the new publication was on Newman's house journal the *Gazette*, and its author was Fr William Darlington, the convert and Dean of Studies, immortalised in the scene in what is now Newman House in both *Stephen Hero* and *A Portrait of the Artist as a Young Man*.[80] This scene takes place above the room in which Newman met the first students of the Catholic University in 1854. Newman's vision of the new university reappears, with some Arnoldian inflections, and in an inverted form, in the consciousness of Stephen Dedalus in the opening episode of *Ulysses*. There, Ireland is re-envisaged both as the centre of the universe and as a marginal presence within it; as the slave of two masters, one Roman Catholic and one British; and Stephen himself seeks refuge from the various afflictions of biological and cultural parentage in a version of the truly Catholic doctrine of the Trinity, which would provide a sense of unity and coherence in an otherwise atomised and heretical condition. He is, certainly in *Portrait*, the most anxious of all the modernist heroes to bear witness to and complete his conversion from doctrinal imposition to aesthetic freedom, while yet retaining the content of the repudiated doctrine in a transposed form. Perhaps the deepest irony in the famous scene in *Portrait* is the recognition that the Newman convert, the Dean of Studies, possesses the English language in a manner not available to Stephen. Out of that recognition, which was part of the ethos and point of the Catholic University as Newman imagined it, emerged a new literature, not Catholic nor English but a converted or tranmsogrified version of each. Nevertheless, the imagined career of Stephen Dedalus and the intellectual career of his creator are closely bound up with the educational experiment Newman launched and of which Joyce was and is the most famous beneficiary.

APPENDIX
Note on A Sale Catalogue of Burke's Library, 7–14 November 1833, London

This catalogue of Edmund Burke's library has attracted a good deal of attention before now. Professor Carl B. Cone has an article, 'Edmund Burke's Library' in *Papers of the Bibliographical Society of America*, 44 (1950), and Professor Thomas Copeland and other editors of the Burke *Correspondence* have referred to it on several occasions as a useful aid in establishing various points on Burke's reading and reviewing. The catalogue is in the British Museum, s-c.e.49.(1). There are other copies in the New York Public Library and in the Bodleian.

We know from James Prior, Burke's most reliable early biographer, that John Nugent, his brother-in-law, inherited the library on Burke's death, and that the pieces of sculpture which ornamented the house at Beaconsfield were sold by auction at Christie's soon after. (See on this, Carl B. Cone's 'Edmund Burke's Art Collection', *Art Bulletin* 29 [June 1947], 126–31.) Further, although there are many items here obviously acquired after Burke's death – like the interesting and now quite rare, although conventionally scurrilous, *Life of Voltaire* by Frank Hall Standish (1821), lot 474 – the catalogue is substantially that of Edmund Burke's library as it stood. His son Richard, who died in 1794, left his own books to his uncle Richard Burke and only a few items from that collection survive here. There is another catalogue of Burke's books in the Phillipps MS.16798, a manuscript of sixty-eight pages listing the items for the sale of 17 August 1813. It has been recorded as lot 273 at Sotheby's for Tuesday 3 July 1873. In addition, Frits Lugt's *Répertoire des catalogues de ventes vol. I 1600–1825* (la Haye, 1938), notes two items which are of interest here. Item 8195 notices the 5 June 1812 sale of what are called Edmund Burke's paintings, etc., and item 8129 for the 19 June 1812 sale of Mr. Burke's art objects, etc., lists forty-two books for sale.

John Morley tells us that Burke and his friend and political colleague William Windham conversed 'as often on old books, as on Hastings or Pitt' during their Scottish tour of 1785. And Windham, Morley continues, provides in contrast to Burke, an extraordinary 'example of the remorse of a bookman impeded by affairs'. Burke was not given to the same regrets as Windham; he did sometimes regret that he had not devoted more of his time to study and to books but, given his involvements and their deep complications, we can only wonder that he devoted so much. Certainly, even the most cursory study of this catalogue shows to what degree Burke incorporated into his own thought and action the standard authorities whose works filled his shelves. It allows us to see to some degree the intellectual commitments that underpinned the different phases of his career.

Apart from general literature, the largest single group of books here recorded is historical. England, France, Ireland and India, in that order, are the countries in whose history he was most deeply read. Travel literature is also heavily represented and includes a valuable collection of books on Chile (a country with which Burke's name is not usually associated), as well as reports, accounts and adventures of various kinds. Lot 539, *Arte de Lengua General del Reyno de Chile* (Lima, 1765) deserves its catalogue description of 'extremely rare' and lots 606 (*Recopilacion de Leyes de los Reynos de las Indias* [Madrid, 1641]) and 607 (*Recopilacion de la Leyes d'estos Reynos* 3 vols. [Madrid, 1640]) are also noteworthy compilations. The great range of Burke's interests and the labour with which he pursued them is also attested by the number of dictionaries, grammars of foreign languages, encyclopaedias and miscellaneous reference works – in all, thirty-two items. All the great names in international law and jurisprudence are represented; and in the antiquarian field, where Burke's interest was directed in the main towards Ireland, there are some notable items, particularly the fine fifteen-volume Francis Grose (lot 333) and the first edition of William Dugdale's *Antiquities of Warwickshire* (with Burke's autograph, lot 219). Unsurprisingly for an aesthetician like Burke and in a century like the eighteenth, there is a considerable collection of works on painting, architecture and general aesthetics; and this grouping naturally links with the antiquarian books in volumes like James Stuart's *Antiquities of Athens* (lot 617), to which Burke was a subscriber.

A good deal of contemporary material relating to the French Revolution survives here, although it is evident that Burke felt no inclination to collect the multitude of pamphlets which appeared in opposition to or in favour of his 'Reflections' between 1791 and 1793. One notes the presence of the Abbé Barruel's disreputable work, *Memoirs of Jacobinism* (lot 28), to the English translation of which Burke contributed a prefatory note. That is the work's outstanding claim to our attention now, unless one also considers the impression it left on the young Shelley. The Enlightenment is in fact, in terms of major works, better represented than the Revolution, although it is salutary to see that for Burke it had obviously as heavily a Scottish as a French flavour. Hume, Robertson, Ferguson and James Beattie are as prominent as Montesquieu, Voltaire, Rousseau and others. Perhaps the very strong representation of contemporary thought is in part explained by the fact that Burke reviewed many of these books for the *Annual Register*, twenty-seven volumes of which appear as lot 17. Similarly, the various collections of state papers are standard items in the library of a man as industrious and as practically informed as Burke.

He was not a collector of rare books; his finances were under such strain during his whole life that such an avocation would have been unthinkable for him. But there are various items worth noting, some of them of great value indeed. Lot 300, Constantine Lascaris's *Grammatica Graeca* of 1547, François Mézeray's illustrated *Histoire de France* of 1634–51 in three volumes (lot 429), Malone on the Shakespeare Forgery, with an autograph dedication by Edmond Malone to Burke (lot 478), the collection of *Curious Old Tracts*, including (lot 515) John Sanford's *Plutarch's Amorous and Tragicall Tales*, 1567, and *Galeni Opera*, Aldus, 1525, with manuscript corrections (lot 395), all stand out from the otherwise very conventional collection of classical, European and English literature. Thomas Hollis is represented by one of his presentation copies of Toland's *Life of Milton* (lot 504) and, in that connection, one notes that in 1817 his first edition of Thomas Spence's *Polymetis*, 1747, sold for £10. 10s. 0d, while in 1833, Burke's copy went for a mere £1. 15s. 0d. But then Burke was never in luck, not even posthumously, where money was concerned. As a man who, in the words of Thomas Copeland, 'lived on loans, gifts and windfalls', he collected a library which was largely made up of a typical combination of review copies, presentation copies, and some isolated items of great value. Yet, for all that, his great learning and amazing vigour in a variety of fields is exhibited here in a solid collection of books and papers which obviously extends from his undergraduate reading at Trinity College, through his attemps to break into the literary world and thence to his great and complicated political crusades.

ABBREVIATIONS

DA	Alexis de Tocqueville, *Democracy in America 2 vols.*, ed. Phillips Bradley (New York, 1945; repr. 1990)
LFR	J.E.E.D. Acton, *Lectures on the French Revolution,* eds. J.N. Figgis and R.V. Laurence (London, 1910)
LMH	J.E.E.D. Acton, *Lectures on Modern History,* eds. J.N. Figgis and R.V. Laurence (London, 1906; repr. 1930)
PW	*Prose Works of Jonathan Swift* 14 vols., ed. Herbert Davis (Oxford, 1939–68)
SW	*Selected Writings of Lord Acton* 3 vols., ed. J. Rufus Fears (Indianapolis, 1985–88)
WS	Edmund Burke, *The Writings and Speeches of Edmund Burke* 9 vols., gen. ed. Paul Langford (Oxford, 1981–2000)
	I, *The Early Writings*, ed. T.O. McLaughlin and James T. Boulton (1997)
	II, *Party, Parliament, and the American Crisis 1766–1771,* ed. Paul Langford (1981)
	III, *Party, Parliament and the American War 1774–1780,* eds. Warren M. Elofson with John A. Woods (1996)
	V, *India: Madras and Bengal 1774–1785,* ed. P.J. Marshall (1981)
	VI, *India: The Launching of the Hastings Impeachment 1786–1788,* ed. P.J. Marshall (1991)
	VII, *The Hastings Trial 1789–1794,* ed. P.J. Marshall (2000)
	VIII, *The French Revolution 1790–1794,* ed. L.G. Mitchell (1989)
	IX, 1 *The Revolutionary War 1794–1797;* 2 *Ireland,* ed. R.B. McDowell (1991)

NOTES

1. Liberty

1. Luke Gibbons, *Edmund Burke and Ireland: Aesthetics, Politics and the Colonial Sublime* (Cambridge, 2003)
2. See Thomas Docherty, 'Newman, Ireland and Universality', *boundary 2* (Spring, 2004), 73–92
3. Richard Bourke, 'Liberty, Authority, and Trust in Burke's Idea of Empire' *Journal of the History of Ideas* 61, 3 (July 2000), 453–71, (454)
4. *WS*, 'Speech on Opening of Impeachment' (February, 1788), VI: 351
5. Francis Jeffrey, *Contributions to the Edinburgh Review* (New York, 1866), 610–16
6. Germaine de Staël, *Œuvres complètes* 2 vols. (Paris, 1836), II: 258. 'My ambition would be to speak of the time we have lived through as though it were already distant from us.'
7. See J.W. Burrow, *A Liberal Descent: Victorian Historians and the English Past* (Cambridge, 1981); Mark Salber Phillips, 'Historical Distance and the Historiography of Eighteenth-Century Britain', in Stefan Collini, Richard Whatmore and Brian Young (eds.), *History, Religion, and Culture: British Intellectual History 1750–1950* (Cambridge, 2000), 31–47; and on France, see Ann Rigney, *The Rhetoric of Historical Representation: Three Narrative Histories of the French Revolution* (Cambridge, 1990)
8. On the Irish situation see Tom Bartlett, *The Fall and Rise of the Irish Nation* (Dublin, 1992); David Dickson, Dáire Keogh, and Kevin Whelan (eds.), *The United Irishmen: Republicanism, Radicalism, and Rebellion* (Dublin, 1993); James Livesey, *Making Democracy in the French Revolution* (Cambridge, Mass., 2001), 78–81; 196–97.
9. For a contemporary view of this relation, see Francis Plowden, *An Historical Disquisition Concerning the Rise, Progress, Nature and Effects of the Orange Societies in Ireland* (Dublin, 1810), 132, where he says the British government 'kept on foot the Society of Orangemen as a *corps de reserve*, and constituted them a body guard to the Irish party, which under the religious cant of *Protestant ascendancy*, stipulated for the continuance of their own monopoly of civil power.'
10. See Clare O'Halloran, *Golden Ages and Barbarous Nations: Antiquarianism and Cultural Politics in Ireland, 1750–1800* (Cork/Field Day, 2004)
11. See Edward Ledwich, 'On the Romantic History of Ireland', in *The Antiquities of Ireland*, 2nd ed. (Dublin, 1804), 10; other notable examples would include William Webb, *An Analysis of the History and Antiquities of Ireland* (Dublin, 1791) and Thomas Campbell, *Strictures on the*

Ecclesiastical and Literary History of Ireland from the Most Ancient Times (Dublin, 1799)

12. Philip Bobbitt, *The Shield of Achilles: War, Peace, and the Course of History* (New York, 2002), 153
13. *WS*, 'Speech on Conciliation with America', III: 132–33
14. *WS* III: 158
15. See John Toland (ed.), *The Oceana of James Harrington, Esq; and His Other Works* (Dublin, 1737), 45; see also Harrington's *The Prerogative of Popular Government,* Book I, Ch. II, 240
16. *WS*, 'Reflections on the Revolution in France', VIII: 193
17. *WS* II: 241–323
18. *WS* VII: 256–57
19. *WS* VII: 231
20. *WS* VII: 240 and 63

2. Swift and Burke

1. Anthony Ashley Cooper, Third Earl of Shaftesbury, *Characteristics of Men, Manners, Opinions, Times*, ed. J.M. Robertson (New York, 1964), 221–22.
2. ibid., 222
3. ibid., 223–4
4. ibid., 227–8
5. ibid., 228–9
6. Francis Hutcheson, *An Inquiry Into The Original of Our Ideas of Beauty and Virtue*, 4th ed. (London, 1738), Treatise II, Section IV, 207
7. *Inquiry*, 208
8. See Ian McBride, 'The School of Virtue; Francis Hutcheson, Irish Presbyterians and the Scottish Enlightenment' in D. G. Boyce et al. (eds.), *Political Thought in Ireland since the Seventeenth Century* (London and New York, 1993), 73–99;Terry Eagleton, *Heathcliff and the Great Hunger: Studies in Irish Culture*, (London, 1995), 104–23; *Crazy John and the Bishop and Other Essays on Irish Culture* (Cork/Field Day, 1998), 94–101; Daniel Carey, 'Swift among the Freethinkers', *Eighteenth-Century Ireland* 12 (1997), 89–99; on Swift, Hutcheson and Burke, see Thomas Duddy, *A History of Irish Thought* (London and New York, 2002), 143–202
9. Hutcheson, *Inquiry*, 236
10. Alasdair Macintyre, *Whose Justice? Which Rationality?* (London, 1988), 260–80
11. Hutcheson, *Inquiry*, 297
12. Knud Haakonssen, *Natural Law and Moral Philosophy: From Grotius to the Scottish Enlightenment* (Cambridge, 1996), 77
13. Cf. N. McKendrick, John Brewer, and J.H. Plumb, *The Birth of a Consumer Society: The Commercialization of Eighteenth-Century England*

(London, 1982); J.G.A. Pocock, 'Virtue and Commerce in the Eighteenth Century', *Journal of Interdisciplinary History* 3, 1 (1972), 119–34

14. Bernard Mandeville, *A Modest Defense of Publick Stews* (London, 1723); *The Fable of the Bees* 2 vols., ed. F.B. Kaye (Oxford, 1924), I: 182. On Mandeville's Epicureanism and libertinism, see S. Rashid, 'Mandeville's *Fable*: Laissez-Faire or Libertinism?' *Eighteenth-Century Studies* 18 (1985), 313–30
15. See D.D. Raphael, *The Moral Sense* (London, 1947), 16
16. See McKendrick, Brewer, and Plumb, *The Birth of a Consumer Society*, 51–53; J.G.A. Pocock, *The Machiavellian Moment: Florentine Political Thought and the Atlantic Republican Tradition* (Princeton,1975), 465–66
17. *The Fable of the Bees*, I: 86
18. E.M. Johnston, *Ireland in the Eighteenth Century* (Dublin, 1974), 77–98; Patrick Kelly, 'The Politics of Political Economy in Mid-Eighteenth Century Ireland', in S.J. Connolly (ed.), *Political Ideas in Eighteenth-Century Ireland* (Dublin, 2000), 105–29
19. See, for instance, Hazlitt's *Remarks on the Systems of Hartley and Helvétius* (London, 1805)
20. Letter to *The Dublin Journal* (1726). Berkeley was of the same opinion and attacked Mandeville in *Alciphron* (1732), to which Mandeville responded in *A Letter to Dion* (1732).
21. David Berman, 'The Irish Counter-Enlightenment', in R. Kearney ed. *The Irish Mind* (Dublin, 1985), 119–40
22. Hutcheson, *Inquiry*, 164–65
23. See Phillip Harth, *Swift and Anglican Rationalism* (Chicago and London, 1961)
24. *PW X*: 66
25. David Nokes, *Jonathan Swift: A Hypocrite Reversed: A Critical Biography* (Oxford, 1985), 111
26. *PW* V: 6.
27. *PW* V: 8
28. *PW* V: 94
29. Also the author of *Ormonds Curtain Drawn* (1646), a slanderous attack on the Duke of Ormond
30. *WS* I: 479
31. *WS*, 'Reflections on the Revolution in France' VII: 97
32. See *The Letter to a Member of the National Assembly*, in *WS* VIII: 314–20
33. J.L. De Lolme, *The Constitution of England in which it is compared with the Republican Form of Government and occasionally with the other Monarchies in Europe* (1776: London, 1823), 359–60
34. *A New and Enlarged Collection of Speeches by the Right Honourable John Philpot Curran . . .* (London, 1819), 122
35. Arno J. Mayer, *The Furies: Violence and Terror in the French and Russian Revolutions* (Princeton, 2000), 26

36. See John Toland (ed.), *The Oceana of James Harrington, Esq; and His Other Works* (Dublin, 1737), 45
37. Katherine O'Donnell, '"Whether the White People Like It or Not": Edmund Burke's Speeches on India – *Caoineadh's Cáinte*', *Éire-Ireland* (Fall/Winter 2002), 187–205; 'The Image of a Relationship in Blood: *Párliament na mBan* and Burke's Jacobite Politics', *Eighteenth-Century Ireland* 15 (2000), 98–119
38. Harrington, *Oceana*, 'The Preliminaries', 58
39. See Quentin Skinner, *Liberty Before Liberalism* (Cambridge, 1997); Philip Pettit, *Republicanism: A Theory of Freedom and Government* (Oxford, 1997)
40. *WS*, 'Letter to Sir Hercules Langrishe' (1792), *WS*, IX: 598
41. *WS* V: 152

3. Montesquieu and Burke

1. Francis Hardy, *Memoirs of the Political and Private Life of James Caulfield, Earl of Charlemont* (London, 1810), 36
2. See C.P. Courtney, *Montesquieu and Burke* (Oxford, 1963; repr. Westport, Connecticut, 1975), 167–69
3. ibid., 27–38
4. Louis Cullen, 'The Blackwater Catholics and County Cork Society and Politics in the Eighteenth Century', in Patrick O'Flanagan and Cornelius G. Buttimore (eds.), *Cork. History and Society. Interdisciplinary Essays on the History of an Irish County* (Dublin, 1993), 535–84
5. ibid., 574
6. *WS* IX: 594–639
7. *WS* IX: 602–03
8. Cullen, 'Blackwater Catholics', 573
9. See J.G.A. Pocock, 'Political Thought in the English-Speaking Atlantic, 1760–1790. Part I: The Imperial Crisis. Part 2: Empire, Revolution and the end of Early Modernity', in J.G.A. Pocock (ed.), with the assistance of G.J. Schochet and L.G. Schwoerer *The Varieties of British Political Thought 1500–1800* (Cambridge, 1993), 246–317
10. The most interesting sustained treatment of Burke's outsider status is Isaac Kramnick, *The Rage of Edmund Burke: Portrait of an Ambivalent Conservative* (New York, 1977)
11. Montesquieu, *Œuvres de Montesquieu – 2 vols.*, ed. R. Caillois (Paris, 1956–58), II, *L' Esprit des Lois* XI: v. 'There is one nation in the world whose constitution has political liberty as its basic aim. We are going to examine the principles on which it is founded. If these principles are good, liberty will appear there as in a mirror.' On Montesquieu and the British constitution, see J. Dedieu, *Montesquieu et la tradition politique anglaise en France* (Paris, 1909); F.T.H. Fletcher, *Montesquieu and English*

Politics (1750–1800) (London, 1939); G. Bonno, *La constitution britannique devant l'opinion française de Montesquieu à Bonaparte* (Paris, 1932).

12. Montesquieu, *Lois XI: vi.* 'In most kingdoms in Europe, the government is moderate, because the prince, who has the first two powers, leaves it to his subjects to exercise the third. Among the Turks, where the three powers are united in the person of the Sultan, an atrocious despotism reigns.' See also Louis Althusser, *Politics and History: Montesquieu, Rousseau, Hegel and Marx,* trans. B. Brewster (London, 1972), 87–95.
13. *Lois XI: vi.* 'the necessary motion of things', 'an harmonious fusion'
14. *Lois* V: xiv. 'In contrast, a despotic government leaps to view, so to speak; it is uniform throughout; as only passions are needed to establish it, everyone is good enough to do that.'
15. *WS*, 'Reflections on the Revolution in France', VIII: 176
16. See Franco Venturi, *Italy and the Enlightenment: Studies in a Cosmopolitan Century* (London, 1972), 44–51
17. *WS*, 'Impeachment Proceedings: Speech in Reply', VII: 263
18. *Lois* XIX: iv. 'Many things govern human beings: climate, religion, laws, the maxims of the government, examples of past things, mores, and manners; a general spirit is formed as a result.'
19. *Lois XIX: vi.* 'May we be left as we are.'
20. *Lois* XIX: xi. 'I have not said this to in any way reduce the infinite distance between vices and virtues: God forbid! I have only wanted to make it understood that not all political vices are moral vices and that not all moral vices are political vices, and those who make laws that run counter to the general spirit should know this.'
21. *Œuvres. Réflexions sur la monarchie universelle,* 11: 34 'Europe is no more than one Nation composed of many; France and England need the wealth of Poland and Muscovy just as one of their provinces needs the others; and the State that hopes to increase its power by the ruin of its neighbour generally weakens itself thereby.'
22. Lois XXV: iv
23. *Lois* XXIV: v
24. See Seamus Deane, *The French Revolution and Enlightenment in England* 1789–1832 (Cambridge, Mass., 1988), 27–31; Martin Thom, *Republics, Nations and Tribes* (London, 1995), 45–56, 200–11
25. Edmund Burke, *Further Reflections on the Revolution in France,* ed. Daniel Ritchie (Indianapolis, 1992), 'An Appeal from the New to the Old Whigs', 195
26. *WS* IX: 629. Cf. 601: 'They who are excluded from votes . . . are excluded, not from the *state,* but from *the British constitution* . . . *The* popular part of the constitution must be to them, by far the most odious part of it. To them it is not *an actual,* and if possible, still less a *virtual* representation. It is indeed the direct contrary!

27. *WS* V: 220. See also the distinction between the 'moral' and the 'geographical' France that governs Burke's argument in 'Remarks on the Policy of the Allies' (1793), WS VIII: 452–99 (esp. 465)
28. *WS* VIII: 485–86
29. *WS* VIII: 320
30. *Lois* XXIV: iii
31. *WS* VII: 86
32. *WS* II: 259
33. On these issues, see D. Lieberman, *The Province of Legislation Defined: Legal Theory in Eighteenth-Century Britain* (Cambridge, 1989).
34. *WS* VIII: 145–46
35. *WS* VIII: 189
36. Edmund Burke, *The Correspondence of Edmund Burke* 10 vols., eds. T. Copeland et al. (Cambridge and Chicago, 1958–78), VI: 215
37. *Lois* III: x. 'No tempering, modification, accommodation, terms, alternatives, negotitations, remonstrances . . . Man is a creature that obeys a creature that demands.'
38. *WS* IX: 32
39. *WS* IX: 667
40. *WS* VIII: 462
41. *WS* IX: 601
42. *WS* IX: 603
43. *WS* IX: 615
44. Alexis de Tocqueville, *The Old Regime and the Revolution,* eds. François Furet and Françoise Mélonio, trans. by Alan S. Kahan (Chicago and London, 1998), 153
45. ibid., 107
46. *WS* VIII: 346
47. *WS* VIII: 347
48. E.E. Crowe, *Yesterday in Ireland* 3 vols. (London, 1829), I: 29–30

4. Virtue, Travel and the Enlightenment

1. 'For to travel is almost the same as conversing with people of other times. It is good to know something of the customs of different peoples in order to judge our own more wisely and to prevent us thinking that anything contrary to our conventions is ridiculous and irrational – which is what people who have seen nothing do. But when you spend too much time travelling, in the end you become a foreigner in your own country. And when you become too curious about the practices of past centuries, you generally become profoundly ignorant of the practices of the present.'
2. Edward Gibbon, *History of the Decline and Fall of the Roman Empire* 4 vols., ed. J.B. Bury (London, 1902), I: 58

3. See J.G.A. Pocock, *Virtue, Commerce and History* (Cambridge, 1985; repr. 1988), 103–23
4. David Hume, *Enquiries Concerning the Human Understanding and Concerning the Principles of Morals*, 2nd. ed., ed. L.A. Selby-Bigge (Oxford,1902), 341
5. ibid., 343
6. Adam Smith, *An Inquiry into the Nature and Causes of the Wealth of Nations*, ed. E. Cannan (New York, 1937), 735–36
7. Quoted in John Barrell, *English Literature in History 1730–80: An Equal, Wide Survey* (London, 1983), 47
8. ibid., 47
9. See Smith's discussion in *The Wealth of Nations*, 746–48 (Volume II, Book V, Ch. I, Part III, Article 3d) of the 'strict or austere' system of morality favoured by the common people and the 'liberal or . . . loose system' favoured by people of rank. He also argues that religious sects begin with the common people and refine on the austere system with 'excessive rigour'. 'The morals of those little sects, indeed, have frequently been rather disagreeably rigorous and unsocial.'
10. Jonathan Swift, *The Drapier's Letters to the People of Ireland*, ed. H. Davis (Oxford, 1965), 128
11. Jean-Jacques Rousseau *Discours sur les sciences et les arts, Lettre à d'Alembert*, ed. J. Varloot (Paris, 1957), 261. 'I don't at all understand . . . how can one be virtuous without religion?'
12. Denis Diderot, *Œuvres philosophiques* ed. P. Vernière (Paris, 1956), 515. 'We should speak out against foolish laws until they are reformed, and meanwhile we should obey them.'
13. See Carole Blum, *Diderot: The Virtue of a Philosopher* (London, 1974), 127–39
14. See M.M. Goldsmith, 'Liberty, Luxury and the Pursuit of Happiness', in A. Pagden (ed.), *The Languages of Political Theory in Early Modern Europe* (Cambridge, 1987), 225–51
15. Barrell, *English Literature in History* 23–24 and 108–09
16. See John Lucas, *England and Englishness: Ideas of Nationhood in English Poetry 1688–1900* (London, 1990), esp. 55–70
17. *PW* XII: 9
18. *PW* XII: 9–10
19. *PW* XII: 12
20. D. Bongie, *David Hume, Prophet* of Counter-Revolution (Oxford, 1965), xii and 33–34
21. See N. McKendrick, John Brewer, and J.H. Plumb, *The Birth of a Consumer Society: The Commercialization of Eighteenth-Century England* (London, 1982), esp. 51–53
22. See R. Perry, 'Radical Doubt and the Liberation of Women', *Eighteenth-Century Studies* 18 (1985), 465–93; David Simpson, *Romanticism,*

Nationalism and the Revolt Against Theory (Chicago and London, 1993), 104–25; Linda Colley, *Britons: Forging the Nation 1707–1837* (New Haven and London, 1992), 237–81.

23. See Mary Poovey, *The Proper Woman and the Woman Writer: Ideology as Style in the Works of Mary Wollstonecraft, Mary Shelley, and Jane Austen* (Chicago and London, 1984), 48–113
24. Godwin saw himself as the rational man taught to feel by the more sentimental and less rational woman. Wollstonecraft's death in giving birth to the child who was to become Mary Shelley undermined faith in the sovereignty of detached reason. See William Godwin, *Memoirs of Mary Wollstonecraft* (1798), ed. W. Clark Dunant (London and New York,1927)
25. *WS*, 'Reflections on the Revolution in France', VIII: 182
26. *WS* VIII: 183, 176
27. *WS* VIII: 131
28. *WS* VIII: 137
29. *WS* VIII: 141
30. *WS* VIII: 127

5. Philosophes and Regicides

1. This chapter draws on earlier essays of mine, 'Burke and the French Philosophes' *Studies in Burke and His Time* 10, 2 (Winter, 1968–69), 1113–37; 'John Bull and Voltaire: The Emergence of a Cultural Cliché', *Revue de Littérature Comparée* 45 (Octobre-Decembre, 1971), 582–94; 'The Reputation of the French Philosophes in the Whig Reviews between 1802 and 1824', *The Modern Language Review* 70, 2 (April, 1975), 271–90; and on *The French Revolution and Enlightenment 1789–1832* (Cambridge, Mass., 1988), esp. 21–42.
2. Edmund Burke, *The Correspondence of Edmund Burke* 10 vols., eds. Thomas Copeland et al. (Cambridge and Chicago, 1958–78), VII: 420–21: '. . . in that you have composed a famous work to overthrow and utterly destroy the fictions of the new philosophers of France'.
3. For the whole conspiracy theory and Barruel's role in it, see Fernand Baldensperger, *Le Mouvement des ideés dans l'émigration française (1789–1815)* 2 vols. (Paris, 1925), II: 15–20; Daniel Mornet, *Les Origines intellectuelles de la révolution française* (Paris, 1933), 363–64; R.R. Palmer, 'World Revolution of the West, 1763–1801', *Political Science Quarterly* 69 (1954), 6–7; Bernard N. Schilling, *Conservative England and the Case against Voltaire* (New York, 1950), 218–77; R.A. Soloway, *Prelates and People: Ecclesiastical Social Thought in England 1783–1852* (London and Toronto, 1969), 34–45; J.M. Roberts, *The Mythology of the Secret Societies* (London, 1972); Amos Hofman, 'The Origins of the Theory of the *Philosophe* Conspiracy', *French History* 2 (1988), 152–72; Darrin M.

McMahon, *Enemies of the Enlightenment: The French Counter-Enlightenment and the Making of Modernity* (Oxford, 2001), 77–83, 110–14.

4. Lucyle Werkmeister, *The London Daily Press, 1772–1792* (Lincoln, Nebraska, 1963), 344. On the reviews and magazines on this and related issues, see Stuart Andrews, *The British Periodical Press and the French Revolution, 1789–99* (Basingstoke and New York, 2000), 148–50, 156–62.
5. See S. Skalweit, *Edmund Burke und Frankreich* (Cologne and Opladen, 1956), 64ff; Marjorie Weiner, *The French Exiles (1789–1815)* (London, 1960), 82–83; Colin Lucas, 'Edmund Burke and the Emigrés', in K.M. Baker, C. Lucas and F. Furet (eds.), *The French Revolution and the Creation of Modern Political Culture* 4 vols. (Oxford, 1987–94), III: 101–14; Kirsty Carpenter, *Refugees of the French Revolution: Émigrés in London, 1789–1802* (London, 1999)
6. See Burke, *Correspondence* (15 September 1793), VII: 426
7. Thomas Copeland, *Our Eminent Friend Edmund Burke: Six Essays* (London, 1949), 165
8. *WS* VIII: 160; see also the 'History of Europe' sections in the *Annual Register 1790* (London, 1793), 9–18, 40–58, which gives a very Burkean account of the role of the men of letters in the Revolution, of the 'licentiousness of the press', the events of October 6, 1789 and the assaults on Marie Antoinette.
9. *Application of Barruel's 'Memoirs of Jacobinism' to the Secret Societies of Ireland and Great Britain* (London, 1798), 'Advertisement'; see also Burke, *Correspondence* IX: 319–20; Barruel's *Memoirs of Jacobinism* 4 vols., trans. John Clifford (London, 1796)
10. The *British Critic*, for instance, chose to review Barruel's *Memoirs* and Robison in sequence, 'that one may, as much as possible, illustrate and explain the other.' 10 (August, 1798), 410. Other notable reviews of both are to be found in the *Monthly Review* 25 (January–February, 1798), 315, 510; *The Eclectic Review*, 'Retrospect of French Literature' (March, 1805), I: 232–33; and the wide coverage given to John Adolphus's *Biographical Memoirs of the French Revolution* 4 vols. (London, 1799) and his *The History of France from 1790 till the Peace of 1802* (London, 1803), in which the conspiracy theory was given further prominence; see, for example, the *Critical Review*, third series, 2 (August, 1804), 383.
11. Christopher Reid, *Edmund Burke and the Practice of Political Writing* (Dublin and New York, 1985), 24
12. *WS* IX: 277
13. See *WS*, '*Thoughts on French Affairs*' (1791), VIII: 351–52 and 'Third Letter on a Regicide Peace' (1797), IX: 337–40
14. See, for example, R. Bisset, *The History of the Reign of George III* 6 vols. (London, 1803; repr. 1820), IV: Ch. 43, 176; John Bowles, *Reflections on the Political and Moral State of Society at the Close of the Eighteenth Century*

(London, 1800–01), 125. For a general view, see Hedva Ben-Israel, *English Historians of the French Revolution* (Cambridge, 1968). The classic statement of the evils of French fiction, dominated by Rousseau, on sexual morals is John Wilson Croker's essay 'French Novels', *Quarterly Review* 56, 111 (April, 1836), esp. 66–72.

15. See Lynn Hunt, *The Family Romance of the French Revolution* (Berkeley and Los Angeles, 1992), 101–07, 111–13; 'The Many Bodies of Marie Antoinette: Political Pornography and the Problem of the Feminine in the French Revolution' in Lynn Hunt (ed.), *Eroticism and the Body Politic* (Baltimore and London, 1991), 108–130. Burke also attributed her undeserved unpopularity to the political hostility towards Austria aroused in 1770 by her marriage to the dauphin, later Louis XVI; this made her 'the object of an implacable rancour, never to be extinguished but in her blood' (*WS*, 'Second Letter on a Regicide Peace' (1796), IX: 285).
16. *WS* IX: 113
17. Sara Maza, 'The Diamond Necklace Affair Revisited (1785–1786): The Case of the Missing Queen', in Hunt (ed.), *Eroticism and the Body Politic*, 63–89
18. See Robert Darnton, *The Forbidden Best-Sellers of Pre-Revolutionary France* (London, 1996); Roger Chartier, *The Cultural Origins of the French Revolution*, trans. Lydia G. Cochrane (Durham and London, 1991), 178–81
19. See John Barrell, *Imagining the King's Death: Figurative Treason, Fantasies of Regicide 1793–1796* (Oxford, 2000), 90–100 and *passim*
20. *WS*, 'First Letter on a Regicide Peace' (1796), IX: 237. See also 196, 204, where he says the government 'began to throw out lures, oglings and glances for peace'; 'threw out oglings and glances of tenderness'.
21. *WS* IX: 76
22. *WS* IX: 60
23. *WS* IX: 240–49; see also J.G.A. Pocock, *Virtue, Commerce, and History* (Cambridge, 1985; repr. 1988), 197–204
24. *WS* IX: 309
25. *WS* IX: 310
26. *WS* IX: 219
27. *WS* IX: 52, 55, 69, 70. The writer of the pamphlet is also snidely referred to as 'the (Noble) Remarker', 'the (Noble) Negotiator' – see 90, 92, 94, 95, 97, 100.
28. Thomas Carlyle, *The French Revolution* (1837), II, Book V, Ch. V, *The Works of Thomas Carlyle* 30 vols. (London, 1898), III: 228: 'Great Burke has raised his great voice long ago; eloquently demonstrating that the end of an Epoch is come, to all appearance the end of Civilised Time.'
29. Carlyle, *The French Revolution*, II, Book I, Ch. IV, III: 28: 'But it is all gone; Today swallowing Yesterday, and then being in its turn swallowed

of Tomorrow, even as Speech ever is. Nay what, O thou immortal Man of Letters, is Writing itself but Speech conserved for a time?'

30. *WS* IX: 48–49
31. *WS* IX: 107–08
32. *WS* IX: 46–47
33. *WS* IX: 331–32
34. *WS* IX: 206. Cf. 'Letter to a Noble Lord' (1796), IX: 180. Burke imagines the 'Sans culotte Carcase Butchers and the Philosophers of the shambles' measuring out the body of 'his Grace' into 'rumps, and sirloins, and briskets.'
35. Cf. the passage in the 'First Letter on a Regicide Peace', *WS* IX: 202, in which Burke mocks the dress of a French minister of the time: 'A strange uncouth thing, a theatrical figure of the opera, his headed shaded with three-colored plumes, his body fantastically hatted, strutted from the back scenes, and after a short speech, in the mock-heroic falsetto of stupid tragedy, delivered the gentleman . . . into the custody of a guard . . .'
36. *WS* VIII: 454–67; see also IX: 50, 60, 277, 248–49, 293, 338–39
37. *WS* IX: 246
38. *WS*, 'Fourth Letter on a Regicide Peace', IX: 56
39. *WS*, 'Third Letter on a Regicide Peace' IX: 384
40. *WS* IX: 386
41. *WS* IX: 113–14
42. *WS* IX: 242
43. *WS* IX: 291–92; for the earlier accounts, see VIII: 158–63, 346–48, and IX: 39–40
44. See James Chandler, 'Poetical Liberties: Burke's France and the "Adequate Representation" of the English' in F. Furet and M. Ozouf (eds.), in *The French Revolution and the Creation of Modern Political Culture* vol. 3, *The Transformation of Political Culture 1789–1848* (Oxford and New York, 1988), 45–57
45. *WS* IX: 240–49
46. *WS* IX: 113
47. Occasionally, Rousseau, Franz Anton Mesmer, Joseph Balsamo Cagliostro and the German Illuminati and freemasons were linked together, along with some of Rousseau's followers, as a specific element in the great conspiracy. See, for example, Lady Charlotte Blennerhassett, *Madame de Staël: Her Friends and Her Influence in Politics and Literature* 3 vols., trans. J.E. Gordon Cumming (London 1889), I: 157–58
48. A point made by Mme de Staël in *De la Littérature considérée dans ses rapports avec les institutions sociales* 2 vols. (London, 1800), II: 65 '. . . the sentiment of equality, both in its majesty and in its meanness, is pourtrayed in every line of the writings of Rousseau, and gains entire possession of mankind as well by means of the virtues as the vices of his nature'.
49. *WS* VIII: 312–13

50. Mary Wollstonecraft, *Vindication of the Rights of Woman; with Strictures on Political and Moral Subjects* (London, 1792), 204, 31
51. Mary Wollstonecraft, *An Historical and Moral View of the Origin and Progress of the French Revolution and the Effect it Has Produced in Europe* (London, 1794), 499–500
52. Mary Wollstonecraft, *A Vindication of the Rights of Men in a Letter to the Right Honourable Edmund Burke Occasioned by his Reflections on the Revolution in France* (London, 1790), 5–6, 102
53. *WS* VIII: 315
54. *WS* VIII: 318
55. *WS* VIII: 315–17
56. Brooke Boothby, *A Letter to the Right Honourable Edmund Burke* (London, 1791), 21–22
57. *WS* VIII: 143–44
58. *WS* VIII: 145
59. John Quincy Adams ('Agricola'), *Observations on Paine's 'Rights of Man'* (Edinburgh, 1792), 18
60. Jean-Jacques Rousseau, *On the Social Contract*, ed. R. Masters, trans. J. Masters (New York, 1978), II: 7, 69: 'One who dares to undertake the founding of a people should feel that he is capable of changing human nature, so to speak; of transforming each individual, who by himself is a perfect and solitary whole, into a part of a larger whole from which this individual receives, in a sense, his life and being.'
61. See Mona Ozouf, 'La Révolution française et l'idée de l'homme nouveau' in Colin Lucas (ed.), *The Political Culture of the French Revolution* (Oxford and New York, 1988), 213–32
62. *WS* VIII: 480–81
63. See *WS*, 'Letter to William Elliot' (1795), IX: 42
64. *WS*, 'Reflections on the Revolution in France', VIII: 144
65. *WS*, 'First Letter on a Regicide Peace', IX: 188

6. Factions and Fictions

1. J.E.E.D. Acton, *Lectures on the French Revolution*, eds. J.N. Figgis and R.V. Laurence (London, 1910); Tom Furniss, *Edmund Burke's Aesthetic Ideology: Language, Gender and Political Economy in Revolution* (Cambridge, 1993); Lynn Hunt, *The Family Romance of the French Revolution* (Berkeley and Los Angeles, 1992), Ch. 1; Leo Strauss, *Natural Right and History* (Chicago, 1953)
2. A powerful example is Matthew Arnold, *Edmund Burke on Irish Affairs* (London, 1881); the more feeble modern instances would include Russell Kirk, *The Conservative Mind from Burke to Santayana* (Chicago, 1953); Conor Cruise O'Brien, *The Great Melody: A Thematic Biography of Edmund Burke* (London, 1992).

3. One of the subtlest of recent accounts of Burke's understanding of history and of 'prejudice' is in David Bromwich, *A Choice of Inheritance: Self and Community from Edmund Burke to Robert Frost* (Cambridge, Mass., and London, 1989), 43–59.
4. *WS*, 'Thoughts on French Affairs' (1791), VIII: 341, 344 (italics in original). On the extension of the idea that revolutionary proselytism was a recurrence of earlier religious 'enthusiasm', see J.G.A. Pocock, 'Edmund Burke and the Definition of Enthusiasm: The Context as Counter-Revolution', in Furet and Ozouf (eds.), *The French Revolution and the Creation of Modern Political Culture* vol. 3 *The Transformation of Political Culture, 1789–1848* (Oxford and New York 1989), 19–43; and his 'Political Thought in the English-Speaking Atlantic, 1760–1790 Part 2: Empire, Revolution and the End of Early Modernity' in J.G.A. Pocock (ed.), with the assistance of G.J. Schochet and L.G. Schwoerer, *The Varieties of British Political Thought, 1500–1800* (Cambridge, 1993), 283–317.
5. *WS* I: 183. Henry St John, first Viscount Bolingbroke, gave intellectual distinction to the Tory party in *The Idea of a Patriot King* (1749) and *Letters on the Study of History* (1752).
6. *WS* I: 236. See also, 216: 'Whatever is fitted in any sort to excite the ideas of pain and danger; that is to say, whatever is in any sort terrible, or is conversant about terrible objects, or operates in a manner analogous to terror, is a source of the *sublime* . . . .'
7. *WS* I: 217
8. *WS* I: 221–22
9. *WS* I: 222
10. *WS* I: 221
11. *WS* I: 222
12. *WS* I: 224
13. *WS* I: 225
14. *WS* I: 220–21
15. *WS* I: 225
16. *WS* I: 311
17. *WS* I: 317
18. *WS* I: 223
19. *WS* I: 317
20. *WS* I: 319
21. *WS* I: 232–33
22. For a penetrating analysis of Burke's view of tragedy and of the accompanying problematic of representation, see Peter de Bolla, *The Discourse of the Sublime: Readings in History, Aesthetics and the Subject* (Oxford, 1989), 281–91.
23. See Burke on Robespierre and his murderers in 'Fourth Letter on a Regicide Peace' (1795), *WS* IX: 84–85. On Rousseau, see 'Letter to a Member of the National Assembly' (1791), VIII: 312–19

24. *WS*, 'Tracts Relating to Popery Laws' (1765), *WS*, IX: 454–55. See F.P. Lock, *Edmund Burke: Volume I; 1730–48* (Oxford, 1998), 194–95. Burke did emphasise the supremacy of the Natural Law more in this work than elsewhere.
25. *WS* IX: 455
26. *WS* IX: 452
27. *WS* IX: 464. For further commentary on Burke and Ireland, see Louis Cullen, 'The Blackwater Catholics and County Cork: Society and Politics in the Eighteenth Century', in Patrick O'Flanagan and Cornelius G. Buttimer (eds.), *Cork: History and Society. Interdisciplinary Essays on the History of an Irish County* (Dublin, 1993), 535–84; Michel Fuchs, *Edmund Burke, Ireland, and the Fashioning of Self* (Oxford, 1996); Seamus Deane, *Strange Country: Modernity and Nationhood in Irish Writing since 1790* (Oxford, 1997), 1–48; Luke Gibbons, *Edmund Burke and Ireland: Politics and the Colonial Sublime* (Cambridge, 2003); T.O. McLoughlin, 'Burke's Dualistic Vision in the *Tracts on the Popery Laws*', *Études anglaises* 34, 2 (1981), 180–91; W.J. McCormack, *From Burke to Beckett: Ascendancy, Tradition and Betrayal in Literary History,* (Cork, 1994); Katherine O'Donnell, 'Edmund Burke and the Heritage of Oral Culture' (Unpublished Ph.D. thesis, National University of Ireland, 1999).
28. *WS* IX: 461
29. *WS* II: 274. See Frank O'Gorman, *The Long Eighteenth Century: British Political and Social History 1688–1832* (London, 1997), 210
30. See James Kelly, 'The Genesis of Protestant Ascendancy: The Rightboy disturbances of the 1780s', in Gerard O'Brien (ed.), *Parliament, Politics and People: Essays in Eighteenth-Century Irish History* (Dublin, 1989), 93–127; W.J. McCormack, *The Battle of the Books: Two Decades of Irish Cultural Debate* (Gigginstown, 1986), 75–76
31. *WS* III: 107
32. *WS* III: 316
33. *WS* VI: 275
34. Cf. Sara Suleri, *The Rhetoric of English India* (Chicago and London, 1992), 45
35. *WS* VI: 271, 459
36. *WS* VI: 93
37. *WS* VI: 109
38. *WS* V: 401–02
39. *WS*, 'Letter to Sir Hercules Langrishe' (1792), IX: 614–15
40. See, among many examples, 'Speech on Opening of Impeachment' (1788), *WS* VI: 346, 350, 354
41. *WS* VI: 283–84
42. *WS* VI: 285–86
43. *WS*, 'Reflections on the Revolution in France' (1790), VIII: 192
44. *WS*, 'Tracts Relating to Popery Laws' (1765), IX: 478–79

45. *WS*, 'Speech on the Opening of Impeachment' (1788), VI: 351–57
46. *WS*, Reflections', VIII: 176–77; and on France being treated 'exactly like a country of conquest', 230
47. *WS*, 'Letter to Richard Burke' (1792), IX: 654–55
48. *WS*, 'Opening of Impeachment', VI: 381–82
49. *WS*, 'Reflections', VIII: 188–212
50. *WS*, 'Opening of Impeachment', VI: 316–17
51. *WS*, 'Letter to Langrishe' (1792), IX: 600–01
52. *WS*, 'Speech on Fox's India Bill', V: 402
53. *WS*, 'Remarks on the Policy of the Allies', VIII: 480; 'Reflections', VIII: 242–43
54. *WS*, 'Opening of Impeachment', VI: 316–17
55. *WS* IX: 657
56. *WS*, 'Letter to Richard Burke', IX: 652–53
57. *WS*, 'Fourth Letter', IX: 50–51
58. *WS* IX: 264
59. *WS* IX: 265, 267
60. *WS* IX: 106
61. *WS*, 'Opening of Impeachment', VI: 351
62. *WS*, 'First Letter on a Regicide Peace' (1796), IX: 199
63. *WS*, 'Fourth Letter', IX: 105
64. ibid., *WS* IX: 101
65. ibid., *WS* IX: 87
66. ibid., *WS* IX: 101
67. Deane, *Strange Country,* 10–17
68. *WS*, 'Fourth Letter', IX: 103
69. *WS*, 'To Unknown' (1797), IX: 676
70. *WS*, 'Fourth Letter' (1795), IX: 114
71. *WS*, 'Speech on Nabob of Arcot's Debts' (1785), V: 547
72. *WS*, 'Fox's India Bill', IX: 402. A favourite trope; see, for instance, 'Fourth Letter', IX: 56, of the Jacobin republic: 'To be sure she is ready to perish with repletion; she has a *Boulimia*, and has hardly bolted down one State, than she calls for two or three more.'
73. On Marie Antoinette, see *WS*, 'Reflections', VIII: 126–32; on Keppel, see 'Letter to a Noble Lord' (1796), IX: 181–87; on the new titles for French assassins, see 'Fourth Letter', IX: 111–14
74. *WS*, 'Letter to a Member of the National Assembly' (1791), VIII : 312–19
75. *WS*, Cf. Suleri, *English India,* 41–48
76. *WS*, 'Fourth Letter', IX: 83
77. 'Letter to a Noble Lord', IX: 173

7. Burke and Tocqueville

1. Daniel Roche, *France in the Enlightenment*, trans. by Arthur Goldhammer (Cambridge, Mass., and London, 1998), 422. In opposition to the

Tocquevillean view of the enclosure of the literary intellectuals, see Keith Michael Baker, *Interpreting the French Revolution* (Cambridge, 1990), 12–27; Dena Goodman,*The Republic of Letters: A Cultural History of the French Enlightenment* (Ithaca and London, 1994), 300–04. Robert Darnton, *The Forbidden Best-Sellers of Pre-Revolutionary France* (London, 1996), 194–97, both agrees and disagrees with Tocqueville about the 'elaboration of a common culture' in the eighteenth century and the function of 'literature, which had done so much to legitimize absolutism in the seventeenth century, [and] now became the principal agent of its delegitimation'.

2. A well-known example would be Mallet du Pan, 'Du Degré d'influence qu'a eu la philosophie française sur la révolution', *Mercure Britannique,* 13 (25 February 1799), 342–70
3. This was recognised by both Mme de Staël and Tocqueville. See Franco Venturi, *The End of the Old Regime in Europe 1768–1776: The First Crisis*, trans. R. Burr Litchfield (Princeton, 1989), 280–81
4. Alexis de Tocqueville, *The Old Régime and the Revolution*, ed. François Furet and Françoise Mélonio, trans. Alan S. Kahan (Chicago and London, 1998), Book 1, Ch. 5, 107
5. Simon Schama's *Citizens: A Chronicle of the French Revolution* (London and New York, 1989) develops this element of Tocqueville's argument 'further than his account allows it to go'. (xv).
6. See François Furet, 'Tocqueville', in François Furet and Mona Ozouf (eds.), *A Critical Dictionary of the French Revolution,* (Cambridge, Mass., and London, 1989), 1021–32. The most thorough extension and transformation of Tocqueville's claim that the Revolution completed rather than reversed the centralising processes of the absolutist regime that preceded it is in Immanuel Wallerstein, *The Modern World-System III: The Second Era of Great Expansion of the Capitalist World-Economy, 1730–1840s* (London, 1989), 52: 'The transformation of the state structure was merely the continuation of a process that had been going on for two centuries. In this regard Tocqueville is correct. Thus, the French Revolution marked neither basic economic nor basic political transformation. Rather, the French Revolution was, in terms of the capitalist world-economy, the moment when the ideological superstructure finally caught up with the economic base. It was the consequence of the transition, not its cause nor the moment of its occurrence.'
7. Jean-Etienne Marie Portalis, *De l'Usage et de l'abus de l'esprit philosophique pendant le dix-huitième siècle* 2 vols. (Paris, 1827), II: 446, 336, 434
8. Tocqueville, *The Old Régime and the Revolution*, 208–09
9. *DA* I, First Book, Ch. XVII, 305. On the idea of limitation in Tocqueville, see Marcel Gauchet, 'Tocqueville' in Mark Lilla (ed.), *New French Thought: Political Philosophy* (Princeton, 1994), 91–111.

10. *DA* II, Second Book, Ch. XIII, 138–39. This compares interestingly with Mme de Staël's claim that the English are more melancholy than the French because the achievement of political liberty and virtue requires reflection and reflection leads one to dwell on serious matters. See *De la Littérature considérée dans ses rapports avec les institutions sociales* (London, 1800), *Œuvres complètes* 2 vols. (Paris, 1836), I: 267. Notable among various anticipations of this view is J.-H. Meister, *Souvenirs d'un voyage en Angleterre* (Paris, 1791), 167–68.
11. *DA* II, Second Book, Ch. III, 101
12. For an interesting discussion of Burke's view of the American, British, French and Irish national characters and their relation to policy, see Frederick A. Dreyer, *Burke's Politics: A Study in Whig Orthodoxy* (Ontario, 1979), 60–67.
13. See Jack P. Greene, 'Empire and Identity from the Glorious Revolution to the American Revolution', in P.J. Marshall (ed.), *The Oxford History of the British Empire; Volume II: The Eighteenth Century* (Oxford and New York, 1998), 208–30
14. *DA* I, Ch. II, 43
15. *DA* I, Ch. 1, 25; Ch. II, 35
16. See Sheldon Wolin, *Tocqueville between Two Worlds: The Making of a Political and Theoretical Life* (Princeton and Oxford, 2001), 229–40
17. Tocqueville's point that America had no feudal past to repudiate is important for the so-called 'Atlantic' thesis about the French Revolution, in which it is seen as part of a general revolution of the Western World in the late eighteenth century. See Jacques Godechot, *Les Révolutions (1770–1799)* (Paris, 1965); R.R. Palmer, *The Age of the Democratic Revolution: A Political History of Europe and America, 1760–1800* 2 vols. (Princeton, 1959). According to this interpretation, the French Revolution had an American moment – up to the Constituent Assembly – which was then followed by the 'dérapage' into the Terror and proto-socialism. This 'true' revolution was resumed in July 1830. Tocqueville is certainly the most influential source for this view, although it was not of course unique to him. See also, R.R. Palmer (ed.), *The Two Tocquevilles, Father and Son: Hervé and Alexis de Tocqueville and the Coming of the French Revolution* (Princeton, 1987); Alan Kahan, 'Tocqueville's Two Revolutions', *Journal of the History of Ideas* 5, 46 (October, 1985), 585–96.
18. *DA*, Introduction, 14
19. Heine went so far as to give his refutation of de Staël's book the same title; see *De l'Allemagne* (Paris, 1833), 7, where he calls her 'this grandmother of doctrinaires' who has 'spread abroad in France so many erroneous ideas' about 'the intellectual revolution in my country'.
20. One of the classic statements of Cold War liberalism in France is that of Raymond Aron; see especially 'Alexis de Tocqueville', in *Main Currents*

in Sociological Thought 2 vols., trans. by Richard Howard and Helen Weaver (London, 1965), I: 183–231; for more recent versions, see François Furet, *Penser la révolution française* (Paris, 1978); Pierre Manent, *Tocqueville et la nature de la démocratie* (Paris, 1982); *An Intellectual History of Liberalism* trans. Rebecca Balinski (Princeton, 1995), 103–13; *Modern Liberty and Its Discontents*, ed. and trans. Daniel J. Mahoney and Paul Seaton (Lanham, New York and Oxford, 1998), 65–77.

21. The great 'liberal' narrative of glamorous individuality is Jacob Burckhardt's *Civilization of the Renaissance in Italy* (1860).
22. *DA*, II, Second Book, Chs. VII–XI, 115–33
23. *DA* II, Second Book, Ch. XIV, 142
24. *DA*, II, First Book, Ch. XXI, 93
25. *DA*, II, Third Book, Ch. XVII, 228
26. *DA*, II: 229
27. See Albert O. Hirschmann, *The Passions and the Interests: Political Arguments for Capitalism before Its Triumph* (Princeton, 1977), 122–25
28. Pierre Nora, *Realms of Memor: The Construction of the French Past* Vol. II *Traditions*, trans. Arthur Goldhammer (New York, 1997), 435–39
29. See John Patrick Diggins, *Politics and the Spirit of Tragedy* (New York, 1996), 1–16. On Weber and melancholy, ennui, and anxiety, see Fredric Jameson, 'The Vanishing Mediator; or, Max Weber as Storyteller', in *The Ideologies of Theory: Essays 1971–1986; Volume 2: The Syntax of History* (London, 1988), 4–12; see also, Irving Babbitt, *Rousseau and Romanticism* (1919), Ch. 9, (Cleveland and New York, 1955), 236–67.
30. George Armstrong Kelly, *The Humane Comedy: Constant, Tocqueville and French Liberalism* (Cambridge, 1992), 227
31. The novel in the nineteenth century also changed to include this belief in the inexorable processes of law, destiny, economics, etc., and the loss of 'individuality'. See Franco Moretti, *The Way of the World: The* Bildungsroman *in European Culture* (London, 1987), 102–03.
32. On the question of the process of centralisation and Tocqueville's dislike for what seemed an inevitable but particularly French phenomenon, see *The Recollections of Alexis de Tocqueville* trans. Alexander Teixeira de Mattos, ed. J.P. Mayer (London, 1948), 202: 'In France, there is only one thing we can't set up: that is, a free government; and only one institution we can't destroy: that is, centralisation.' See also Hugh Brogan, *Tocqueville* (London, 1973), 72–76.
33. This was a question asked in these very terms in the first decade of the Revolution. See, for example, the writings of Burke's German translator and disciple, Friedrich von Gentz, translated in *Mercure Britannique*, 17 (23 April 1799), 3–34, esp. 28, and 20 (10 June 1799), 197–217.
34. See Hedva Ben-Israel, *English Historians of the French Revolution* (Cambridge, 1968), 219–21

35. Tocqueville, *Recollections,* 3; for an extension of this reading of 1830 to that of 1848, see 86–88
36. From the 1843 essay, 'The Emancipation of Slaves' in *Alexis de Tocqueville: Writings on Empire and Slavery*, ed. and trans. Jennifer Pitts (Baltimore and London, 2001), 207
37. This is Gustave de Beaumont's view even more than it is Tocqueville's. See Seymour Drescher, *Tocqueville and England* (Cambridge, Mass., 1964), 116–17. According to Beaumont, 'Britain might still, through Ireland, be concretely fitted into the world-wide democratic movement.'
38. Gustave de Beaumont, *Ireland: Social, Political and Religious* 2 vols. (London, 1839), I: 316. On Tocqueville, see *Journeys to England and Ireland*, ed. and trans. J.P. Mayer (London, 1958) and *Alexis de Tocqueville's Journey in Ireland*, ed. and trans. Emmet Larkin (Dublin, 1990)
39. *Tocqueville's Journey in Ireland*, 83
40. See Beaumont, Ireland, I: 276–83; II: 55, 312–13; Larkin's Introduction to *Tocqueville's Journey in Ireland*, 7–12. The commentary on Orange provocation is extensive; see, for instance, John O'Driscol, *Views of Ireland, Moral, Political and Religious* 2 vols. (London, 1823), II: 127–35; John Gamble, *Sketches of History, Politics and Manners, in Dublin, and the North of Ireland in 1810* (London, 1826), 269–71; Francis Plowden, *An Historical Disquisition Concerning the Rise, Progress, Nature and Effects of the Orange Societies in Ireland* (Dublin, 1810).
41. *DA* I, Ch. XVII, 300–01
42. See Saree Makdisi, *Romantic Imperialism: Universal Empire and the Culture of Modernity* (Cambridge, 1998), 100–06; Immanuel Wallerstein, *After Liberalism* (New York, 1995), 93–102
43. Tzvetan Todorov, *On Human Diversity: Nationalism, Racism, and Exoticism in French Thought*, trans. Catherine Porter (Cambridge, Mass., and London, 1993), 198–201
44. See Todorov, *On Human Diversity*, 191–206. Soldiers under Bugeaud's command killed all the occupants of a house in the Rue Transnonian on 15 April 1834, in the course of quelling a republican insurrection in the Marais district of Paris. Honoré Daumier commemorated the event in a lithograph. See also Walter Benjamin, *The Arcades Project*, trans. Howard Eilkand and Kevin McLaughlin (Cambridge, Mass., and London, 1999), 699–700, 717. Lamoricière, a relative of Tocqueville, makes an unflattering appearance in the *Recollections*, 256
45. *Writings on Empire and Slavery*, 92
46. ibid., 122
47. ibid., 70
48. ibid., 78. See also, 244, 45n.
49. ibid., 146.
50. Philip Bobbitt, *The Shield of Achilles: War, Peace, and the Course of History* (New York: 2002), 153

51. Jurgen Habermas, *The Structural Transformation of the Public Sphere: An Inquiry into a Category of Bourgeois Society*, trans. Thomas Burger and Frederick Lawrence (Cambridge, Mass., 1991), Part IV, Ch. 15, 129–40
52. See Robert J.C. Young, *Postcolonialism: An Historical Introduction* (Oxford, 2001), 88–100, 293–307. The most powerful analysis of the contradictions of the British liberal position and its relation to Burke's writings, particularly on India, is Uday Singh Mehta, *Liberalism and Empire: A Study in Nineteenth-Century British Liberal Thought* (Chicago and London,1999).

8. Freedom Betrayed

1. Cited in Gertrude Himmelfarb, 'The American Revolution in the Political Theory of Lord Acton', *Journal of Modern History* 21, 4 (December, 1949), 293–94. See F.A. Hayek, 'Individualism: True and False', in *Individualism and Economic Order* (London, 1949), 1–32.
2. See *Letters of Lord Acton to Mary Gladstone*, ed. Herbert Paul (New York and London, 1904), 92: 'That is the foreign effect of Adam Smith – French Revolution and Socialism.'
3. Mary Drew, *Acton, Gladstone and Others* (London, 1924; repr. Freeport, New York, 1968), 10
4. James Bryce, *Studies in Contemporary Biography* (London, 1903), 397
5. J.E.E.D. Acton ed. *Selected Writings of Lord Acton* 3 vols., (Indianapolis, 1985–88), I, *Essays in the History of Liberty*, 137
6. J.W. Burrow, *A Liberal Descent: Victorian Historians and the English Past* (Cambridge, 1981), 88–89, 197
7. There were two lists, the first sent to Mary Drew and published in L. March-Phillips and B. Christian (eds.) in *Some Hawarden Letters, 1878–1913, Written by Mary Drew* (London, 1917), 187–91; for the second, see Clement Shorter, 'Lord Acton's Hundred Best Books', *Pall Mall Magazine* 36, 147 (July, 1905), 3–10.
8. *SW* III (1988), *Essays in Religion, Politics, and Morality*, 'Review of Cross's *George Eliot's Life*', 484
9. *LMH*, 'Luther', 105
10. *LMH*, 'Frederic the Great', 290
11. *LMH*, 'The Counter-Reformation', 117
12. *SW*, (1986), *Essays in the Study and Writing of History*, 'German Schools of History', II: 331
13. *SW* I: 118
14. *SW* I: 47
15. *SW* III: 539
16. *SW*, 'The American Revolution', I: 194
17. *SW* I: 271
18. *SW* I: 7

19. *SW* I: 22
20. *SW* I: 428
21. *LMH*, 'Beginning of the Modern State', 51
22. *SW* I: 449
23. Quentin Skinner, 'Meaning and Understanding in the History of Ideas', *History and Theory* 8 (1969), 3–53; revised version in *Visions of Politics Volume I; Regarding Method* (Cambridge, 2002), 57–89 (85)
24. Hugh A. MacDougall, *The Acton–Newman Relations: The Dilemma of Christian Liberalism* (New York, 1962), 154–85
25. J.E.E.D. Acton, *Historical Essays and Studies*, eds. J.N. Figgis and R.V. Laurence (London, 1907), 'A History of the French Revolution', 494–95
26. Acton, *Letters to Mary Gladstone*, 57
27. ibid., 60–61
28. *SW* III: 463
29. Thomas Moore, *Memoirs of the Life of the Right Honourable Richard Brinsley Sheridan* (London, 1825), 453–54. See also Acton's note: 'Keep Burke in two – Burke as a Liberal – Burke as a continuist', cited in G.E. Fasnacht, *Acton's Political Philosophy* (London, 1952), 63.
30. Himmelfarb, 'American Revolution in the Political Theory of Lord Acton', 293–312
31. *SW*, 'The History of Freedom in Christianity', I: 50. 'From the elements of that crisis Burke built up the noblest political philosophy in the world.'
32. *LFR*, 'The Influence of America', 31
33. *SW* I: 137
34. *SW* I: 140
35. Acton, *Letters to Mary Gladstone* 49. The famous lines on Burke in Goldsmith's poem 'Retaliation' (1774, are: 'Who, born for the Universe, narrow'd his mind, /And to party gave up, what was meant for mankind.'
36. ibid., 56–57
37. See the selections from the Add. MSS printed in *SW* III: 539–41, in which, for instance, he further distinguishes party and principle: . . . 'party is above country, as principles are above interests'.
38. *LMH,* 'The Hanoverian Settlement' 276.
39. G.P. Gooch, *History and Historians in the Nineteenth Century*, (rev. ed. Boston, 1959), 364
40. *LFR*, 204
41. *LFR*, 76
42. *SW*, 'The History of Freedom in Christianity', I: 51
43. *LFR*, 'The Fourth of August', 97: 'France might be transformed after the likeness of England; but the very essence of the English system was liberty founded on inequality. The essence of the French ideal was democracy, that is, as in America, liberty founded on equality.'

44. *LFR*, 48: 'By arresting the preponderance of France, the Revolution of 1688 struck the first real blow at Continental despotism . . . But it neither introduced nor determined any important principle.'
45. Acton, *Essays on Church and State*, ed. Douglas Woodruff (London, 1952), 404 (Review of J.G. Philmore's *History of England during the Reign of George III*)
46. *SW*, 'Review of Bryce's *American Commonwealth*', I: 399
47. *LFR*, 47: 'The greatest writers of the Whig party, Burke and Macaulay, constantly represented the statesmen of the Revolution as the legitimate ancestors of modern liberty. It is humiliating to trace a political lineage to Algernon Sidney . . . Lord Russell, Shaftesbury. . . Halifax . . . Marlborough, Locke, whose notion of liberty involves nothing more spiritual than the security of property, and is consistent with slavery and persecution; or even to Addison . . .'
48. Acton, *Historical Essays and Studies* 'A History of the French Revolution', 492
49. Add. 4967.74
50. Add. 4967.80
51. See Add. 4967.81: 'Never thinks out his thoughts. Want of moral courage. Secret of his wife's religion. St. Omer's. Adventurers about him. Never quite independent. When his opportunity came . . . he lost it. Irishman. Hence so vague about America. Half tones. No such thing as political science.' Other notes on Burke's Catholic attachments are to be found in Add. 4967.14, 16, 19.
52. *LFR*, 'Appendix', 358–59
53. *SW*, 'Sir Erskine May's Democracy in Europe', I: 74
54. *The Correspondence of Lord Acton and Richard Simpson* 3 vols., J. Altholtz, D. McElrath and J.C. Holland (eds.) (Cambridge, 1971–75), I, 6–7; see R.L. Schuettinger, *Lord Acton: Historian of Liberty* (La Salle, Illinois, 1976), 77–80
55. See David Mathew, *Acton: The Formative Years* (London, 1946), 99–105
56. *SW*, 'The Study of History', II: 507
57. *SW* I: 97
58. Cf. Add. 4967.101,102: 'Burke's principles. Defence of prejudice. This is the definition of dishonesty, [and] Burke's fondness for prejudice – That is, unavoidably, a fondness for untruth – The Question of sincerity thereby fails.'
59. See Peter Iver Kaufman, '"Unnatural" Sympathies? Acton and Döllinger on the Reformation', *Catholic Historical Review* 70 (1984), 547–59
60. See the review of Macknight's life of Bolingbroke in *Home and Foreign Review* 2, 4 (April 1863), 634–37
61. See Lionel Kochan, *Acton on History* (London, 1954), esp. 77–97
62. *SW* I: 74. For an acute discussion of Acton's view of the importance of the Quakers and the Pennsylvania constitution, see John Nurser, *The*

Reign of Conscience: Individual, Church, and State in Lord Acton's History of Liberty (New York and London, 1987), 84–90
63. *LFR*, 'The Fourth of August', 97
64. *LFR*, 'The Influence of America', 27
65. *LFR*, 'The Fourth of August', 97
66. *Home and Foreign Review* 2, 4 (April, 1863), 635
67. See *SW*, 'Report on Current Events, July 1860', I: 496–97, 'The Civil War in America: Its Place in History', I: 263–79
68. *SW* I: 274
69. *SW*, 'Review of Blankenburg's *Die innern Kämpfe der nordamerikanischen Union*', I: 372–33
70. *SW* I: 266–67
71. *SW* I: 363
72. *SW*, 'Sir Erskine May's *Democracy in Europe*', I: 72
73. *SW* I: 270–71. As conclusion to the debate between Jefferson and Hamilton, Acton says 'Absolute power and restrictions on its exercise cannot exist together' and 'We understand liberty to consist in exemption from control. In America it has come to mean the right to exercise control.'
74. *SW*, 'Cavour', I: 442–43: 'The theory of liberty insists on the independence of the Church; the theory of liberalism insists on the omnipotence of the State as the organ of the popular will.'
75. *SW* I: 399
76. Add. 4967.76. For a markedly similar opinion, see Leslie Stephen, *English Literature and Society in the Eighteenth Century* (London, 1920), 198.
77. *SW*, 'Review of Flint's *Historical Philosophy*', II: 501
78. Cf. *SW*, 'History of Freedom in Christianity', I: 51, where Acton claims that for forty years socialism 'has been associated with envy and hatred and bloodshed, and is now the most dangerous enemy lurking in our path'.
79. *SW*, 'The Civil War in America', I: 278
80. *SW* I: 427–28. See Gertrude Himmelfarb, *Lord Acton: A Study in Conscience and Politics* (London, 1952), 183; Hugh Tulloch, 'Lord Acton and German Historiography' in B. Stuchtey and P. Wende (eds.), *British and German Historiography 1750–1950: Traditions, Perceptions and Transfers* (Oxford, 2000), 162–72
81. *SW* I: 426
82. *The Rambler*, new series, 2 (March, 1860), review of *Lectures on Ancient and Modern History* by James Burton Robertson, 397
83. Acton, *Essays on Church and State*, 456–57
84. *SW*, 'Nationality', I: 413
85. *SW*, 'The American Revolution', I: 190
86. Paul Smith, 'Historian in the Seat of God', *London Review of Books* (10 June 1999), 29–30

87. See the essay 'Bureaucracy', possibly part-written by Acton and by his colleague Richard Simpson, *SW* I: 518–30, with its closing footnote on Burke as the opponent of the bureaucratic vision of the state in England.
88. See Roland Hill, *Lord Acton* (New Haven and London, 2000), 82–5, 348–50; Owen Chadwick, *Acton and History* (Cambridge, 1998), 139–85
89. See the political programme he presented in the *Chronicle* (15 February 1868), 147–48
90. *Chronicle* (4 January 1868), cited in Guy A. Ryan OFM, 'The Acton Circle 1864–1871: *The Chronicle* and *The North British Review*' (Unpublished Ph.D. thesis, Notre Dame, 1969), 96
91. Ryan, 'The Acton Circle', 87
92. *The Rambler* 'Irish Education', new series 3 (September 1860), 418–19
93. *LMH*, 'Henry IV and Richelieu', 171
94. *SW* III: 611
95. Cited in *SW* III: 585 from V. Conzemius (ed.), *Döllinger, Johann Ignaz von,* Briefwechsel 3 vols. (Munich, 1963–71), III: 356–58
96. See his caustic review of Sylvester Malone's *Church History of Ireland* in *Home and Foreign Review* 4, 8 (April, 1864), 712
97. *SW* II: 77–78, 84
98. *SW* II: 86; for the essay, see 98–131
99. See *Lord Acton: The Decisive Decade 1864–1874: Essays and Documents*, eds. Damian McElrath et al. (Louvain, 1970), 44
100. *SW*, 'Ultramontanism' (written in collaboration with Richard Simpson), III: 176
101. *SW* III: 171
102. See *Lord Acton: The Decisive Decade*, 9–12, 20–35
103. 'Letters to the Editor of the *Times*' (8 November–9 December 1874), *SW* III: 363–84
104. John Henry Newman, *A Letter Addressed to His Grace the Duke of Norfolk on Occasion of Mr. Gladstone's Recent Expostulation* (London, 1875), 15, 20, 58, 106
105. *SW* I: 183
106. *SW* I: 182
107. Excerpt from *The Rambler* (1862), in *Essays on Church and State*, 457–8
108. *SW* I: 178
109. *SW*, 'The Count de Montalembert', III: 15–16
110. As in Marx's 1853 essay 'The British Rule in India' in Karl Marx and Friedrich Engels, *On Colonialism* (London, 1976), 41: '. . . whatever may have been the crimes of England she was the unconscious tool of history in bringing about that revolution'.
111. Marx and Engels, *On Colonialism*, 130–213
112. Schuettinger, *Lord Acton: Historian of Liberty*, ix
113. See H.C.G. Matthew, *The Liberal Imperialists: The Ideas and Politics of a Post-Gladstonian Élite* (Oxford, 1973), 150–51

114. See Uday Singh Mehta, *Liberalism and Empire: A Study in Nineteenth-Century British Liberal Thought* (Chicago and London, 1999), 180–96
115. Frederick G. Whelan, *Edmund Burke and India: Political Morality and Empire* (Pittsburgh, 1996), 309
116. Bury's own idea of progress owed a great deal to the theory of evolution and to his awareness of Acton's idea of freedom. See Harold Temperley (ed.), *Selected Essays of J.B. Bury* (Cambridge, 1930). x and 58
117. *SW*, 'Buckle's Philosophy of History', III: 443–59
118. *SW*, 'The Catholic Academy', I: 61–63; 'The classical revival was the conquest of an unknown world. The mediaeval revival is a pilgrimage to the homes of our fathers . . .'
119. *SW*, 'Introduction to Burd's Edition of *Il Principe* by Machiavelli', II: 484–85
120. *Chronicle* 2 (11 January 1868), 31–32
121. *SW*, Add. MSS. 4954, III: 582

9. Newman

1. On Gibbon and Newman, see Brian Young, 'Gibbon, Newman and the religious accuracy of the historian' in David Waverley ed., *Edward Gibson: centenary essays* (Oxford, 1997), 309–30. See also J.G.A. Pocock, *Barbarism and Religion* 2 vols. (Cambridge, 1999)
2. Lytton Strachey, *Eminent Victorians* (London, 1986), 23
3. Patrick J. Corish, 'Gallicanism at Maynooth: Archbishop Cullen and the royal visitation of 1853', in Art Cosgrove and Donal McCartney (eds.), *Studies in Irish History presented to R. Dudley Edwards* (Dublin, 1979), 176–89; Dermot S. Roantree, 'William Monsell M.P. and the Catholic Question in Victorian Britain and Ireland' (Unpublished Ph.D. thesis, University College Dublin, 1990), 154–66; see also Newman's retrospective account, written in 1870–73, of his disagreements with Cullen, especially on the employment as professors of men who had been Young Irelanders: 'Memorandum about My Connection with the Catholic University', in *John Henry Newman: Autobiographical Writings* ed. Henry Tristram (London and New York, 1956), 326–30.
4. John Henry Newman, *Apologia pro Vita Sua: Being a History of His Religious Opinions*, ed. Martin J. Svaglic (Oxford, 1967), 117: 'I had an unspeakable aversion to the policy and acts of Mr. O'Connell, because, as I thought, he associated himself with men of all religions and no religions against the Anglican Church, and advanced Catholicism by violence and intrigue.'
5. *The Catholic University Gazette,* no. 36, (1 February 1855), 321–22. See Fergal McGrath, *Newman's University: Idea and Reality* (Dublin, 1951), 333–34. Many of the *Gazette*'s accounts of the early developments were republished in Newman's *My Campaign in Ireland* (Aberdeen, 1896).

6. See McGrath, *Newman's University*, 319; Thomas Wall, 'Catholic Periodicals of the Past. The Catholic University Gazette', *Irish Ecclesiastical Record*, fifth series, 102 (1964), 206–23
7. Excerpts were reprinted in Newman's *My Campaign in Ireland*; other excerpts can be found in Donal McCartney and Thomas O'Loughlin (eds.), *Cardinal Newman: The Catholic University. A University College Dublin Commemorative Volume. A Selection from Newman's Dublin Writings* (Dublin, 1990). See Vincent Ferrer Blehl SJ, *John Henry Newman, Bibliographical Catalogue of His Writings* (Charlottesville, 1978). See also *The Works of Cardinal Newman: Birmingham Oratory Millennium Edition,* Volume III, *Rise and Progress of Universities and Benedictine Essays*, ed. Mary Katherine Tillman (Leominster and Notre Dame, 2001).
8. Ireland's unique position as an English-speaking and predominantly Catholic country was much noticed in the nineteenth century; scarcely any comment was made on the links between Catholicism and the Irish language. See James Godkin, *The Religious History of Ireland* (London, 1873), quoting Macaulay, 199: 'It is a most significant circumstance that no large society of which the tongue is not Teutonic has ever turned Protestant, and that wherever a language derived from that of ancient Rome is spoken, the religion of modern Rome prevails.'
9. *Gazette* no. 18, (28 September 1854), 141–42: 'On the Lesson to be Gained from the aforesaid Characteristic of the Popes', retitled 'Moral of that Characteristic of the Popes: Pius IX', in *Rise and Progress*, Tillman (ed.), and *Historical Sketches* 3 vols. (London, 1856, 1872–73, repr. 1913), III: 147–48
10. *Gazette* no. 2 (8 June 1854), 10. Later titled 'What is a University?' in *Rise and Progress*, Tillman (ed.), 6
11. *Gazette* no. 3, (15 June 1854), 23–24; reprinted as 'Site of a University', in *Rise and Progress*, Tillman (ed.), and *Historical Sketches* 3 vols. (London, 1856, 1872–73, repr. 1913), III: 31–32,
12. *Historical Sketches*: 71–72; *Rise and Progress*, Tillman (ed.) 74. Newman did, of course, see the new University's foundation as an opportunity to renew the battle he had been engaged in at Oxford in the 1830s. See *Letters and Diaries* XIV: 389–90: 'Curious it will be if Oxford is imported into Ireland, not in its members only, but in its principles, methods, ways, and arguments. The battle there will be what it was in Oxford 20 years ago. Curious too . . . that while I found my tools breaking under me in Oxford, for Protestantism is not so susceptible of so high a temper, I am renewing the struggle in Dublin, with the Catholic Church to support me. It is very wonderful – Keble, Pusey, Maurice, Sewell, etc. who have been able to do so little against Liberalism in Oxford, will be renewing the fight, alas, not in their persons, in Ireland.'
13. *Gazette* no. 16 (September 1854), 'The Isles of the North', 126; *Rise and Progress*, Tillman (ed.) 128; *Historical Sketches* III: 128–29

14. *Rise and Progress*, Tillman (ed.); *Historical Sketches* III: 129
15. See the conversation on England's loss of 'the dogmatic structure' and the English lack of the gift of faith, between Charles Reding and the Roman Catholic priest on the train journey from Oxford to London in *Loss and Gain*, Part III, Ch.VI (London, 1919), 383, 385.
16. A. Dwight Culler, *The Imperial Intellect: A Study of Newman's Educational Ideal* (New Haven and London, 1955), 258–59
17. *Gazette* no. 43 (3 May 1855), 436; see *Idea of a University,* Discourse VI. 'Knowledge Viewed in Relation to Learning', Section 9, 128–29. It is in this light that he states his preference for the Oxford of sixty years before, with no teaching, no examinations, merely the bringing of young men together for three to four years, over a place with exams but no residence or tutorials. Even with 'a heathen code of ethics', Oxford can boast of a succession of great men, 'who have made England what it is, – able to subdue the earth, able to domineer over Catholics'.
18. See Biancamaria Fontana, *Rethinking the Politics of Commercial Society: The* Edinburgh Review *1802–1832* (Cambridge, 1985); Thomas A. Boylan and Timothy P. Foley, *Political Economy and Colonial Ireland: The Propagation and Ideological Function of Economic Discourse in the Nineteenth Century* (London and New York, 1992)
19. See Norman Vance, 'Improving Ireland: Richard Whately, Theology and Political Economy' in Stefan Collini, Richard Whatmore and Brian Young (eds.), *Economy, Polity, and Society: British Intellectual History 1750–1950* (Cambridge, 2000), 181–202
20. Wilfrid Ward, *The Life of John Henry Cardinal Newman, based on His Private Journals and Correspondence* 2 vols. (London, 1912), I: 306
21. *Gazette* no. 27 (30 November 1854), 'Colleges the Correction of the Deficiencies of the University Principle', 214; *Rise and Progress*, Tillman (ed.); *Historical Sketches* III: 222
22. *Gazette* no. 23 (2 November 1854), 181; *Rise and Progress*, Tillman (ed.); *Historical Sketches* III, 204–05
23. *Gazette* no. 23, 184; *Rise and Progress*, Tillman (ed.); *Historical Sketches* III, 212. In the later version, Newman adds to this the concluding sentence, 'Nor does the Holy See simply lend an ear to the project of others: it originates the undertaking.' In the *Gazette* no. 24 (9 November 1854), 191, Newman also remarks that the new foundations at Louvain, Quebec and the Seminario Pio in Rome, as well as Dublin, 'seem to suggest to us that a change of policy is in progress at Rome on the subject of methods of education. We are not then concerned in an isolated, experimental, or accidental attempt, but sharing in a great movement, which has the tokens of success in its deliberateness and extent.'
24. *Gazette* no. 29 (14 December 1854), 'Abuses of the Collegiate System', 228: *Rise and Progress*, Tillman (ed.); *Historical Sketches* III: 229

25. The contrary view is standard. See, for instance, Bill Readings, *The University in Ruins* (Cambridge, Mass., 1996), 74. For a more challenging account, see Thomas Docherty, *Criticism and Modernity: Aesthetics, Literature, and Nations in Europe and its Academies* (Oxford, 1999), 214–22; 'Newman, Ireland and Universality', *boundary* 2 (Spring, 2004), 73–92.
26. For instance the *Gazette* records the destinations of missionary priests from All Hallows, in no. 35 (25 January 1855), 308–09. One of Newman's closest supporters, Dr David Moriarty, had been Head of All Hallows until 1854, when he was made Coadjutor Bishop of Kerry. He was the celebrant of the High Mass on 4 June 1854, at the inauguration of the Catholic University, at which Newman took the oaths of the office of Rector. The *Gazette* no. 3 (15 June 1854), 17, records this. See McGrath, *Newman's University*, 153, 314.
27. See *Gazette* no. 1 (1 June 1854), 1: 'The principal object of the Meeting was that of taking steps immediately necessary for the establishment and commencement of the new Catholic University. For that purpose, following the pattern of the Belgian Bishops twenty years ago, in the erection of the University of Louvain, their lordships, after recording their past nomination, made by means of the University Committee, and already confirmed by his Holiness, of the Very Rev Dr Newman, Priest of the Oratory of St. Philip Neri, to the office of Rector, proceeded to commit to him the execution of the great work which it will be, in years to come, the glory of their Lordships' time to have designed: that is, under their control and with their sanction, and with an annual meeting to receive and to consider the Rector's report.' In the *Gazette* no. 32 (4 January 1855), 251–52, the editor announced an enlargement in the scope of its coverage of university education and, specifically of Catholic University education, once more identifying Louvain as its example: 'We hope in particular to draw frequent attention to the progress and development of the University of Louvain, which was pointed out in so marked a manner by the Holy Father for our imitation, when in his wisdom he first suggested the idea of the Catholic University of Ireland.' Louvain, an ancient university foundation, was restored as a Catholic university in 1835.
28. See the *Gazette* no. 35 (25 January 1855), 309–10 and no. 36 (1 February 1855), 325–28, for the reprinting of the Apostolic Letters on the foundation of the new seminary.
29. *Gazette* no. 39, (22 February 1855), 362. The address is reprinted in the column written by Newman.
30. *Gazette* no. 3 (15 June 1854), 18
31. *Gazette* no. 39, 362
32. See John Milner, *An Inquiry into Certain Vulgar Opinions Concerning the Catholic Inhabitants and the Antiquities of Ireland in a series of Letters from*

thence, addressed to a Protestant Gentleman in England (London, 1808), 3–7, 112–26. Richard Simpson, 'Milner and His Times', *Home and Foreign Review* 2 (April 1863), 531–57.

34. 'Fall of De la Mennais' in Newman, *Essays Critical and Historical* (London, 1871), 140
34. ibid., 154–60
35. Thomas Wyse, *Historical Sketch of the late Catholic Association of Ireland* 2 vols. (London, 1829), I: 247–57. The most renowned and detailed of the French accounts of the Catholic political reawakening and the system of Protestant injustice is Gustave de Beaumont, *Ireland: Social, Political and Religious* 2 vols. (London, 1839).
36. *L'Avenir* nos. 77–79 (1–3 January 1831). See Part II; see also Part III, in his final address to the priests and laity of France respectively, where Montalembert claims that 'Liberté et pauvreté' are the basis of Irish and of Catholic Christianity and power; and that Irish Catholicism has been moulded and maintained by two forces that France also will come to know: 'd'un coté la persécution, et de l'autre la foi' (on the one hand, persecution, and on the other, faith).
37. Comte de Montalembert, *Catholic Interests in the Nineteenth Century* (London, 1852), 22. O'Connell's version is different. See his *A Memoir on Ireland Native and Saxon* (Dublin, 1843), 33: 'WELLINGTON and PEEL – blessed be heaven – we defeated you. Our peaceable combination, bloodless, unstained, crimeless, was too strong for the military glory – bah! of the one, and for all the little arts, the debasing chicanery, the plausible delusions, of the other. Both at length conceded, but without dignity, without generosity, without candour, without sincerity. Nay, there was a littleness in the concession almost incredible, were it not part of public history. They emancipated a people, and by the same act they proscribed an individual. PEEL and WELLINGTON, we defeated and drove you before us into coerced liberality, and you left every remnant of character behind you, as the spoil of the victors.'
38. O'Connell, *A Memoir*, 22–23
39. Newman, *Apologia pro Vita Sua*, 254
40. See 'Fall of De la Mennais', 158–59; 'Here again is a clear connexion between his [Lammenais's] theology and the popular philosophy of the day. He is a believer in the gradual and constant advance of the species, on the whole, in knowledge and virtue, and here he does but faithfully represent the feeling, nay, the teaching of his own Church. They who look at Antiquity as supplying the rule of faith, do not believe in the possibility of any substantial increase of religious knowledge; but the Romanist believes in a standing organ of Revelation, like the series of Jewish prophets, unfolding from time to time fresh and fresh truths from the abyss of the divine counsels.'

41. Newman, *An Essay in Aid of a Grammar of Assent* (London, 1917), Part II, Ch.VI, 175–77
42. Newman, *Essays Critical and Historical*, 347
43. ibid., *Essays*, 348, 349, 350
44. George Moore, *A Letter to M. le Comte de Montalembert, on his late review of the Government of England* (Dublin, 1859), 15. See also Lord Acton, 'The Count de Montalembert' (1858) in *Selected Writings of Lord Acton*, 3 vols., ed. J. Rufus Fears (Indianapolis, 1988), III: 9–16, in which Acton objects to Montalembert (in his book *De l'Angleterre* [Paris, 1854]) 'recommending the forms of our government to a nation [France] incapable of its spirit . . .' (12)
45. Newman, *An Essay on the Development of Christian Doctrine* (London, 1920), Ch. II, Section II, 91
46. Newman's identification of liberalism and Protestant evangelicalism is harshly represented in Frank M. Turner, *John Henry Newman: The Challenge to Evangelical Religion* (New Haven and London, 2002).
47. In Newman, *Essays Critical and Historical* I: 102–37
48. See, for example, Newman, *Grammar of Assent*, Ch. VII, 'Certitude', 210–58
49. See Newman, *Apologia pro Vita Sua,* Introduction, xx–xxxvii
50. Christopher Dawson, *The Spirit of the Oxford Movement* (1933; London, 1945), 9
51. This was the burden of Newman's sermon, 'Intellect, the Instrument of Religious Training' at the opening of University Church on Stephen's Green on 1 May, 1856. See McCartney and O'Loughlin (eds.), *Cardinal Newman: The Catholic University*, 101–08
52. See Newman's references to Gothic fiction in *Lectures on the Present Position of Catholics in England* (London, 1918), Lecture III, 'Fable the Basis of the Protestant View', 93–96, 120–42; and for the extended references to Blanco White and Maria Monck, Lecture IV, 'True Testimony Insufficient for the Protestant View', 142–74. See also Victor Sage, *Horror Fiction in the Protestant Tradition* (London, 1988), 26–41.
53. The trial began on 24 June, 1852; the last *Discourse* to be delivered was on 7 June.
54. On the whole question of conversion, see Gauri Viswanathan, *Outside the Fold: Conversion, Modernity, and Belief* (Princeton, 1998), esp. 44–72.
55. 'Memorandum about My Connection with the Catholic University', in *Autobiographical Writings*, 329–30: '. . . English Catholics felt no interest in the University scheme . . . I had gone to Ireland on the express understanding that it was an English as well as an Irish University and nothing else. And . . . the English Catholics had given it up.'
56. Newman, *Callista: A Tale of the Third Century* (London, 1914), Ch. VII, 75
57. Newman, *Essay on the Development of Christian Doctrine*, Introduction, 5

58. ibid., 7
59. Newman, *Present Position of Catholics in England*, Lecture II, 46
60. ibid., 48–49
61. ibid., 56–57
62. See Newman, *Grammar of Assent*, 302–03, on the English prejudice against logic and the association of it with pedantry.
63. ibid., 62
64. ibid., 55
65. W.E. Gladstone, *The Vatican Decrees in Their Bearing on Civil Allegiance: A Political Expostulation* (London, 1874), 12, Propositions 3 and 4: 'That no one can become [Rome's] convert without renouncing his moral and mental freedom, and placing his civil loyalty and duty at the mercy of another. That she [Rome] has equally repudiated modern thought and ancient history.'
66. Newman, *A Letter Addressed to His Grace the Duke of Norfolk on the Occasion of Mr. Gladstone's Recent Expostulation* (London, 1875), 66: '. . . I shall drink . . . to Conscience first, and to the Pope afterwards.'
67. See James D. Bastable (ed.), *Newman and Gladstone: Centennial Essays* (Dublin,1978); Gertrude Himmelfarb, *Lord Acton: A Study in Conscience and Politics* (London, 1952; repr. Chicago, 1962), 155–58; Owen Chadwick, *Acton and History* (Cambridge, 1998), 115–203. Although Acton's letters of 1874 to *The Times* newspaper on the Declaration of Infallibility were more scandalous to Catholics in their tone, they fundamentally agreed with Newman's position that it made no difference to the loyalty of Catholics as British subjects. 'Letters to the Editor of the *Times*' in *SW* III: 363–84. See also Carl Schmitt's discussion of state sovereignty and the challenges to it from trade unions or the Catholic Church, in which the Gladstone and Newman debate is acknowledged, *The Concept of the Political*, trans. George Schwab (Chicago, 1996), 43n.
68. J.E.E.D. Acton, 'George Eliot's Life', *Historical Essays and Studies*, eds. J.N. Figgis and R.V. Laurence (London, 1907), 283, 303
69. Newman, *Idea of a University*, Discourse VIII, Section 10, 185–87; see also the list of the qualities of a gentleman in the *Gazette* no. 2 (June, 1854), 11
70. 'Culture and Anarchy' in *The Complete Prose Works of Matthew Arnold* 11 vols., ed. R.H. Super (Ann Arbor, 1960–77), V: 106–07. See also 'Irish Catholicism and British Liberalism' (1878)VIII: 321–47; his 1879 letter to *The Times*, 'The Irish University Question' IX: 56–60; 'An Unregarded Irish Grievance' (1881), IX: 295–311.
71. 'Higher Schools and Universities in Germany: Preface to the Second Edition', in Arnold, *Complete Prose Works* VII: p. 113
72. 'Christianity and Letters' first appeared under the title 'On the Place held by the Faculty of Arts in the University Course', *Gazette* no. 25, (16 November 1854), 193–200; 'English Catholic Literature' under the title

'On the Formation of a Catholic Literature in the English Tongue' in no. 14 (31 August 1854), 105–09 and again in no. 15 (7 September 1854), 112–19. Lists of books, advertising 'Catholic Literature in the English Tongue' were published in the first 32 numbers of the *Gazette*.

73. 'A Catholic Literature for Ireland' (February 1847), W.J. McCormack ed., 'The Intellectual Revival (1830–50)' in Seamus Deane et al. (eds), *The Field Day Anthology of Irish Literature* 3 vols. (Derry, 1991), I: 1292–97. Duffy was the joint-publisher (with Burns and Lambert of London) of the *Gazette*; the 'Standard Catholic Works' advertised there were sold by him from his shop in Wellington Quay and he published a very high percentage of books recommended in the *Gazette's* lists of items towards a Catholic literature.
74. Cf. the opening of the *Gazette* essay with that in *The Idea of a University*: 'One of the special objects, which the Irish University will subserve, is that of the formation of a Catholic Literature in the English language'; 'One of the special objects which a Catholic University would promote is . . .' See also *The Idea of a University,* 'English Catholic Literature', Part 3, 'In Its Relation to Classical Literature', 267.
75. See John Coulson, *Religion and Imagination, 'in Aid of a Grammar of Assent'* (Oxford, 1981), 3–45
76. Newman, *Idea of a University*, 'Literature', Section 9, 255
77. Arnold, 'Literature and Dogma', in *Complete Prose Works* VI: 411
78. Arnold, 'St. Paul and Protestantism', in *Complete Prose Works* VI: 17–20, 25–27
79. See Michael Tierney (ed.), *Struggle with Fortune: A Miscellany for the Centenary of the Catholic University of Ireland* (Dublin, 1954)
80. On Darlington, see *A Page of Irish History: The Story of University College, Dublin 1883–1909*, compiled by Fathers of the Society of Jesus (Dublin, 1930), 67–126

BIBLIOGRAPHY

Acton, J.E.E.D., *Letters of Lord Acton to Mary Gladstone*, ed. Herbert Paul (New York and London, 1904)

——. *Lectures on Modern History*, eds. J.N. Figgis and R.V. Laurence (London, 1906; repr. 1930)

——. *Historical Essays and Studies*, eds. J.N. Figgis and R.V. Laurence (London, 1907)

——. *Lectures on the French Revolution*, eds. J.N. Figgis and R.V. Laurence (London, 1910)

——. *Essays on Church and State*, ed. Douglas Woodruff (London, 1952)

——. *Lord Acton: The Decisive Decade 1864–1874: Essays and Documents*, eds. Damian McElrath et al. (Louvain, 1970)

——. *The Correspondence of Lord Acton and Richard Simpson*, 3 vols., eds. J. Altholtz, D. McElrath and J.C. Holland (Cambridge, 1971–75)

——. *Selected Writings of Lord Acton*, 3 vols., ed. J. Rufus Fears (Indianapolis, 1985–88)

Acton: Uncollected Reviews and Notices Cited

The Rambler, new series, 2 (March, 1860), 397

Home and Foreign Review 2, 4 (April, 1863), 634–37

Home and Foreign Review 4, 8, (April, 1864), 712

Chronicle (4 January 1868), 96

Chronicle (11 January 1868), 31–32

Chronicle, (15 February, 1868), 147–48

Acton MSS in Cambridge University Library

Add. 4967.81 Add. 4967.14, 16, 19. 74, 80, 81, 101, 102

Adams, John Quincy, ('Agricola'), *Observations on Paine's 'Rights of Man'* (Edinburgh, 1792)

Adolphus, John, *Biographical Memoirs of the French Revolution* 4 vols. (London, 1799)

——. *The History of France from 1790 till the Peace of 1802* (London, 1803)

Althusser, Louis, *Politics and History: Montesquieu, Rousseau, Hegel and Marx*, trans. B. Brewster (London, 1972)

Andrews, Stuart, *The British Periodical Press and the French Revolution, 1789–99* (Basingstoke and New York, 2000)

Arnold, Matthew, *Edmund Burke on Irish Affairs* (London, 1881)

——. *The Complete Prose Works of Matthew Arnold*, 11 vols. ed. R.H. Super (Ann Arbor, 1960–77)

Aron, Raymond, *Main Currents in Sociological Thought* 2 vols., trans. Richard Howard and Helen Weaver (London, 1965)

Babbitt, Irving, *Rousseau and Romanticism* (1919; repr. Cleveland and New York, 1955)

Baker, Keith Michael, *Interpreting the French Revolution* (Cambridge, 1990)
Baldensperger, Fernand, *Le Mouvement des ideés dans l'émigration française (1789–1815)* 2 vols. (Paris, 1925)
Barrell, John, *English Literature in History 1730–80: An Equal, Wide Survey* (London, 1983)
——. *Imagining the King's Death: Figurative Treason, Fantasies of Regicide 1793–1796* (Oxford, 2000)
Barruel, Abbé, *Memoirs of Jacobinism* 4 vols., trans. J. Clifford (London, 1797)
Bartlett, Tom, *The Fall and Rise of the Irish Nation* (Dublin, 1992)
Bastable, James D. (ed.), *Newman and Gladstone: Centennial Essays* (Dublin, 1978)
Beaumont, Gustave de, *Ireland: Social, Political and Religious* 2 vols. (London, 1839)
Ben-Israel, Hedva, *English Historians of the French Revolution* (Cambridge, 1968)
Benjamin, Walter, *The Arcades Project*, trans. Howard Eilkand and Kevin McLaughlin (Cambridge, Mass., and London, 1999)
Berman, David, 'The Irish Counter-Enlightenment', in R. Kearney ed. *The Irish Mind* (Dublin, 1985), 119–40.
Bisset, R., *The History of the Reign of George III* 6 vols. (London, 1803; repr. 1820)
Blehl, Vincent Ferrer, SJ, *John Henry Newman, Bibliographical Catalogue of His Writings* (Charlottesville, 1978)
Blennerhassett, Charlotte, *Madame de Staël: Her Friends and Her Influence in Politics and Literature* 3 vols., trans. J.E. Gordon Cumming (London, 1889)
Blum, Carole, *Diderot: The Virtue of a Philosopher* (London, 1974)
Bobbitt, Philip, *The Shield of Achilles: War, Peace, and the Course of History* (New York, 2002)
Bongie, D., *David Hume, Prophet of Counter-Revolution* (Oxford, 1965)
Bonno, G., *La Constitution britannique devant l'opinion française de Montesquieu à Bonaparte* (Paris, 1932)
Boothby, Brooke, *A Letter to the Right Honourable Edmund Burke* (London, 1791)
Bourke, Richard, 'Liberty, Authority, and Trust in Burke's Idea of Empire' *Journal of the History of Ideas* 61, 3 (July 2000), 453–71
Bowles, John, *Reflections on the Political and Moral State of Society at the Close of the Eighteenth Century* (London, 1800–01)
Boylan, Thomas A., and Timothy P. Foley, *Political Economy and Colonial Ireland: The Propagation and Ideological Function of Economic Discourse in the Nineteenth Century* (London and New York, 1992)
Brogan, Hugh, *Tocqueville* (London, 1973)
Bromwich, David, *A Choice of Inheritance: Self and Community from Edmund Burke to Robert Frost* (Cambridge, Mass., and London, 1989)
Bryce, James, *Studies in Contemporary Biography* (London, 1903)
Burke, Edmund, *The Correspondence of Edmund Burke* 10 vols., eds. Thomas Copeland et al. (Cambridge and Chicago, 1958–78)
——. *The Writings and Speeches of Edmund Burke* 9 vols., gen. ed., Paul Langford (Oxford, 1981–2000)
——. I, *The Early Writings*, ed. T.O. McLaughlin and James T. Boulton (1997)
——. II, *Party, Parliament, and the American Crisis 1766–1771*, ed. Paul Langford (1981)
——. III, *Party, Parliament and the American War 1774–1780*, eds. Warren M. Elofson with John A. Woods (1996)
——. V, *India: Madras and Bengal 1774–1785*, ed. P.J. Marshall (1981)

——. VI, *India: The Launching of the Hastings Impeachment 1786–1788*, ed. P.J. Marshall (1991)
——. VII, *The Hastings Trial 1789–1794* ed. P.J. Marshall (2000)
——. VIII, *The French Revolution 1790–1794* ed. L.G. Mitchell (1989)
——. IX, 1 *The Revolutionary War 1794–1797*; 2 *Ireland*, ed. R.B. McDowell (1991)
——. *Further Reflections on the Revolution in France*, ed. Daniel Ritchie (Indianapolis, 1991)
Burrow, J.W,. *A Liberal Descent: Victorian Historians and the English Past* (Cambridge, 1981)
Campbell, Thomas, *Strictures on the Ecclesiastical and Literary History of Ireland from the Most Ancient Times* (Dublin, 1799)
Carey, Daniel, 'Swift among the Freethinkers', *Eighteenth-Century Ireland* 12 (1997), 89–99
Carlyle, Thomas, *The Works of Thomas Carlyle* 30 vols. (London, 1898)
Carpenter, Kirsty, *Refugees of the French Revolution: Émigrés in London, 1789–1802* (London, 1999)
Chadwick, Owen, *Acton and History* (Cambridge, 1998)
Chandler, James, 'Poetical Liberties: Burke's France and the "Adequate Representation" of the English' in F. Furet and M. Ozouf (eds.), *The French Revolution and the Creation of Modern Political Culture* vol. 3 *The Transformation of Political Culture 1789–1848* (Oxford and New York, 1988), 45–57
Chartier, Roger, *The Cultural Origins of the French Revolution*, trans. Lydia G. Cochrane (Durham and London, 1991)
Clifford, John, *Application of Barruel's 'Memoirs of Jacobinism' to the Secret Societies of Ireland and Great Britain* (London, 1798)
Colley, Linda, *Britons: Forging the Nation 1707–1837* (New Haven and London, 1992)
Conzemius,V. (ed.), *Döllinger, Johann Ignaz von,* Briefwechsel, 3 vols. (Munich, 1963–71)
Copeland,Thomas, *Our Eminent Friend Edmund Burke: Six Essays* (London, 1949)
Corish, Patrick J., 'Gallicanism at Maynooth: Archbishop Cullen and the Royal Visitation of 1853', in Art Cosgrove and Donal McCartney (eds.), *Studies in Irish History presented to R. Dudley Edwards* (Dublin, 1979), 176–89
Coulson, John, *Religion and Imagination, 'in Aid of a Grammar of Assent'* (Oxford, 1981)
Courtney, C.P,. *Montesquieu and Burke* (Oxford, 1963; repr. Westport, Connecticut, 1975)
Croker, John Wilson, 'French Novels', *Quarterly Review* 56, 111 (April, 1836), 66–71
Crowe, E.E., *Yesterday in Ireland* 3 vols. (London, 1829)
Cullen, Louis, 'The Blackwater Catholics and County Cork: Society and Politics in the Eighteenth Century', in Patrick O'Flanagan and Cornelius G. Buttimore (eds.), *Cork. History and Society. Interdisciplinary Essays on the History of an Irish County* (Dublin, 1993), 535–84
Culler, A. Dwight, *The Imperial Intellect: A Study of Newman's Educational Ideal* (New Haven and London, 1955)
Curran, J.P., *A New and Enlarged Collection of Speeches by the Right Honourable John Philpot Curran* (London, 1819)
Darnton, Robert, *The Forbidden Best-Sellers of Pre-Revolutionary France* (London, 1996)
Dawson, Christopher, *The Spirit of the Oxford Movement* (1933; London, 1945)
de Bolla, Peter, *The Discourse of the Sublime: Readings in History, Aesthetics and the Subject* (Oxford, 1989)

de Lolme, J.L., *The Constitution of England in which it is compared with the Republican Form of Government and occasionally with the other Monarchies in Europe* (1776; London, 1823)

Deane, Seamus, *The French Revolution and Enlightenment in England 1789–1832)* (Cambridge, Mass., 1988)

——. *Strange Country: Modernity and Nationhood in Irish Writing since 1790* (Oxford, 1997)

Dedieu, J., *Montesquieu et la tradition politique anglaise en France* (Paris, 1909)

Dickson, David, Dáire Keogh, and Kevin Whelan (eds.), *The United Irishmen: Republicanism, Radicalism, and Rebellion* (Dublin, 1993)

Diderot, Denis, *Œuvres philosophiques*, ed. P. Vernière (Paris, 1956)

Diggins, John Patrick, *Politics and the Spirit of Tragedy* (New York, 1996)

Docherty, Thomas, *Criticism and Modernity: Aesthetics, Literature, and Nations in Europe and its Academies* (Oxford, 1999)

——. 'Newman, Ireland and Universality', *boundary 2* (Spring, 2004), 73–92

Drescher, Seymour, *Tocqueville and England* (Cambridge, Mass., 1964)

Drew, Mary, *Acton, Gladstone and Others* (London, 1924; repr. Freeport, New York, 1968)

Dreyer, Frederick A., *Burke's Politics: A Study in Whig Orthodoxy* (Ontario, 1979)

du Pan, Mallet, 'Du Degré d'influence qu'a eu la philosophie française sur la révolution', *Mercure Britannique* 13 (25 February 1799), 342–70

Duddy, Thomas, *A History of Irish Thought* (London and New York, 2002)

Duffy, James, 'A Catholic Literature for Ireland' *Duffy's Irish Catholic Magazine* (February 1847), repr. in *The Field Day Anthology of Irish Writing*, Seamus Deane et al. (eds.) (Derry, 1991), II: 1292–97

Eagleton, Terry, *Heathcliff and the Great Hunger: Studies in Irish Culture* (London, 1995)

——. *Crazy John and the Bishop and Other Essays on Irish Culture* (Cork, 1998)

Fasnacht, G.E., *Acton's Political Philosophy* (London, 1952)

Fletcher, F.T.H., *Montesquieu and English Politics (1750–1800)* (London, 1939)

Fontana, Biancamaria, *Rethinking the Politics of Commercial Society: The* Edinburgh Review *1802–1832* (Cambridge, 1985)

Fuchs, Michel, *Edmund Burke, Ireland, and the Fashioning of Self* (Oxford, 1996)

Furet, François, 'Tocqueville', in François Furet and Mona Ozouf (eds.), *A Critical Dictionary of the French Revolution*, (Cambridge, Mass., and London, 1989), 1021–32

——. *Penser la révolution française* (Paris, 1978)

Furniss, Tom, *Edmund Burke's Aesthetic Ideology: Language, Gender and Political Economy in Revolution* (Cambridge, 1993)

Gamble, John, *Sketches of History, Politics and Manners, in Dublin, and the North of Ireland in 1810* (London, 1826)

Gauchet, Marcel, 'Tocqueville', in Mark Lilla (ed.), *New French Thought: Political Philosophy* (Princeton, 1994), 91–111

Gibbon, Edward, *History of the Decline and Fall of the Roman Empire*, 4 vols., ed. J.B. Bury (London, 1902)

Gibbons, Luke, *Edmund Burke and Ireland: Aesthetics, Politics and the Colonial Sublime* (Cambridge, 2003)

Gladstone, W.E., *The Vatican Decrees in Their Bearing on Civil Allegiance: A Political Expostulation* (London, 1874)

Godechot Jacques, *Les Révolutions (1770–1799)* (Paris, 1965)
Godkin, James, *The Religious History of Ireland* (London, 1873)
Goldsmith, M.M., 'Liberty, Luxury and the Pursuit of Happiness', in A. Pagden (ed.), *The Languages of Political Theory in Early Modern Europe* (Cambridge, 1987), 225–51
Gooch, G.P., *History and Historians in the Nineteenth Century*, rev. ed. (Boston, 1959)
Goodman, Dena, *The Republic of Letters: A Cultural History of the French Enlightenment* (Ithaca and London, 1994)
Greene, Jack P., 'Empire and Identity from the Glorious Revolution to the American Revolution', in P.J. Marshall (ed.), *The Oxford History of the British Empire; Volume II: The Eighteenth Century* (Oxford and New York, 1998), 208–30
Haakonssen, Knud, *Natural Law and Moral Philosophy: From Grotius to the Scottish Enlightenment* (Cambridge, 1996)
Habermas, Jurgen, *The Structural Transformation of the Public Sphere: An Inquiry into a Category of Bourgeois Society*, trans. Thomas Burger and Frederick Lawrence (Cambridge, Mass., 1991)
Hardy, Francis, *Memoirs of the Political and Private Life of James Caulfield, Earl of Charlemont* (London, 1810)
Harth, Phillip, *Swift and Anglican Rationalism* (Chicago and London, 1961)
Hayek, F.A., *Individualism and Economic Order* (London, 1949)
Hazlitt, William, *Remarks on the Systems of Hartley and Helvétius* (London, 1805)
Heine, Heinrich, *De l'Allemagne* (Paris, 1833)
Hill, Roland, *Lord Acton* (New Haven and London, 2000)
Himmelfarb, Gertrude, 'The American Revolution in the Political Theory of Lord Acton', *Journal of Modern History* 21, 4 (December, 1949), 293–94.
——. *Lord Acton: A Study in Conscience and Politics* (London, 1952; repr. Chicago, 1962)
Hirschmann, Albert O., *The Passions and the Interests: Political Arguments for Capitalism before Its Triumph* (Princeton, 1977)
Hofman, Amos, 'The Origins of the Theory of the *Philosophe* Conspiracy', *French History* 2 (1988), 152–72
Hume, David, *Enquiries Concerning the Human Understanding and Concerning the Principles of Morals*, 2nd. ed., ed. L.A. Selby-Bigge (Oxford, 1902)
Hunt, Lynn, *The Family Romance of the French Revolution* (Berkeley and Los Angeles, 1992)
——. 'The Many Bodies of Marie Antoinette: Political Pornography and the Problem of the Feminine in the French Revolution', in Lynn Hunt (ed.), *Eroticism and the Body Politic* (Baltimore and London, 1991), 108–30
Hutcheson, Francis, *An Inquiry into the Original of Our Ideas of Beauty and Virtue*, 4th. ed. (London,1738)
Jameson, Fredric, *The Ideologies of Theory: Essays 1971–1986; Volume 2: The Syntax of History* (London, 1988)
Jeffrey, Francis, *Contributions to the Edinburgh Review* (New York, 1866)
Johnston, E.M., *Ireland in the Eighteenth Century* (Dublin, 1974)
Kahan, Alan, 'Tocqueville's Two Revolutions', *Journal of the History of Ideas* 5, 46 (October, 1985), 585–96
Kaufman, Peter Iver, '"Unnatural' Sympathies? Acton and Döllinger on the Reformation', *Catholic Historical Review* 70 (1984), 547–59

Kelly, George, Armstrong, *The Humane Comedy: Constant, Tocqueville and French Liberalism* (Cambridge, 1992)

Kelly, James, 'The Genesis of Protestant Ascendancy: The Rightboy Disturbances of the 1780s', in Gerard O'Brien (ed.), *Parliament, Politics and People: Essays in Eighteenth-Century Irish History* (Dublin, 1989), 93–127

Kelly, Patrick, 'The Politics of Political Economy in Mid-Eighteenth-Century Ireland', in S.J. Connolly (ed.), *Political Ideas in Eighteenth-Century Ireland* (Dublin, 2000), 105–29

Kirk, Russell, *The Conservative Mind from Burke to Santayana* (Chicago, 1953)

Kochan, Lionel, *Acton on History* (London, 1954)

Kramnick, Isaac, *The Rage of Edmund Burke: Portrait of an Ambivalent Conservative* (New York, 1977)

Ledwich, Edward, *The Antiquities of Ireland*, 2nd. ed. (Dublin, 1804)

Lieberman, D., *The Province of Legislation Defined: Legal Theory in Eighteenth-Century Britain* (Cambridge, 1989)

Lilla, Mark (ed.), *New French Thought: Political Philosophy* (Princeton, 1994)

Livesey, James, *Making Democracy in the French Revolution* (Cambridge, Mass., 2001)

Lock, F.P., *Edmund Burke: Volume I; 1730–48* (Oxford, 1998)

Lucas, Colin, 'Edmund Burke and the Emigrés' in K.M. Baker, C. Lucas and F. Furet (eds.), *The French Revolution and the Creation of Modern Political Culture* 4 vols. (Oxford, 1987–94), III: 101–14

Lucas, John, *England and Englishness: Ideas of Nationhood in English Poetry 1688–1900* (London, 1990)

McBride Ian, 'The School of Virtue: Francis Hutcheson, Irish Presbyterians and the Scottish Enlightenment' in D.G. Boyce et al. (eds.), *Political Thought in Ireland since the Seventeenth Century* (London and New York, 1993), 73–99

McCartney, Donal, and Thomas O'Loughlin (eds.), *Cardinal Newman: The Catholic University. A University College Dublin Commemorative Volume. A Selection from Newman's Dublin Writings* (Dublin, 1990)

McCormack, W.J., *From Burke to Beckett: Ascendancy, Tradition and Betrayal in Literary History,* (Cork, 1994)

——. *The Battle of the Books: Two Decades of Irish Cultural Debate* (Gigginstown, 1986)

——. 'The Intellectual Revival (1830–50)', in Seamus Deane et al. (eds.), *The Field Day Anthology of Irish Literature* 3 vols. (Derry, 1991), I: 1292–97.

MacDougall, Hugh A., *The Acton–Newman Relations: The Dilemma of Christian Liberalism* (New York, 1962)

McGrath, Fergal, *Newman's University: Idea and Reality* (Dublin, 1951)

Macintyre, Alasdair, *Whose Justice? Which Rationality?* (London, 1988)

McKendrick, N., John Brewer, and J.H. Plumb, *The Birth of a Consumer Society: The Commercialization of Eighteenth-Century England* (London, 1982)

McLoughlin, T.O., 'Burke's Dualistic Vision in the *Tracts on the Popery Laws*', *Études Anglaises,* 34, 2 (1981), 180–91

McMahon, Darrin M., *Enemies of the Enlightenment: The French Counter-Enlightenment and the Making of Modernity* (Oxford, 2001)

Makdisi, Saree, *Romantic Imperialism: Universal Empire and the Culture of Modernity* (Cambridge, 1998)

Mandeville, Bernard, *A Modest Defense of Publick Stews* (London, 1723)

——. *The Fable of the Bees* 2 vols., ed. F.B. Kaye (Oxford, 1924)

——. *A Letter to Dion* (London, 1732)

Manent, Pierre, *Tocqueville et la nature de la démocratie* (Paris, 1982)

——. *An Intellectual History of Liberalism*, trans. Rebecca Balinski (Princeton, 1995)

——. *Modern Liberty and Its Discontents*, ed. and trans. Daniel J. Mahoney and Paul Seaton (Lanham, New York and Oxford, 1998)

March-Phillips, L., and B. Christian (eds.), *Some Hawarden Letters, 1878–1913, Written by Mary Drew* (London, 1917)

Marx, Karl, and Friedrich Engels, *On Colonialism* (London, 1976)

Mathew, David, *Acton: The Formative Years* (London, 1946)

Matthew, H.C.G., *The Liberal Imperialists: The Ideas and Politics of a Post-Gladstonian Élite* (Oxford, 1973)

Mayer, Arno J., *The Furies Violence and Terror in the French and Russian Revolutions* (Princeton, 2000)

Maza, Sara 'The Diamond Necklace Affair Revisited (1785–1786): The Case of the Missing Queen', in Lynn Hunt (ed.), *Eroticism and the Body Politic*, (Baltimore and London, 1991), 63–89

Mehta, Uday Singh, *Liberalism and Empire: A Study in Nineteenth-Century British Liberal Thought* (Chicago and London, 1999)

Meister, J.-H., *Souvenirs d'un voyage en Angleterre* (Paris, 1791)

Milner, John, *An Inquiry into Certain Vulgar Opinions Concerning the Catholic Inhabitants and the Antiquities of Ireland in a series of Letters from thence, addressed to a Protestant Gentleman in England* (London, 1808)

Montalembert, Charles, Comte de, 'Du Catholicisme en Irlande', *L'Avenir* 1–3 January 1831, 77–79

——. *Catholic Interests in the Nineteenth Century* (London, 1852)

——. *De l'Angleterre* (Paris, 1854)

Montesquieu, Charles-Louis Secondat, *Œuvres de Montesquieu* 2 vols. ed. R. Caillois (Paris, 1956–58)

Moore, George, *A Letter to M. le Comte de Montalembert, on his late review of the Government of England* (Dublin, 1859)

Moore, Thomas, *Memoirs of the Life of the Right Honourable Richard Brinsley Sheridan* (London, 1825)

Moretti, Franco, *The Way of the World: The* Bildungsroman *in European Culture* (London, 1987)

Mornet, Daniel, *Les origines intellectuelles de la révolution française* (Paris, 1933)

Newman, John Henry, *An Essay on the Development of Christian Doctrine* (London, 1845; 1920)

——. *Lectures on the Present Position of Catholics in England* (London, 1851; 1918)

——. *Callista: A Tale of the Third Century* (London, 1856; 1914)

——. *An Essay in Aid of a Grammar of Assent* (London, 1870; 1917)

——. *Essays Critical and Historical* (London, 1871)

——. *Historical Sketches* 3 vols. (London, 1856, 1872–73, repr. 1913)

——. *A Letter Addressed to His Grace the Duke of Norfolk on the Occasion of Mr. Gladstone's Recent Expostulation* (London, 1875)

——. *My Campaign in Ireland* (Aberdeen, 1896)

——. *Loss and Gain* (London, 1919)

——. *John Henry Newman: Autobiographical Writings*, ed. Henry Tristram (London and New York, 1956)

——. *The Letters and Diaries of John Henry Newman* vols.1–8 ed. I. Ker et al. (Oxford, 1978–84); Vols. 11–31 ed. C.S. Dassein et al. (Oxford, 1961–72)

——. *Apologia pro Vita Sua: Being a History of His Religious Opinions*, ed. Martin J. Svaglic (Oxford, 1967)

——. *The Idea of a University: defined and illustrated in nine discourses delivered to the Catholics of Dublin in occasional lectures and essays addressed to the members of the Catholic university*, ed. and introduced by Martin J. Svaglic (Notre Dame, 1982)

——. *The Works of Cardinal Newman*: Birmingham Oratory Millennium Edition, Volume I, *Lectures on the Present Position of Catholics in England*, ed. and introduced by Andrew Nash (Leominster and Notre Dame, 2000); Volume III, *Rise and Progress of Universities and Benedictine Essays*, ed. Mary Katherine Tillman (Leominster and Notre Dame, 2001)

——. (ed.), *The Catholic University Gazette* (1854–55)

Nokes, David *Jonathan Swift: A Hypocrite Reversed: A Critical Biography* (Oxford, 1985)

Nora, Pierre, *Realms of Memory: The Construction of the French Past*, Volume II, *Traditions*, trans. Arthur Goldhammer (New York, 1997)

Nurser, John, *The Reign of Conscience: Individual, Church, and State in Lord Acton's History of Liberty* (New York and London, 1987)

O'Brien, Conor Cruise, *The Great Melody: A Thematic Biography of Edmund Burke* (London, 1992)

O'Connell, Daniel, *A Memoir on Ireland Native and Saxon* (Dublin, 1843)

O'Donnell, Katherine, '"Whether the White People Like It or Not': Edmund Burke's Speeches on India – *Caoineadh's Cáinte*' *Éire-Ireland* (Fall/Winter 2002), 187–205

——. 'The Image of a Relationship in Blood: *Párliament na mBan* and Burke's Jacobite Politics', *Eighteenth-Century Ireland* (2000), 98–119

——. 'Edmund Burke and the Heritage of Oral Culture' (Unpublished Ph.D. thesis, National University of Ireland, 1999)

O'Driscol, John, *Views of Ireland, Moral, Political and Religious* 2 vols. (London, 1823)

O'Gorman, Frank, *The Long Eighteenth Century: British Political and Social History 1688–1832* (London, 1997)

O'Halloran, Clare, *Golden Ages and Barbarous Nations: Antiquarianism and Cultural Politics in Ireland, 1750–1800* (Cork, 2004)

Ozouf, Mona, 'La Révolution française et l'idée de l'homme nouveau' in Colin Lucas (ed.), *The Political Culture of the French Revolution* (Oxford and New York, 1988), 213–32

——. A *Page of Irish History: The Story of University College, Dublin 1883–1909, A*, compiled by Fathers of the Society of Jesus (Dublin, 1930)

Palmer, R.R., 'World Revolution of the West, 1763–1801', *Political Science Quarterly* 69 (1954), 1–21

——. *The Age of the Democratic Revolution: A Political History of Europe and America, 1760–1800* 2 vols. (Princeton, 1959)

——. (ed.), *The Two Tocquevilles, Father and Son: Hervé and Alexis de Tocqueville and the Coming of the French Revolution* (Princeton, 1987)

Perry, R., 'Radical Doubt and the Liberation of Women', *Eighteenth-Century Studies* 18 (1985), 465–93

Pettit, Philip, *Republicanism: A Theory of Freedom and Government* (Oxford, 1997)

Phillips, Mark Salber, 'Historical Distance and the Historiography of Eighteenth-Century Britain', in Stefan Collini, Richard Whatmore and Brian Young (eds.),

History, Religion, and Culture: British Intellectual History 1750–1950 (Cambridge, 2000), 31–47

Plowden, Francis, *An Historical Disquisition Concerning the Rise, Progress, Nature and Effects of the Orange Societies in Ireland* (Dublin, 1810)

Pocock, J.G.A., 'Virtue and Commerce in the Eighteenth Century', *Journal of Interdisciplinary History* 3, (1972), 119–34

——. *The Machiavellian Moment: Florentine Political Thought and the Atlantic Republican Tradition* (Princeton, 1975)

——. *Virtue, Commerce and History* (Cambridge, 1985; repr. 1988)

——. 'Edmund Burke and the Definition of Enthusiasm: The Context as Counter-Revolution', in F. Furet and M. Ozouf (eds.), *The French Revolution and the Creation of Modern Political Culture* Vol. 3 *The Transformation of Political Culture, 1789–1848* (Oxford, 1988), 19–43

——. 'Political Thought in the English-Speaking Atlantic, 1760–1790. Part I: The Imperial Crisis. Part 2: Empire, Revolution and the End of Early Modernity', in J.G.A. Pocock (ed.), with the assistance of G.J. Schochet and L.G. Schwoerer *The Varieties of British Political Thought 1500–1800* (Cambridge, 1993), 246–317

——. *Barbarism and Religion* 2 vols. (Cambridge, 1999)

Poovey, Mary, *The Proper Woman and the Woman Writer: Ideology as Style in the Works of Mary Wollstonecraft, Mary Shelley, and Jane Austen* (Chicago and London, 1984)

Portalis, Jean-Etienne, Marie *De l'Usage et de l'abus de l'esprit philosophique pendant le dix-huitième siècle* 2 vols. (Paris, 1827)

Raphael, D.D., *The Moral Sense* (London, 1947)

Rashid, S., 'Mandeville's *Fable*: Laissez-Faire or Libertinism?', *Eighteenth-Century Studies* 18 (1985), 313–30

Readings, Bill, *The University in Ruins* (Cambridge, Mass., 1996)

Reid, Christopher, *Edmund Burke and the Practice of Political Writing* (Dublin and New York, 1985)

Rigney, Ann, *The Rhetoric of Historical Representation: Three Narrative Histories of the French Revolution* (Cambridge, 1990)

Roantree, Dermot S., 'William Monsell M.P. and the Catholic Question in Victorian Britain and Ireland' (Unpublished Ph.D. thesis, University College Dublin, 1990)

Roberts, J.M., *The Mythology of the Secret Societies* (London, 1972)

Robison, John, *Proofs of a Conspiracy against all the Religions and Governments of Europe* (London, 1797)

Roche, Daniel, *France in the Enlightenment*, trans. Arthur Goldhammer, (Cambridge, Mass., and London, 1998)

Rousseau, Jean-Jacques, *Discours sur les sciences et les arts, Lettre à d'Alembert* ed. J. Varloot (Paris, 1957)

——. *On the Social Contract* ed. R. Masters, trans. J. Masters (New York, 1978)

Ryan, Guy A., OFM *The Acton Circle 1864–1871: the* Chronicle *and the* North British Review (Unpublished Ph.D. thesis, Notre Dame, 1969)

Sage, Victor, *Horror Fiction in the Protestant Tradition* (London, 1988)

Schama, Simon, *Citizens: A Chronicle of the French Revolution* (London and New York, 1989)

Schilling, Bernard N., *Conservative England and the Case against Voltaire* (New York, 1950)

Schmitt, Carl, *The Concept of the Political*, trans. G. Schwab (Chicago, 1996)
Schuettinger, R.L., *Lord Acton: Historian of Liberty* (La Salle, Illinois, 1976)
Shaftesbury, Anthony Ashley Cooper, Third Earl of, *Characteristics of Men, Manners, Opinions, Times*, ed. J.M. Robertson (New York, 1964)
Shorter Clement, 'Lord Acton's Hundred Best Books', *Pall Mall Magazine* 36, 147 (July, 1905), 3–10
Simpson, David, *Romanticism, Nationalism and the Revolt against Theory* (Chicago and London, 1993)
Simpson, Richard, 'Milner and His Times', *Home and Foreign Review* 2 (April, 1863), 531–57
Skalweit, S., *Edmund Burke und Frankreich* (Cologne and Opladen, 1956)
Skinner, Quentin, *Liberty before Liberalism* (Cambridge, 1997)
——. *Visions of Politics Volume I; Regarding Method* (Cambridge, 2002)
Smith, Adam, *An Inquiry into the Nature and Causes of the Wealth of Nations*, ed. E. Cannan (New York, 1937)
Smith, Paul, 'Historian in the Seat of God', *London Review of Books* (10 June 1999), 29–30
Soloway, R.A., *Prelates and People: Ecclesiastical Social Thought in England 1783–1852* (London and Toronto, 1969)
Staël, Germaine de, *De la Littérature considérée dans ses rapports avec les institutions sociales*, 2 vols. (London, 1800)
——. *Œuvres complètes* 2 vols. (Paris, 1836)
Stephen, Leslie, *English Literature and Society in the Eighteenth Century* (London, 1920)
Strachey, Lytton, *Eminent Victorians* (London, 1986)
Strauss, Leo, *Natural Right and History* (Chicago, 1953)
Suleri, Sara, *The Rhetoric of English India* (Chicago and London, 1992)
Swift, Jonathan, *Prose Works of Jonathan Swift* 14 vols., ed. Herbert Davis, (Oxford, 1939–68)
——. *The Drapier's Letters to the People of Ireland*, ed. Herbert Davis (Oxford, 1965)
Temperley, Harold (ed.), *Selected Essays of J.B. Bury* (Cambridge, 1930)
Thom, Martin, *Republics, Nations and Tribes* (London, 1995)
Tierney, Michael (ed.), *Struggle with Fortune: A Miscellany for the Centenary of the Catholic University of Ireland* (Dublin, 1954)
Tocqueville, Alexis de, *Democracy in America* 2 vols., ed. Phillips Bradley (New York, 1945; repr. 1990)
——. *The Recollections of Alexis de Tocqueville*, trans. Alexander Teixeira de Mattos, ed. J.P. Mayer (London, 1948)
——. *Journeys to England and Ireland* ed. and trans. J.P. Mayer (London, 1958)
——. *Alexis de Tocqueville's Journey in Ireland*, ed. and trans. Emmet Larkin (Dublin, 1990)
——. *The Old Régime and the Revolution*, eds. François Furet and Françoise Mélonio, trans. Alan S. Kahan (Chicago and London, 1998)
——. *Alexis de Tocqueville: Writings on Empire and Slavery*, ed. and trans. Jennifer Pitts (Baltimore and London, 2001)
Todorov, Tzvetan, *On Human Diversity: Nationalism, Racism, and Exoticism in French Thought*, trans. Catherine Porter (Cambridge, Mass., and London, 1993)
Toland, John (ed.), *The Oceana of James Harrington, Esq; and His Other Works* (Dublin, 1737)

Tulloch, Hugh, 'Lord Acton and German Historiography', in B. Stuchtey and P. Wende (eds.), *British and German Historiography 1750–1950: Traditions, Perceptions and Transfers* (Oxford, 2000), 159–72

Turner, Frank M., *John Henry Newman: The Challenge to Evangelical Religion* (New Haven and London, 2002)

Vance Norman, 'Improving Ireland: Richard Whately, Theology and Political Economy', in Stefan Collini, Richard Whatmore and Brian Young (eds.), *Economy, Polity, and Society: British Intellectual History 1750–1950* (Cambridge, 2000), 181–202

Venturi, Franco, *Italy and the Enlightenment: Studies in a Cosmopolitan Century* (London, 1972)

——. *The End of the Old Regime in Europe 1768–1776: The First Crisis*, trans. R. Burr Litchfield (Princeton, 1989)

Viswanathan, Gauri, *Outside the Fold: Conversion, Modernity, and Belief* (Princeton, 1998)

von Gentz, Friedrich, 'De la marche de l'opinion publique en Europe relativement à la révolution française', *Mercure Britannique* 17 (23 April 1799), 3–34; 20 (10 June 1799), 197–217

Wall, Thomas, 'Catholic Periodicals of the Past. The Catholic University Gazette', *Irish Ecclesiastical Record*, 5th series, 102 (1964)

Wallerstein, Immanuel, *The Modern World-System III: The Second Era of Great Expansion of the Capitalist World-Economy, 1730–1840s* (London, 1989)

——. *After Liberalism* (New York, 1995)

Ward, Wilfrid, *The Life of John Henry Cardinal Newman, based on His Private Journals and Correspondence* 2 vols. (London, 1912)

Webb, William, *An Analysis of the History and Antiquities of Ireland* (Dublin, 1791)

Weiner, Marjorie, *The French Exiles (1789–1815)* (London, 1960)

Werkmeister, Lucyle, *The London Daily Press, 1772–1792* (Lincoln, Nebraska, 1963)

Whelan, Frederick G., *Edmund Burke and India: Political Morality and Empire* (Pittsburgh, 1996)

Wolin, Sheldon, *Tocqueville between Two Worlds: The Making of a Political and Theoretical Life* (Princeton and Oxford, 2001)

Wollstonecraft, Mary, *A Vindication of the Rights of Men in a Letter to the Right Honourable Edmund Burke Occasioned by his Reflections on the Revolution in France* (London, 1790)

——. *Vindication of the Rights of Woman; with Strictures on Political and Moral Subjects* (London, 1792)

——. *An Historical and Moral View of the Origin and Progress of the French Revolution and the Effect it has Produced in Europe* (London, 1794)

Wyse, Thomas, *Historical Sketch of the late Catholic Association of Ireland* 2 vols. (London, 1829)

Young, Brian, 'Gibbon, Newman and the religious accuracy of the historian' in David Waverley ed., *Edward Gibson: centenary essays* (Oxford, 1997), 309–30

Young, Robert J.C., *Postcolonialism: An Historical Introduction* (Oxford, 2001)

INDEX